THE CHALLENGE
OF THE PRIMITIVES

Robin Clarke and Geoffrey Hindley

The Challenge
of the Primitives

McGraw-Hill Book Company
New York   St. Louis   San Francisco

123456789BPBP798765

Library of Congress Cataloging in Publication Data
Clarke, Robin
The challenge of the primitives.
  1. Society, Primitive. 2. Civilization, Modern.
I. Hindley, Geoffrey, joint author. II. Title.
GN320.C49   301.2   75-6907
ISBN 0-07-011234-7

Contents

For Janine and Diana

Introduction

As our technological society rushes headlong towards its dubious future, a new interest in primitive peoples has sprung to life. Television, radio and magazines are finding that extended features on those few unsullied tribes that still exist, and on the many more that once covered the globe, are sure-fire winners. Their tone is one of wonder and inquiry, increasingly mixed with feelings of envy. The implication is that the primitive may have found a more satisfactory answer to the problem of life than we have.

This book takes that assumption for its starting point. It picks its information from those societies, not with the ambition of making final statements on the nature of primitive life or of discovering behind the data that illusive artefact called human nature, but rather in an attempt to suggest fruitful ways in which we can begin to rebuild a wholesome and life-enhancing society in the wasteland of the modern technological world. There have been thousands of societies on this planet and some of them hold secrets that we could well learn from. It is those secrets we are looking for.

It is also our conviction that, interesting as it may be, research into animal life and societies, so fashionable with the scientific establishment as a source for comparisons and insights into social organization, can never provide more than peripheral comments on the human condition. Granted that approximations can be found in the non-human realm to tool-using, to affection, to communication, even speech, in no serious way has even the most impressive collection of statistics or learned papers been able to dislodge the well founded conviction held by all men and women that they are in important ways distinct from the other species on the planet. Our problems are human and, while they may be illuminated by reference to other species, they will never be solved that way. Whatever rats may do in the research laboratory's maze, they remain rats. It is by looking at how other human societies have arranged themselves that we may learn a few pointers to the resolution of our dilemmas. Conventional wisdom allows vast credence to the statistics derived from the behaviour of fruit flies or rabbits, but the statistics from societies, the tools of the anthropologist, enjoy rather less currency. Sometimes it seems that we find it easier to register the differences between us and the New Guinea tribesman than those between us and the guinea-pig.

Not so long ago there was a tribe living in New Guinea, good farmers and brave warriors, who over countless generations had evolved a pattern of life, perfectly adapted to their social needs and to the landscape in which they lived. They are no longer there. An international mining corporation discovered rich mineral deposits under their territory and armed with 'authorizations' and bulldozers easily ploughed down the villages and cleared the land. The warriors now pass their days spending money provided by the company in the beer halls provided by the company, and their nights in the prefabricated dwellings built by the company. After thousands of years of being people, the tribesmen are now a social problem—their land stolen, their culture destroyed and their self-respect sacrificed to Western man's insatiable demand for raw materials.

As Western men we should not be unduly disturbed by the story. After all, modern civilization rests squarely on foundations such as this. In the last century it cannibalized the souls of its own people and scarred the bosom of its own landscape in the name of progress and in this century it is merely extending the process. That nineteenth-century doctrine of progress has been scouted so often since, that it might be thought to have been finally discredited; but it has not been. In one form or another it is the one fundamental principle of action that our culture acknowledges; yoked to the ideology of self-help and the dream of a leisured, technology-based society of the future, it inspires our planners and politicians to investment in machinery that far outstrips any corresponding investment in social engineering or the much debated 'quality of life'.

It begins to seem as though, by its very nature, Western civilization is being ineluctibly drawn to a pointless, exhausting, unobtainable and, in the last analysis, destructive goal of what one might call 'ultimate superiority'. The productive process, the research process and the knowledge industry have all entered upon exponential growth curves, so that we, willy-nilly, are drawn up, clutching half-heartedly at our humanity as we go. Alone of the world's civilizations we seemed able to realize the dreams that once gave hope to the secular world. But as the dreamers made the dreams come true, they found them to be quite insubstantial. The journey to the moon was once a poetic fancy and only fools thought it possible; now that they have been proved right they have been shown to be fools, none the less. There are the other age-old dreams of men—dreams of a just society, of peace on earth and goodwill, of liberty, equality and fraternity—that not even the fools of our modern generation have attempted to make real. With a relentless and blinkered logic we pin our hopes to the triune deity of profit, efficiency and self-interest, believing that it will provide all the conditions of the good life and allow it to spring up, unattended, by some kind of parthenogenesis.

But the virgin soil of universal material well-being, were it ever to materialize, would still need to be fertilized by convictions about the nature of our humanity. On the monitors of social cohesion and achievement, the dials are everywhere registering retrogression rather than advance. Today the West can no longer escape doubt. Even on the superficial level of economic organization, historic convictions are faltering. Capitalist governments are mounting programmes of state intervention that to the old guard look like the foundations of state socialism; the struggle for fuel and food to maintain the industrial system is sparking off the first conflicts in a new series of trade wars; indeed, the desperate need of the advanced nations for fuel oil is forcing them gradually to abandon old lines of foreign policy and is already inhibiting the grand, contemptuous stance of independent manœuvre which used to characterize their dealings with the underdeveloped world.

As the idea that endless material advance may prove to be a chimera filters out to the population at large, discontent is beginning to mount and attitudes to change. We can observe the slow formulation of a new orthodoxy. At the upper end of the social spectrum the notion is beginning to shape that a man proves his prestige not by the possession of goods, but by the cultivation of his experience of life. The battle against drugs is the more difficult because society's opinion-formers and even the families of its politicans are seeking to deepen their experience by this mode. The rich bourgeoisie finds its relaxation in holiday camps on the Mediterranean where the age-old ideals of communal living are being revived because of their practical merits for the modern servantless family. While, again on the economic front, American entrepreneurs are making a multi-million dollar business from, of all things, barter exchanges. The ideas of the primitives are being ushered in at the front door, though the hosts may not realize the full and revolutionary implications of the new fashions. The primitive lives in a society that he labours to keep in being with hard work; Western man lives in a social structure which he sees, like everything else, only as a zone of exploitation.

For too many generations we have been pursuing with all possible speed the shadows of material well-being and have discounted the human attributes and activities that give them meaning. In the words of the anthropologist Paul Bohannan, 'We have shown a lamentable tendency to exclude from productive work, activities leading to products that maintain a way of life itself.'[1]

And that 'ultimate superiority' which is our unspoken goal; is it not also an indefinable goal? So far we have kept our sanity by being careful to consider only the next challenge on the planner's programme or the designer's drawing-board. Past experience has taught us that there will always be new and bigger such challenges and that, with luck, we might never have to ask, let alone face, that tedious and cliché'd old question 'What is it all for?'. Science, our austere and veiled religion, long ago ruled the question 'Why?' out of order, and most people have been willing, like obedient acolytes, not to press it.

But if we do begin to ask that question, we are confronted by a yawning emptiness inside ourselves. Used for so long to worship the god Change, we can find no clue as to how to live in a world that stands still and expects us to be men rather than money-earners. And we now observe a curious and terrifying fact about ourselves. It is that our civilization has overcome the natural environment with such success that the continued existence of that environment itself seems threatened. Where are we to find help in coming to terms with these two fatal facts of our situation: the emptiness within and the danger from without?

The theme of this book is that Western man is lost in a search for happiness, and may begin to find his way again only if he is prepared to look into the world of the primitives; a world that he is fast destroying. The objectives of that primitive world have been different from ours. Our quest for progress has led us to dedicate the energies of our society to maintaining imbalance and tension as a motive force. The primitive society, on the other hand, devotes its resources to the maintenance and nurturing of a social equilibrium, inherited from the past but always adaptable to the present. Aware of the fragility of human institutions and their crucial role in his struggle for survival in the world, primitive man has made it his business to ensure the continuance of social patterns that have proved successful.

But we, over a period that now stretches back almost two centuries, have been busy overturning and dismantling social structures inherited from the past. Urged on by the god of profit, the first stage of the programme entailed the decanting of huge sections of the population out of a traditional rural environment into disgusting industrial towns—hurriedly run up for the purpose—and their anti-human factories.

It would be hard to conceive a process better designed to break up a social structure, yet, incredible as it may appear, there are people who, lamenting the fragmentation of modern society, wonder how it came about. In view of our experience it is no longer quite so obvious that the conservatism of the primitives is mistaken.

The objectives of their world have been different from those of the West in another respect. As important as the conservation of a proved and comfortable social structure has been the conscious and constant effort to harmonize their own living with the natural environment. While the distinguishing attitude of Western man in his dealings with nature is one of dismissive superiority, that of the primitive has been a mixture of fear and humility. He acts in the belief, given body by religious strictures, that he is a part of nature, not outside it or superior to it, and in the belief also that to deny this will bring dire consequences ascribed to the intervention of the angry gods. As we begin to reap the grim, dead harvest of generations of ignorant and thoughtless exploitation, there is nothing that we can offer from our wisdom to say that the primitives are wrong.

Western man has broken out of the cycle that locked the species into its environment and gave it a place in the world. It seemed like a great leap forward. Today something of the glamour has gone and we are tempted, instead, to see that historical breakthrough only as the logical outcome of a development, a development made possible by the agricultural revolution of the neolithic age and the discovery of metal technology. Why it should have been with us that the tree bore its dread fruit is another speculation, but now it seems we are doomed. The course of historical evolution seems to many an irreversible process; it is our destiny, we have come to think, to travel faster, build bigger and live more extravagantly. We still look back on a nostalgic past where life seems to have been orderly and to have had its rhythms, yet we still work for a future of socially destructive materialism.

One of the seven wonders of the ancient world was the temple of the goddess Diana, at Ephesus. In the year 356 B.C. it was burned down by a certain Herostratus who wished that his name might be remembered by posterity 'if only for the perpetration of some appalling crime'.

Our destruction of the few primitive cultures surviving shows a vandalism worthy to be compared with that of Herostratus. As we eliminate the last traces of the once infinitely varied polyphony of human social structure we should remember that we, like Herostratus, will undoubtedly be remembered by posterity if only for the perpetration of an appalling crime. But, whereas the citizens of Ephesus hastened to rebuild the temple of Diana even more gloriously than before, there is no one to rebuild the human structures nursed through the centuries of sensitive, intelligent and mature men, once we have destroyed them. Let us learn what we can from their rich example before it is too late.

1

The World of Nature

1 The First Affluent Society

Man has existed on this planet for some two million years. For all of that time he has survived by winning food from the land, and for 99 per cent of it he has done so by hunting fish and animals and by gathering plant materials. Agriculture is little more than ten thousand years old, industrial society only three hundred years old. And of the eighty thousand million human beings estimated ever to have lived on the Earth, 90 per cent have been hunters and gatherers, six per cent agriculturalists and the remaining four per cent industrialists dependent on agriculture.

Seen in this light, our way of life is atypical. If the length of human history were represented by the height of St Paul's, our modern form of society would be represented only by the thickness of ink on a postage stamp placed on top of the dome. It is hardly correct, then, to dub the hunters and gatherers – as Desmond Morris has done – 'remote cultural backwaters so atypical and unsuccessful that they are nearly extinct'.[1] On the contrary, hunting and gathering has been the almost universal response to the challenge of human life on the Earth and future historians or archaeologists will record our own deviation from it as a period of admittedly great productivity but unparalleled brevity. Technological society, as it has been practised for three hundred years, has at most another two centuries to run. What will replace it remains unknown, but there appear to be only two possibilities. One is that the end of our way of life will be marked by catastrophe, with a drastic reduction in population and a return to traditional forms of hunting, gathering and primitive agriculture. The other, less cataclysmic future is that we shall succeed in mutating our industrial way of life to a form which is compatible with long-term survival – a form, in other words, which does not mortgage the future of humanity by depending for its existence on the one-way use in a few decades of resources which have taken the planet billions of years to accumulate.

Either way, human society a hundred years from now will be as different from today's as ours is from the way of life in the prehistoric period. By definition, our new way of life will also have had to regain the stability that marked primitive life. That our ancestors, and those few of them we have permitted to continue their traditions to this day, had found a stable relationship with nature is beyond doubt; the survival of the primitive, over such long periods of time and over such vast geographical areas, is the proof of the utility of the cake which he baked. We do not romanticize primitive life by attributing to it an ecological awareness which we have long since lost. In asserting that, we are merely stressing the facts of history; if it were not true, we would not be here today.

What, then, are we to make of the stereotyped view of primitive life? It holds that until the industrial age, life was 'nasty, brutish and short'. Man was engaged in a perpetual struggle for survival and a battle for food which cost him all his waking hours. Many if not most children died at birth or shortly afterwards and those lucky (or unlucky) enough to survive could expect to reach at most their fortieth birthday. Their life span was marked by pain and disease and by unceasing hard work and physical discomfort. Superstition and fear were the order of the day, ruthlessly exploited by political elites who alone were able to survive in a manner which we would recognize as 'living'. Hunger, pestilence and war were the chains of mankind and held him captive throughout a long adolescence which reached maturity only with the revolutionary effects of agriculture, urbanization and industrialization. Until then human life was no better than an animal's; even as great a scientist as Charles Darwin, when he first met the Fuegians of South America, described the baboon as a 'much more wholesome fellow'.

To challenge this caricature is not only to challenge our own myth of progress but it is also to challenge the last two hundred years of anthropology. Throughout that period it was the social customs of primitive society that presented the intellectual challenge. Until a decade or so ago, no anthropologist would waste his valuable time in the field studying the primitive's physical relationship with the environment. It occurred to no one to measure the mortality statistics of a tribe, to study their methods of population control, their calorific intake, their ecological concepts, their botanical knowledge or their work-loads. It had been pre-decided that life was tough and chancy, and the anthropologist's job was to study the social and political devices that had presumably arisen to deal with all the varying emergencies of being a primitive.

All this, of course, reflected the interests of our own society at that time. It can be no coincidence that the early death, hard work and commonness of disease that were said to mark primitive society were also the pathologically distinguishing features of early industrial society. By a device made distressingly familiar to us through the Cold War, our own society was at least partly attributing to the 'enemy' those very deficiencies from which it itself was suffering. At the same time these characteristics were casually brushed aside and intellectual interest was focused on the social and political upheavals of the period. It was this interest that was carried abroad by the anthropologist and was thus destined to become his principal field of study.

Within the past decade, that focus of interest has changed. We have been reawakened, as never before, to concepts connected with ecology, population growth, demography and natural resources. We find our own future threatened by these new concepts and, sure enough, the pattern of anthropological study and writing has also changed. The messages now coming back from the tropical forests, the arid deserts and the Arctic wilderness are quite different. Primitive life has been measured and found to be not so wanting as was once thought. Life spans are longer, hunger rarer, the work load lighter and disease less in evidence than had always been assumed.[2] As we shall see, the new biological facts being revealed by ecological and bio-anthropologists lend little support to the idea of the 'nasty brutish and short' life-style of the primitive. And even this term is now being seen for the contradiction that it really is. If life ever was nasty and brutish, its brevity must surely have counted as an advantage. As Alex Comfort has wittily pointed out, an equally valid description of our own way of life might be 'nasty, brutish and long' – but if that were the case, we could hardly count its extra length as 'progress'.

But a qualification still needs to be made. Today's hunters and gatherers exist only in the remotest areas of the Earth – in inhospitable desert, inaccessible tropical forest and undesirable Arctic pack-ice. Most of our information about primitive gatherers comes from these people and these people alone. They do not represent a good sample of how most men lived for most of history. We have used our new technology to occupy those portions of the Earth that present us with a pleasing face and which were, in fact, least in need of technological control. We have relegated the primitive to those areas which even we, with our mighty control of nature, have deemed unlivable. Had we used our technology to adapt ourselves to the Arctic, the desert and the tropical forest – and left the temperate zones to those who wished to hunt and to fish and to farm – we would certainly have been fairer to the primitive. We might also have had a different picture of his way of life; for if, as we shall see, the Bushmen of the Kalahari desert have only to work a fifteen-hour week to provide themselves with an adequate diet, those who sought a similar way of life on the American plains, the European steppes and the Asian plateaux must have formed an affluent society in the real meaning of that word.

The :Kung Bushmen of the northern Kalahari Desert in southern Africa provide the finest example to date of what life can be like in a simple hunting and gathering community. They were studied extensively by a team of anthropologists including Irven deVore and Richard B. Lee from August 1963 to January 1965 – a period which included the second year of an extremely severe drought.[3] In spite of this it was found that the Bushmen had an always adequate and varied diet, achieved through a weekly workload which amounted to less than one-third of the average in Western society.

The Kalahari is not a particularly hospitable environment. A parched sandy soil overlying limestone rock is fed by at most ten inches of rain a year and heated to a temperature which can reach

110° F. in the shade. Night temperatures in the winter can fall below freezing-point. There is, however, a surprising amount of vegetation and hence water rather than food requirements determine the Bushmen's camp-sites. Around the few water-holes that exist are clustered the camp-sites, ranging in size from sixteen to ninety-four people. It was at one of these water-holes, called Dobe, that the anthropologists made their now classic study.

The :Kung Bushmen were found to know and have named some two hundred different plant species and more than two hundred and twenty animal species. Of these, eighty-five plants were eaten together with fifty-four different types of animals. Anyone who believes that primitive nutrition rarely ventures outside two or three staple species might find it interesting to calculate how many different animal and vegetable species go to make up his own diet.

Yet, like us, the Bushmen have their likes and dislikes. The plants are strictly ordered in a hierarchy of desirability which appears to allow for taste, nutritional value, abundance and ease of collecting. The same is true of the animals, of which only ten are highly regarded: the wart-hog, kudu, diuker, steenbok, gemsbok, wildebeeste, spring hare, porcupine, ant bear and common hare. But the mongongo nut, the staple diet of the region, far exceeds these in importance.

These nuts are the focus of the day's food collection and the ease of the Bushman's life is regulated by the distance between his water supply and the nearest mongongo trees. During the dry season, when water is more difficult to find, nut collection becomes more arduous and the return journey may involve a hike of two to sixteen miles. When the distance between water and nuts becomes more than three miles in the rainy season, the Bushman usually decides it is time to move camp to an area where standing water is closer to the nuts. It is this factor which determines his semi-nomadic life-style.

Lee and deVore made a very detailed analysis over a four-week period of just how much work was involved in collecting and hunting food. About 65 per cent of the population worked in finding food; despite the rigours of desert life, about fifteen hours' work a week were all that were required of each member to provide the basic food-stuffs. If affluence in a society is defined by the amount of leisure time involved, the :Kung Bushmen were affluent indeed. The Bushman had a 4½-day weekend which he spent mainly in visiting other camps, entertaining friends and dancing.

Measures of the nutritional value of the food eaten are also revealing. The Bushmen are fortunate in that the staple food of mongongo nuts has a high calorific and protein content. This item of diet alone produced a daily calory intake of 1,260 calories and a protein intake of 56 grammes, equivalent to eating the calories contained in 2½ pounds of rice or the protein in 14 ounces of lean beef.

During the same one-month period, 18 game animals were killed which provided 454 pounds of edible meat. This, in turn, worked out at just over 9 ounces of uncooked meat per day per person which yielded about 35 grammes of animal protein per person per day. This is, if anything, slightly more than the average amount of meat protein eaten per day by the average American. It is three times more than the average amount of all animal protein, including fish and eggs, eaten by people of the Third World at the present time. The overall results of the study show the average Bushman consuming 2,140 calories and 93·1 grammes of protein a day. The protein figure is remarkably high and according to records is only exceeded by some half a dozen countries in the modern world.

Calculations also show that, allowing for the typical weight of the Bushman and his normal activities, his diet was roughly equivalent to the amount of energy consumed — in fact, he seemed to eat about 165 more calories than he needed and about 33 grammes of protein per day more than absolutely necessary. It might be thought that there was little margin for error here but that would be to misunderstand the nature of a hunting and gathering society. The concept of surplus does not exist among the Bushmen; no food is kept for more than forty-eight hours and the whole 'economy' is geared to the simple expedient of going out and getting more food when it is required. As might be expected, the Bushmen have no set meal-times; they eat either when they are hungry or when food is brought in.

Not surprisingly, the anthropologists making this study found no evidence of the commonest disease of malnutrition in Africa, kwashiorkor. Neighbouring agricultural societies, by contrast, were having a particularly bad time during the drought in which this study was made. Their crops having failed for three years running, and more than one hundred thousand head of cattle having died, the World Food Programme was providing famine relief for 30 per cent of the people of Botswana. And although this programme did not reach as far as the Dobe area of the Kalahari, local non-Bushmen women were able to provide for their families by joining in with the Bushmen gathering expeditions.

Not only were the hunters and gatherers of the Bushman society able to support these extra mouths but they also supported a considerable percentage of their own population. Neither the young nor the old nor the sick are unnecessarily co-opted in the search for food. On average three searchers provide the food for themselves as well as for two dependents. In such a society, what we would call in economic terms 'surplus accumulation' is referred to as hoarding and is deeply despised. Bushman food is shared not only between families but also between camps. If the system breaks down in any way, individuals or families simply rearrange their lives to be with people who share more equitably; there is great social mobility within the Bushman society.

It follows from all this that the concept of scarcity is virtually unknown, at least in the sense in which we use the term. Food is always available and the variable is simply the ease with which it is obtainable. Contrary to the picture that has always been drawn of the life-style of the hunter and gatherer, the Bushman is not pushing against the limits of his food supply. Much of the mongongo nut supply is simply never picked up; it is left to lie on the ground and eventually rot. If the production of the land more nearly equated demand for food, the Bushmen could not live without the concept of scarcity and without drastic cycles of hunger and famine. It is a sobering thought that the whole of the West's economic system is based on the concept of scarcity and the balancing of supply and demand. In view of this, it is not surprising that our own way of life has now been discovered to be so ecologically unstable.

But to what extent are the Bushmen really typical of a hunting and gathering way of life? Could they not be the one freak exception that proves the rule of famine and struggle for other similar societies? It seems unlikely. We should not be deceived as to the real hostility of the environment of the Kalahari Desert. Although the Bushmen there may make life appear easy, we, even with our advanced technology, would be hard put to survive more than forty-eight hours. Those who lived in wetter and more comfortable surroundings must surely have found life no more difficult than do the Bushmen. And even their response to the desert environment may not be unique. In 1841 George Grey returned from an expedition to the Australian desert where he studied the way of life of the Aboriginals of the south-west coast.[4] He listed their diet as including:

ANIMAL FOODS

6 sorts of kangaroo
5 marsupials smaller than
   rabbits
2 species of opossum
9 species of marsupial
   rats and mice
   dingoes
1 type of whale
2 species of seal
   birds of every kind
   including emu and wild
   turkey
3 types of turtle
11 kinds of frog
7 types of iguanas and
   lizard
8 sorts of snake
   eggs of every species of
   bird and lizard

PLANT FOODS

29 kinds of root
4 kinds of fruit
2 species of cycad nuts
   seeds of several legu-
   minous plants
2 kinds of mesembrian-
   themum
7 types of fungus
4 sorts of gum
2 kinds of manna
   flowers of several
   species of Banksia

ANIMAL FOODS—*continued*

29 kinds of fish
all salt water shellfish
except oysters
4 kinds of freshwater
shellfish
4 kinds of grub

More recent observations, in other parts of Australia, have since confirmed the immense diversity of the Aboriginal diet. This is a point, it seems, on which we have no choice but to concede the fact that the primitive diet includes as much if not more variation than our own. But what of its desirability?

To a Western palate, most of the list above does not include 'food'—we do not eat, nor probably could we force ourselves to do so, the eggs of lizards, the meat of marsupial mice or any kinds of grub, frog or snake. But that this is not a biological rule can be determined even within the confines of modern Europe. The French do indeed eat the legs of frogs and the meat of snails—not through necessity but as a result of a gastronomic decision to regard such things as great delicacies. The Ifugao eat three species of dragon-fly, the powdered flesh of locusts, crickets, flying ants, red ants, water bugs and many kinds of beetle. In what sense are their tastes for food to be judged less informed than our own (which incidentally include the limited consumption of ants coated at great expense in chocolate)? For us, milk is a staple food; yet in much of Asia it is regarded as a mucous discharge just about as attractive as the secretions from the nasal orifice.

In truth, there is only one biological fact that determines food habits: most parts of nearly all plants and nearly all animals can be ingested by human beings as food. The poisonous exceptions are rare and are universally known throughout primitive society. Moreover, many of them are eaten in large quantities after first having been elaborately treated to render them harmless. The staple crop of the Boro Indians of the Amazon, for instance, is a kind of manioc which contains the extremely poisonous prussic acid. To prepare it, the Boro slice the manioc roots and soak them for a day with a piece of rotten manioc to promote fermentation.

The roots are grated and squeezed out, and then powdered by hand into flour which is heated and stirred to remove more of the poisons. The flour is kneaded with water and made into unleavened bread; the juice is boiled to a paste and used as a sauce for cassava after seasoning with peppers and fish. Even the manioc leaves are boiled, powdered very fine and seasoned with such fish, worms and insects as are available.[5] What is remarkable about this is not that the Boro feed off a staple crop which we would regard as poisonous but that they use all the plant and go to such lengths to prepare so many different types of food from it. A Boro cookbook would surely have much in common with those verbose and lengthy Victorian recipes which are now coming back into vogue in our own society. The primitive, it seems, has as much respect for food as we have but is prepared to go to considerably greater lengths than are we, to find what he regards as tasty and to prepare it in ways which are acceptable to his own society. As we shall see, food consumption in primitive society is regulated by elaborate rituals and taboos which we have now almost lost. A primitive would regard our own casual mixing of different types of food as extremely degenerate; and he would be appalled that at every meal members of both sexes and all different age groups ate roughly the same foods. In his society such things are controlled by tradition and cultural practices which attribute to certain cuts of meat and certain types of plant values which we now choose to ignore.

In Bushman society, as in most others, it is on the meat that most ritual centres. For the Bushman, and for us, meat is rarer, more highly prized and more costly than plant food. When the Bushman study was made there were eleven men in the camp, of whom four never went hunting. The remaining seven spent a total of seventy-eight man-days hunting, and killed and caught some eighteen animals. Their chance of a catch on any one day, in other words, was about one in four. When the women went gathering, by contrast, the chance of their returning with food was 100 per cent. A calorific analysis reveals also that every hour spent gathering produced 2·4 times as many calories as every hour spent hunting. Hunting is thus a riskier and less productive activity than is gathering. This is why in nearly all hunting and gathering communities most of the food eaten comes from plants, even though most cultural interest may centre on the game killed. The Bushman chooses, in other words, leisure over larger portions of meat. As Richard B. Lee has put it, the Bushmen 'eat as much vegetable food as they need, and as much meat as they can'.[6]

It would be tempting to conclude that this was a quirk of the Bushman diet dictated by the poverty of the environment. But if we turn to the Hadza, who live in eastern Africa just south of the equator, we find similar evidence. The Hadza live in an area which may appear somewhat barren but which is teeming with wild game—elephant, rhinoceros, giraffe, eland, zebra, wildebeeste, waterbuck, impala, baboon, leopard, and many other smaller animals such as porcupine and hare are there for the taking. Perhaps nowhere in the world supports as much game and has recently supported a hunting and gathering society. Yet, reports Dr James Woodburn, 'the Hadza rely mainly on wild vegetable matter for their food. Probably as much as 80 per cent of their food by weight is vegetable while meat and honey together account for the remaining 20 per cent.'[7] This is in spite of a great preference among the Hadza for meat and the fact that the Hadza restrict their consumption of plants mainly to ten species. Yet, Woodburn adds, 'for a Hadza to die of hunger, or even to fail to satisfy his hunger for more than a day or two, is almost inconceivable'. Woodburn estimates that an average of two hours a day is spent in obtaining food in Hadza society. The rest of the time is spent in a variety of activities, of which gathering among the men is the most important.

In this respect, as well as nutritionally, the Hadza have an easier life than do neighbouring agricultural tribes. In a 1960 survey of sixty-two Hadza children, a medical team reported: 'The clinical nutritional status of all the children was good by tropical standards; in particular, the syndromes of kwashiorkor and nutritional marasmus, rickets, infantile scurvy and vitamin B deficiency syndromes were not seen.' This is a result, it should be noted, of a society that attaches more importance to 'games of chance than it does to the chances of game'. Similar estimates can be made of Aboriginal society, where the Australian native has been calculated to spend between two and four hours a day in the combined activities of food gathering and preparation. 'A fair case can be made,' writes Marshall D. Sahlins, 'that hunters often work much less than we do, and rather than a grind the food quest is intermittent, leisure is abundant, and there is more sleep in the daytime per capita than in any other conditions of society.'[8]

The type of societies studied by Sahlins are more accurately described as hunters/gatherers than merely hunters; as we have seen, gathering is usually the most significant and rewarding of the two activities. Richard B. Lee has tried to test this idea. Using data from fifty-eight societies that earned their living from hunting, gathering and fishing exclusively, he found that twenty-nine of them depended mainly on gathering, eighteen on fishing (which is of course a much less chancy activity than hunting game) and only eleven (or one-sixth) mainly on hunting.[9]

Even more intriguing was the relationship of these eleven societies to latitude. Lee's sample included eight groups from the Arctic and of these, six were mainly dependent on hunting. In the temperate latitudes fishing was dominant in fourteen out of twenty-two cases, with the other eight being split equally between gathering and hunting. And in the tropics and warmer regions generally, gathering was dominant for twenty-five out of twenty-eight societies, with only one depending mainly on hunting. And yet, with only one exception, all societies at all latitudes derived at least 20 per cent of their diet by weight from the hunting of mammals. The average percentage of the diet that was meat was found to be 35 per cent for all the societies examined, a figure remarkably close to the 37 per cent of the :Kung Bushmen.[10]

All this must reflect the fact that hunting is such a chancy activity. And indeed when we examine known stories of massive starvation and deprivation in primitive society, we find that they concern mainly the Eskimo, and particularly those tribes living so far north that their diet is restricted almost exclusively to animals and some fish. Under such conditions, the variations in the supply of game that are a natural feature of animal life across the world can be catastrophic for the northern Eskimo. Hunger strikes, and it strikes cruelly, for the Eskimo has no alternative to fall back on save what little meat he has kept frozen in the snow and, as a last resort, the flesh of his brothers. But for the Eskimo, cannibalism is the most shameful activity to which he can be driven. If forced to it, he is pitied for years by his colleagues for having had to taste human flesh.

At certain times, then, and in certain regions of the northern Arctic, Eskimo life may approximate to the harsh stereotype of primitive life with which we started this chapter. But even this should not prevent us from a fair comparison with the world as it functions today. In the exploitation of the Third World that has gathered momentum since 1945, the 1,000 million people living in the rich countries have increased their animal protein consumption from 36 to 44 grammes per person a day. The luckless 2,200 millions—the majority of the world population—have seen their share fall from 11 grammes to a mere 8. The world is fast on the way to starvation, and millions more people die from starvation or its side-effects now than they did when all the world was a hunter and a gatherer. However many justifications and qualifications one cares to heap on to this stark fact, the ultimate position remains unaltered: the world is worse fed now than it was in the days of our ancestors.[11]

2 Food Farmers and Dollar Farmers

'Swithen' or 'swivven' is an old northern English word meaning 'to burn, sweal or singe, as heather'. It is used now, in the form 'swidden', to denote a kind of agriculture better known as 'slash-and-burn' which was once practised from Scandinavia to Melanesia. In a primitive economy it is by far the most common form of agriculture. And as it differs so markedly from modern ideas of farming, it has for long been a target of special abuse for those concerned with agricultural development in the Third World.

Essentially, the technique is used in forest and scrubland. First, a small area is cleared with simple axes or machetes, the larger timber taken out for firewood or fencing, and the smaller brushwood laid out on the clearing and allowed to dry for perhaps a couple of months. Meanwhile the garden clearing is fenced and then the area is ignited. Everything is burnt and the garden is then planted out, using the ash as fertilizer. Nothing is added except seed and labour and after a few months the first produce is collected. The garden is replanted as many times as useful food can be obtained from it—the first crop is usually good, the second much poorer and the third often negligible. After two or three years, then, the garden is abandoned and a new clearing is made. When the forest has regenerated, in as little as ten years in some tropical regions, the process may be repeated.

This practice has been an easy target for both anthropologists and Western agriculturalists. A vast literature exists explaining how this very primitive, simple and easy technique of food production must be stamped out, and stamped out quickly. The charges are that it wastes enormous volumes of timber; that most of the nutrients are lost into the air during burning; that it leads rapidly to soil erosion; that the fires often spread much wider than the original clearing, destroying vast tracts of otherwise exploitable forest; that the new forest which grows up is always different from and poorer than the original; that the technique can be used to support only very low population levels; that it can only be used by nomads, and thus prohibits the setting up of a centralized, urban society; that it does not make use of the principle of crop rotation; that the crops are of poor quality and, worse, that they have no commercial value. Further—and this to the Western eye may be the most heinous crime of all—such a system of agriculture cannot be relied upon to cultivate the concept of private property.[1]

Pitting his modern mind against the problem of how to wrest maximum production from the land, civilized man, it is usually argued, has found the real solutions. First, small plots of workable land have been systematically replaced by vast prairie tracts of unbroken pasture and arable land. By using just one crop over areas of perhaps several hundred acres, the work input to agriculture can be minimized and its mechanization and profitability maximized. With the help of the chemical industry and the tractor combines, productivity per acre has been raised and raised every year. New strains of high-yielding plants have been produced and have spread their net globally. By turning food production into an industry, massive world-wide famine has been avoided, it is claimed, and a system of agriculture instituted which will in time feed the four billions we will soon have on the Earth's surface. The land has been conquered, and if somewhat more than half the world population still feels (and knows) that it is hungry, then we have only to tighten our belts (or rather they have to tighten theirs) for a few more years until agro-business has taught even the most illiterate the proper way to grow their food and get rich at the same time.

To be sure, these stereotypes of swidden and modern farming have a certain basic relationship to reality. But stereotypes they certainly are. And in the past decade a new attempt has been made to re-examine the basis of swidden farming from a more ecological point of view. The result has been surprising, for many if not all the old critiques of the process have been judged either faulty or at best partially true.

One of the key points at issue is ecological stability. Today, it is widely accepted that the monoculture form of agriculture is perhaps the most profitable but the most ecologically unstable. This is basically because it turns land into an ecological system about as far removed from the natural one as can be imagined. Plants are not simple biological organisms which can be successfully grown simply with the right mix of chemicals and a suitable supporting medium. Each species depends for its health on the presence of other living organisms, plants and animals, both up and down the ecological ladder. A healthy eco-system is one in which there is therefore great diversity and a steady-state situation between the individual species and the natural environment. Were it not for the chemicals and mechanical equipment now used in farming, our own monocultures would be perilously unstable, subject every year to one disease or predator which would always wipe them out—as indeed still happens with crops such as maize in the United States in spite of all our technical efforts. But a swidden garden is something quite different, as Harold C. Conklin has written:

> At the sides and against the swidden fences there is found an association dominated by low, climbing or sprawling legumes (asparagus beans, sieva beans, hyacinth beans, string beans and cow-peas). As one goes into the center of the swidden, one passes through an association dominated by ripening grain but also including numerous root crops, shrub legumes and tree crops. Pole-climbing yam vines, heart-shaped taro leaves, ground-hugging sweet potato vines, and shrub-like manioc stems are the only visible signs of the large store of starch staples which is building up underground, while the grain crops fruit a meter or so above the swidden floor before giving way to the more widely spaced but less rapidly maturing tree crops. Over the first two years a new swidden produces a steady stream of harvestable food in the form of seed grains, pulses, sturdy tubers, and underground

stems, and bananas, from a meter below to more than 2 meters above the ground. And many other vegetable, spice and nonfood crops are grown simultaneously.[2]

In other words diversity seems to be the key to swidden gardening, which attempts not only to mix different types of plant together but also to utilize their differing depths of growth from below to above ground level in a way which has also earned it the name 'vertical gardening'. All this is evident in the swidden gardener's vocabulary and garden expertise. The Hanunoo of the Philippines, for instance, habitually grow at least forty-eight different species in one swidden which may be two or three acres big, and they recognize four hundred and thirty different kinds of cultivated plant. In the first year in a swidden they may plant up to one hundred and fifty specific crop types.

In this way, the most characteristic form of primitive agriculture seeks not to do away with nature but rather to adapt, to provide a harvest more utilizable by man than the natural one. It has been said that the swidden gardener turns the natural forest into a harvestable one, and in doing so of course he reaps the benefits that accrue from not disturbing nature too profoundly. Were he, for instance, to attempt to grow a single crop over large areas in a cleared tropical forest, experience has shown there is one inevitable result. First, the weeding problems quickly get out of hand in a hot and humid environment where growth can be extremely rapid—in the tropics a bamboo can grow as much as thirty inches in a single day. But more important than this, the poor tropical soil is quickly leached out by the burning sun and the heavy rain, leading to a process of soil erosion known as laterization. Laterized soils are often impossible to work and are to be found wherever the forest has been deprived of its natural cover. They are now a common feature in Vietnam where spraying with defoliants has wreaked an ecological damage which will last several decades at least.

The harvestable forest of a swidden garden avoids this effect, or keeps it to a minimum, and allows the soil quickly to regain its natural state when the swidden reverts to natural forest. And the fertilizer for the swidden itself is not so much extracted from the poor soil but from the ash formed when the clearing is burnt. In this way the natural process of growth and decay is merely accelerated in time, and not altered grossly in character. Proof of this comes from the observation that in areas where altitude prevents the burning of the garden because there is no dry period, rice production from a swidden is only one third to one half that of areas where burning can take place.

By retaining the natural parasol effect of the tropical forest, the swidden garden also helps cut down on weeding. Of course, a swidden garden does need weeding, perhaps two or three times completely, but the work is made much lighter by the presence of green matter between the garden soil and the sun itself. For this reason a large labour force is not required and on average the swidden requires the adult members who depend on it to work between five hundred and one thousand hours a year – in Western terms perhaps between ten and twenty weeks a year. This does not compare badly with Western practice, where perhaps between one-tenth and one-half of the family salary is spent on food. But such a simple comparison is misleading, for it implies that none of us actually works directly any longer to produce food – we merely earn money to pay for it. In fact it is not only the farmers who produce food in our society: far more people are involved in jobs such as chemical engineering, fertilizer production, plant breeding and mechanical agricultural equipment production, maintenance and servicing – not to mention the supply and distribution of fossil fuels on which all these depend. We are wont to think that we have succeeded in drastically reducing the number of man-hours required to produce food. And to some extent we have – but the reduction is much less marked if all the various jobs on which agriculture is dependent are taken into account.

But in fact this kind of justification for swidden farming is not really needed. There is plenty of evidence from the field. For example, the Finno-Ougrian peoples in nineteenth-century Europe are said to have produced a rye yield three to four times as high by slash and burn as is possible with continuously cropped fields.[3] Reports have been made that irrigated rice agriculture is less than half as productive as swidden farming in terms of man-hours.[4] And there are plenty of examples of people who have been persuaded to change their system to continuous cropping, only to revert to swidden farming a few years later when they find the old system more productive in terms of both food quantity and man-hours involved. In some cases in Vietnam agricultural peoples who were traditionally ploughers have given up their ancestral methods in favour of the swidden.[5]

But it does remain a fact that swidden farming can support only a limited population density. In the past, this factor has been grossly exaggerated, and used as an argument for immediate 'advance' to continuous cropping methods. The facts are now better known and generally support the idea that a swidden people need six to seven acres of forest per head of population. Higher densities than this are known, but so are lower ones. For comparison, the world average of arable and pasture land is currently about two and a half acres a head. But what we should remember is that swidden farming is now practised largely in tropical or sub-tropical areas, which are certainly not the areas of tremendous fertility which is their popular image. As we have said, the soil is poor and attempts to introduce other forms of farming have often failed; and though there may be ways to increase the productivity of swidden farming, we have not found them yet. Certainly, we could not immediately increase world food production by ploughing up the tropical forests and planting suitable grain; the result would be a catastrophe, for Western forms of agriculture are quite unsuitable for the tropics. Indeed, it is extremely doubtful that our own form of agriculture is at all suitable for any planet as perilously near starvation as we have been for the past three decades.

The Western world is addicted to meat. For us, no meal is considered a real meal unless it includes animal protein and nearly all our large-scale farming is directed towards meat production in one form or another. Now, we do not intend to indulge in any sentimentality over the question of exploiting and killing animals in this way; neither we nor the primitive could afford any such luxury. But there are many little-known facts that lie behind our obsession with meat-eating which contrast starkly with primitive habits, and with our global demand for better food.

No man needs meat to survive—a perfectly adequate diet can be assembled from plant protein. To do so is, however, technically rather difficult, and a portion of meat in a diet is medically advisable. The great question is how much? Two beefsteaks a day? or meat when you can get it, as in many primitive hunting and gathering societies? or maybe meat twice a week?

One of the golden rules of ecology is that the higher up the food chain one eats the less efficient is the overall process. For maximum efficiency we should be able to convert the sun's energy and carbon dioxide in the air into protein ourselves. Of course we can't—but plants can. And animals obtain their nutrient requirements either by eating plants directly or by eating other animals which themselves are herbivores. The logic of eating well down in the food chain is easy to see from the following figures. For every pound of protein in a hen's eggs, that hen has had to eat 4·3 pounds of plant protein. For milk the figure is 4·4, for chicken meat 5·5, for pig 8·3 and for beef 21.[6] In other words, a given area of farmland can either be used to provide the beef protein necessary for one person, or the equivalent in plant protein for twenty-one people. Thus by concentrating so exclusively on meat we have in a sense thrown away the advantages accruing from the increased production of modern farming.

In the United States the average mix of animal protein eaten is such that one person's diet of protein could have provided the plant protein needed to feed eight people. One acre of cereals will provide five times more protein than if that field were used for beef production. An acre of legumes provides ten times more, an acre of leafy vegetables fifteen times and an acre of spinach twenty-six times more.[7] To cap it all, in a world where water shortage is imminent if not actual, a mixed beef and grain diet requires eight times the volume of water needed for the equivalent diet of grain only.[8]

Yet in the West a journey to the country reveals huge areas of grain ripening in the sun. It would seem that this was a step in the right direction. Not at all, for 78 per cent of that grain is fed directly to animals to provide animal protein in the form of beef and ham and veal. Excluding dairy cattle, in 1968 twenty million tons of edible plant protein were fed to domestic animals in the United States, of which a portion ended up on the dinner-table at a huge protein loss. In fact it has been calculated that if this grain were used directly, the protein saved would have provided 90 per cent of the yearly global protein deficit at that time.[9] As Lyle P. Schertz has put it, 'the billion people in the developed countries use practically as much cereals as feed to produce animal protein as the two billion people in the developing countries use directly as food'.[10] The situation is made worse by the fact that beef cattle are fed for their fat, most of which is then thrown away. Or rather it is exported back to the developing countries as inedible grease in return for edible plant protein or edible fish protein which is then fed to cattle to continue the vicious circle.

The more one investigates this quagmire of waste, the deeper one sinks. To provide the huge output of meat which the West now thinks it requires, it exploits not only the Third World but its own land as well. Pressures on productivity are so acute that over-grazing and over-ploughing are common, with the result that, according to Georg Borgstrom, the United States has now lost one quarter of the top soil it had when the prairies were first ploughed.[11] The savage rape of the land that is now carried out in the name of farming makes a sharp contrast with that of the primitive swidden farmer, whose exuberance in burning down one-third of an acre of forest per man every year, to allow it to grow again after two years, has been attacked as wasteful by our own agriculturalists. Yet the primitive was far nearer a stable and ecologically viable situation than we are. Without so much as the help of an acid indicator kit, he could distinguish ten basic and thirty derivative soil and mineral categories.[12] Today's farmer merely calls in the nearest fertilizer firm to advise him on how much energy-intensive chemicals he should apply this year. And most years the figure quoted is higher than in the previous one.

In fact, this waste is greatest of all when the energy balance is considered. Today the energy input to food production is enormous. Energy is used in making fertilizer; in producing pesticides and herbicides; in fuelling tractors, combine harvesters, drying machines, hedge croppers, ditch diggers, and a thousand other tasks. As a result our productivity has gone up, and to many it appears that we have learned how to use the sun's productivity more efficiently. 'This', writes the ecologist Howard T. Odum, 'is a sad hoax, for industrial man no longer eats potatoes made from solar energy; now he eats potatoes partly made of oil.'[13]

Perhaps there would be little to criticize in this if our energy sources were more carefully chosen than they are. But they still consist mostly of fossil fuel ripped from the Earth's belly with careless cuts, which never heal and which sink deeper every year towards the bottom of a barrel which is already beginning to show. Soon there may be little more where the last lot came from. What then? Odum writes:

> The citizen in the industrialized country thinks he can look down upon the system of man, animals, and subsistence agriculture that provides some living from an acre or two in India when the monsoon rains are favourable. Yet if fossil and nuclear fuels were cut off, we would have to recruit farmers from India and other underdeveloped countries to show the now affluent citizens how to survive on the land while the population was being reduced a hundredfold to make it possible.[14]

Such an idea is not as extraordinary as it may sound. With – until now – access to all the energy it needs, Western agriculture has been slowly but surely turned into a vast industrial business, where profit and loss rule the working day and the planting schedule. We have forgotten that agriculture is basically a means of growing food, utilizing the free energy of the sun. Now that our other energy sources feature so much more importantly in the agricultural equation, there are those who argue that we should forget agriculture altogether. Food – or perhaps it would be better called nutrition – could be grown in factories where the sun never entered because its energy would be replaced by the giant output of a nuclear reactor. If, in the future, such a system becomes more profitable, it may well be adopted; and soon after agriculture would be relegated to the folk museum, along with such antique crafts as cobbling, weaving and smithying.

Any subsequent crisis in energy supply would, of course, then affect much more than the production of automobiles. We would have to learn again, and quickly, the ancient art of farming, with imported instructors who had been lucky, or unlucky, enough not to have had the chance to go nuclear. Even today, such advice might be highly interesting. No doubt a primitive farmer who surveyed our own agricultural practices, and the international trade system on which they were based, would see immediately how we managed such an enormous productivity yet produced so many hungry people.[15] Like Francis Moore Lappé in her *Diets for a Small Planet*, he would direct our attention away from animals and back towards the plants that make so much more efficient use of both land and sun. He would puzzle over the system we had invented for helping the hungry countries, which consists essentially in importing their higher quality proteins and paying for them by returning lower quality proteins. But in the end he would probably single out one very practical guide to the future. 'Stop trying to grow money', he would advise, 'and start trying to grow food.'

3 More Than One Kind of Medicine

One of our most firmly held beliefs is that Western society is fast on the way, in the words of Harvey Brooks, 'to the final conquest of human disease'. In the new millennium that is to come, man will finally be freed from the burden of illness under which he toils. He will die, if at all, from sheer senility; and in passing quietly and with dignity from this life to the next will thus be able to acclaim the final triumph of our technical society. In an alternative interpretation of the myth, death itself will be eliminated, the world population stabilized and birth, childhood and adolescence done away with. The human being—if such he could then be called—will presumably pass his time with 500-year job contracts, living in all the various regions of the Earth in turn to savour the diversity which his new longevity will give him. And so literally is this myth taken in the United States that a number of new 'cryogenic' societies there are now planning to commit the bodies of their members to the deep freeze when they die so that they may be 'revitalized' at some future time when science has finally found the secret of immortality.

It does not need exceptional insight to see that a world without disease, even if desirable, is extremely unlikely. Modern medicine has produced spectacular cures, but they are of much more limited applicability than we generally care to admit. Antibiotics, which can more or less eliminate the chance of death from bacterial infections, have been the greatest triumph. But just as death from those infections has become rare, death in our society from heart disease, from cancer, from thrombosis and from accidents has become not merely common but 'normal'. Against such complaints we still have no protection, and as much is revealed by what to many is a startling medical statistic: life expectancy for a man aged sixty is the same today as it was a hundred years ago. If we ever do find cures for the new afflictions of modern man, it is certain that other ones will be revealed to take their place. Men will continue to die from disease either because their medical ingenuity finally fails them or because, when the cards are down, they begin to count the medical cost too high (as those with kidney disease already know).

Seen in this light, the saying that primitive man was also a diseased man does not shed very much light. All men die, all men die from disease (or accident), and all men die only once. The difference, we have been taught to believe, is that today men live longer and their lives are freer from pain and disease than was formerly the case. It is as well to examine this idea with some care for though in some general sense it is largely true, in many more specific ways its implications are false. To do this we shall have to investigate the health of primitive populations – a much neglected area of research; we shall have to take into account the effects of the population explosion from which we, but not our primitive ancestors, suffer so acutely; we shall have to ask how the aged of our population are allowed to spend the extra years allotted to them; and finally we must ponder on the question of values. If it be granted that modern medicine has proved able to extend life far longer than seemed possible to earlier generations, what advantage does that confer? Is the aim really eternity? Can anyone conceive a life without end and, once the idea has been grasped, does not the idea seem horrifying? We hear much of parameters in modern science, and the parameters of life are birth and death. Without the one, life is impossible; without the other, it is meaningless. 'All men are mortal. Socrates is a man; therefore Socrates is mortal.' So runs the schoolboy syllogism. But the truth is there. A part of our humanity is that we die. If we try to visualize a world where medicine or any other agency had made immortality possible, does anyone doubt that Socrates, rather than being a shining reminder of human devotion to principle and a fire to warm the lives of those who came after him, would be an old and tedious man? The young American genetics researcher, John Beckwith, put the question pithily; 'What benefit is a cure for cancer to man if in the process he loses his humanity?'[2] The humanity which is the subject of this book, and the humanity that all men want to fulfil for themselves, is an equation of which one of the invariables is death.

At first glance life in a primitive society—without qualified doctors, dentists, modern drugs or anaesthetics—seems to us insupportable. But to get any real idea of what that existence could have meant, we have to dispose of some false ideas. Probably no society at any time existed without some form of medical treatment. So accustomed are we to the idea of Western medicine that we tend to dismiss out of hand any claim that any other form of treatment can ever be anything but medical quackery. Quackery exists, to be sure, but that primitive medical remedies were also sometimes effective is equally certain. The doctors of ancient India, for example, listed more than fifteen hundred herbs which they used in therapy. How many had a beneficial physiological— as distinct from psychological—effect remains unknown. But there are plenty of suggestive examples: from such herbs came digitalis for heart treatment, quinine for malaria, citrus fruit for scurvy, and ephedrine for asthma. In ancient India rauwolfia was used as the potent tranquillizer it is and for the treatment of high blood pressure.

If a count were to be made of all the herbs that have been used for medical purposes in primitive society, the tally would reach several hundred thousand. Today numerous research programmes are under way to assess the efficacy of these remedies in Western terms. We can only regret that a full answer will probably never be forthcoming—the subject area is too large and we have left it too late ever to gain a complete understanding. But what is clear is that primitive medical systems were often as detailed and complicated as is our own. The primitive did not believe in the magical cure-all property of one or two selected plants—as do the medical quacks of the Western market stalls. An example from Siberia makes the point clearer. Primitive tribes there used spiders and whiteworms as cures for sterility; squashed cockroach for abscesses; pike's gall for eye complaints; nasal insufflation of the powder of a mummified woodpecker for high fever; and, among the Siberian Bouriate, the flesh of bears was used for seven specific illnesses, the blood for five, the fat for nine and the brains for twelve.[3] Now the point here is not that all these remedies were necessarily effective; it is rather that these Siberian societies— and others in Africa and the Americas—took their medicine extremely seriously. The systematic way in which they classified and organized rivalled and sometimes exceeded ours in its sheer complexity.

Another distinguishing feature of primitive medicine was that it did not rely solely on physiological effect. For the primitive, a psychological approach to medicine was imperative. And here we touch on one of the raw nerves of Western medicine. Few of our doctors would deny that the psychological aspects of therapy are in some poorly understood way of crucial significance. Yet so far we have completely failed to put our finger on what precisely the problem or the solution is. Meanwhile we are fast on the way to eliminating those few aspects of psychological comfort which were formerly a part of Western treatment: the general practitioner disappears and is replaced by the collective, the sterile atmosphere of large hospital reception centres and, ultimately, by the prospect of computer diagnosis by telephone. As each technical advance is chalked up, questions as to the efficacy of mechanical medicine grow stronger. As China enters the United Nations system, we are forced to believe at last in the efficacy of a different system of medicine, based on the placing of small needles under the skin and known as acupuncture. We now know that operations are performed in China using these needles as the only anaesthetic and that the patients remain throughout the operation happy and relaxed—and conscious. We know that the most effective 'cure' for smoking is hypnosis and that the only hope of speedily improving a paralysing back-ache is to sidestep the Western medical system and slip unnoticed into the soothing care of those masseurs whose treatment is effective but whose methods are still far from official recognition.

The primitive world is rich in suggestive parallels. Traditionally, the witch-doctor's powers are vested at least equally in the chemical and the psychological. No cure is ever effected without ritual; and usually the process is long, frequently involving the use of trance, narcotic drugs, self-induced hysteria, deep meditation and a range of very non-Western states of mind. Only now, it seems, is it beginning to be feasible to regard all this as anything more than mere buffoonery. One specific reason for this centres on what in the West is called the autonomic nervous system.

It has been a classic assumption of Western medicine that man has two different kinds of relations with his body. One is the conscious control he can exert over the skeletal muscles. Through the cerebro-spinal nervous system, a human being can command, through a complicated series of nerve connections, his arms to move, his feet to walk, his mouth to open. The second concerns the whole range of other bodily functions — blood pressure, heart rate, the rhythm of waves in the brain and the operation of the glandular system — governed by the autonomic nervous system. These, it was long believed, cannot be manipulated at will. We now know that this dichotomy between conscious and involuntary bodily functions is false. Experiments have shown beyond doubt that the trance-like states of those who practise Yoga and other forms of meditation are as much physiological as they are psychological. Hard scientific evidence is fast accumulating that in these states their practitioners can exert conscious control over such things as visceral and glandular activity, rate of heartbeat and level of blood pressure. Indeed, without meditation, rats have now been trained in such exotic arts as changing the frequency of intestinal contractions, the amount of blood flowing through the stomach wall, the tail and the ear, and even the filtration rate of the kidneys. At Rockefeller University in New York one thirty-three-year-old woman with high blood pressure has been taught to change her blood pressure at will by as much as 25 millimetres of mercury.[4]

In the West this new field of study is generating great excitement. The prospect is being opened up of an alternative type of 'mental medicine'. The vast range of psychosomatic diseases known to Western man — all those diseases which produce bodily reactions as a result of psychological causes — are now being interpreted as cases where patients have learnt at least some partial control over their autonomic nervous systems. The prospect is that mental medicine might be used as a cure in all these cases as well as in high blood pressure, asthma, spastic colitis, ulcer and cardiac difficulties – to mention only a selection.

The general connection between all this and the primitive stress on altered states of mind during medical treatment is obvious enough, even if the specific details still elude us. That the psychology of medicine involves more than bedside manner is now beyond dispute, and that primitive ritual may enable a patient to achieve conscious control of some function that is normally uncontrollable has become a respectable hypothesis.

The anthropologist Gilges, describing a witch-doctor in Northern Rhodesia, wrote: 'How far he was a herbalist and how far a witch-doctor I could never fathom, but I regret that I shall never possess his knowledge of African psychology and his art in the treatment of his fellow men, that, coupled with my scientific medical knowledge, might have made a most useful combination.'[5] Gilges was referring here to practices other than those which may lead to control of the autonomic nervous system. As in so many other areas, medicine to primitive people was not solely concerned with its subject matter. Medical practices are hard, if not impossible, to disentangle from ritual, social and political customs which unite every aspect of primitive behaviour into a whole which defies partial analysis. Though for us different techniques exist to deal with physical illness, social malaise and psychological disturbances, we would expect to find these treatments welded into one in primitive society. And so we do, as the following example from the African Ndembu illustrates.

The story is told by V. W. Turner of a patient complaining of weakness, palpitations and back pains. He was convinced, too, that the other villagers bore him a grudge, and had withdrawn from all social life. The doctor began his treatment by talking over the history of the village, the patient's grievances and those of the other villagers; in this activity everyone was invited to participate. Finally, and after a lengthy time, the doctor drew blood from the patient and, according to custom, drew with it the offending 'tooth' which had caused all the trouble. With the release of blood, everyone gathered joyfully round to congratulate the fainting patient on his recovery.[6] Here, in the words of Mary Douglas, is

> a case of skilful group therapy. The back-biting and envy of the villagers, symbolized by the tooth in the sick man's body, was dissolved in a wave of enthusiasm and solidarity. As he was cured of his physical symptoms they were all cured of social malaise. These symbols worked at the psychosomatic level for the central figure, the sick man, and at the general psychological level for the villagers, in changing their attitudes, and at the sociological level in so far as the pattern of social status in the village was formally altered and in so far as some people moved in and others moved away as a result of the treatment.[7]

Such an approach appears more interesting now than it might have done a few years ago. For today in the West the fashion has swung markedly in favour of group therapy. New treatment centres, for the physically ill as well as the 'alienated' or 'maladjusted', are springing up in many countries. There the treatment is communal, uninhibited discussion of the most personal aspects of the patients' lives is encouraged in front of the whole community, and modes of behaviour are tolerated which are quite different from those that normally prevail. But however aggressively modern this approach may seem, it is as well to remember that it has always formed the essence of primitive medicine. The only surprise, perhaps, is that in our obsessive search for a 'chemical fix' for every ailment, we should have forgotten the therapeutic value of human intercourse and public humility. The witchdoctor's ritual does indeed fail to work miracles; but it may work cures, and it does so in a human and understandable way.

Turning from therapy to disease, almost as many cultural shocks are in store. The unexamined assumption that the burden of disease from which we suffer today was also the incurable lot of the primitive can already be relegated to the realm of historical mythology. If it be claimed that the evidence of our eyes belies this, we must remember that the pathetic fate which is now the lot of those few surviving primitives is far from their historical condition. Today the stories that come back from the Amazonian jungles are those of horrifying epidemics of measles, smallpox and influenza which sweep the few pre-literate socities remaining with a speed and viciousness unknown in the West. Paradoxically, that this is so merely confirms that the diseases exported by civilized man were once unknown in other regions of the world. And in North America, the distribution of smallpox-infected blankets as 'presents' to eighteenth-century Indian chiefs records a form of genocide which our own biological warfare experts have only recently been able to improve on.

More specifically, we know that measles, mumps, chicken-pox, scarlet fever, smallpox, whooping cough, diphtheria and many other viral and bacterial diseases were unknown until the invention of the city. Only then did men congregate in sufficient density to become the obvious target population for infective hosts. Of course, the organisms that cause these diseases have probably always existed — even if in different forms. But until man proved himself the dominant species, asserting his presence in concentrations previously unknown in nature, such infectious organisms had a difficult time in making their living off human material. Other species were to be found in greater concentration and it was they that became the natural focus of the micro-organisms' attention. The classic example is malaria and in a striking piece of research in the 1950s the American scientist Dr F. B. Livingstone was able to determine that in West Africa, at least, malaria was unknown until the invention of agriculture.[8] The need for irrigation that soon followed created large areas of stagnant water. This provided a favourable environment for the malarial mosquito which, in its turn, was forced to adapt to living off human blood as man was the most abundant of the mammals living in the near neighbourhood. From that event much else stemmed. Malaria became the number one disease of most tropical or semi-tropical areas, caused the death of hundreds of millions of human beings and gave rise, at least partially, to the modern necessity of D.D.T. From there it was a short step to the range of ecological contaminations that has since engulfed us.

This does not mean, of course, that primitive man was disease-free. We do know, however, that the range of primitive disease was substantially smaller than is ours. Further, the diseases that did exist — at least the infectious ones — usually produced a less devastating effect than they did in our own society until a few decades ago. Surely one of the greatest medical advantages of primitive society lay in the habit of nomadism, which so greatly reduced the chance of man fouling his own nest. Where today man has to pay meticulous attention to his own sewage system, the role of sewage in a nomadic society was as fertilizer for ground to which the tribe would return only much later when all chance of infection had disappeared.

If agriculture is ecologically connected with a diversification of disease, the new foods it soon made available are even more so. We do not need to dwell here on the now universally known connection between white sugar and dental decay. As sugar was exported with the Western way of life, it proved an irresistible attraction to the primitive. Again, though dental disease was not unknown in primitive society, a full set of healthy teeth even in old age was to be expected. In our society such a phenomenon is almost unknown. And along with sugar went a whole range of new customs: over-eating, freedom from physical work, social stress and great emphasis on cholesterol-rich animal foods. Rather than generalize on the overall impact of these Western modes, it may be more compelling to present actual data from one of the few strictly scientific comparative studies that have been made.

The studies concern two islands in the Pacific — Rarotonga and Pukapuka. There Dr Ian Prior, the director of the Medical Unit of the Wellington Hospital in New Zealand, was able to compare life and health in the relatively Westernized Rarotonga — which operates a cash economy with average incomes of $150 to $200 a year — with the largely primitive existence on Pukapuka, where the inhabitants earn no more than $30 a year. Dr Prior writes:

The difference in health between the two groups of islanders is quite fascinating, though not entirely unexpected. If it is not unexpected, it is purely because of data collected from other islands in the Pacific like New Guinea where the natives are still leading their simple, primitive lives and are almost totally free of the afflictions that are most significant in urban, industrial societies. And the natives from such islands are neither malnourished nor die too young to manifest the degenerative diseases. Quite the contrary.[9]

The Rarotongans suffered from much the same level of cardiovascular and metabolic diseases that we do. The Pukapukans were virtually free of vascular disease. In the first island 30 per cent of the men and 25 per cent of the women were grossly overweight and 21 per cent of the men and 36 per cent of the women had high blood pressure. On Pukapuka only 1 man in 379 and 2·2 per cent of the women were grossly overweight; only 2 per cent of the men and 4·4 per cent of the women had high blood pressure. Dr Prior suggests that these differences stem directly from the more active life of Pukapukans, from their different diet and particularly from their much lower level of salt intake which seem to protect them from high blood pressure.

The idea that bad food leads to degenerative disease has swept the West like wildfire in the past few years. Health food shops and restaurants make their owners small fortunes, ultimately by claiming that such civilized commodities as refined sugar and white flour lead not only to obesity, dental caries and diabetes but also to thrombosis, peptic ulcer, constipation, varicose veins and even piles. On balance, the facts support their claims, leaving us to ponder the absurdity that much of the West's incredibly complicated and costly medical services have arisen largely to treat those diseases which are produced by the Western way of life. One may well wonder whether our medicine is more of a technical triumph than an extremely vicious circle.

Part of the disease-ridden image of the primitive may stem less from facts than from observance of social customs which appear revolting to the Western eye. Thus a Tikopian baby, writes

Dorothy Lee, 'will get premasticated food, warmed with the mother's body warmth and partly digested through her salivary iuices; his mother will put it directly to his mouth with her lips.'[10] An Eskimo woman will wash her hair and her dishes in fresh urine; an Eskimo man, in a kind of Arctic sauna, will urinate on to the back of the man next in line to generate steam—and when ingesting the narcotic fly agaric, Siberian Chutkees will even drink the urine of the next in line to spread a limited amount of the drug round a large circle of friends (much of the active constituent has been found to pass rapidly through the body without undergoing chemical reaction). Most tribes will allow small children to play on the ground, even when it is littered with animal dung, or to suckle at extremely dirty mothers' breasts, breasts which are sometimes used to provide not only babies with milk but also some of the smaller domestic animals. In short, primitive customs relating to food, dirt and excrement exhibit value systems much different from ours; those we have mentioned do not include some of the most powerful taboos of Western society—but others have far stricter taboos than we do.

Some of our obsessions, of course, do far more harm than good. One recent fad—the vaginal deodorant—has heaven knows what psychological effect on the female and is medically valueless. Were we able to compute all the various ways in which the manufacture of such absurdities further weakens our unsteady relationship with the Earth's limited supplies of energy and raw materials, we would certainly find their overall effect on human health was negative. And equally, some of what appear to us to be the most unhygienic habits of the primitive have very positive effects on well-being. As an example, the gamma globulin levels—which give a rough indication of ability to fight off infections from foreign organisms—have been found in the Xavante and Yanomama tribes of South America to be approximately twice as high as the average in civilized populations.[11] These levels undoubtedly result from the practice in both these tribes of allowing even very young infants exposure to all manner of dirt; in effect, the net result is something akin to the results of our extensive vaccination programme.

We would do well to remember, then, that completely sterile conditions are seldom the answer to human health and may in some circumstances lead to dangerous results. Those who claim to be able to kill '99 per cent of known houshold germs' would undoubtedly wreak considerable damage if their products were ever used to do exactly that. Germs are vital to life, even human life, and our digestion, our mastication and our skin health could not survive without them. Health comes not from eliminating germs but from learning how best to live with them. As one of the pithiest poets in the English language has put it

Adam
Had 'em

and it does no disrespect to the primitive to learn that Adam passed his legacy on to succeeding generations.

This he most certainly did. But the result was clearly very far from the popular impression of rampant disease among the primitives which still thrives. In the next chapter we shall see in more detail how healthy primitive man really was, and it will be as well to bear in mind the conclusion of an anthropologist, Professor Neel, who has spent many years in studying the health of South American Indians:

If measles, pertussis and malaria are relatively recent introductions to the Xavantes, in spite of which they maintain very good health, then one is forced to ascribe to 'untouched' primitive man a very high level of physical fitness and resistance indeed ... Our thinking about the health of primitive man has been influenced too much by the observations of medical missionaries and civilian administrators on demoralized and crowded agriculturalists and pastoralists.[12]

4 Population and Population Control

Even if we acknowledge that primitive medicine was sometimes ingenious, often efficacious and psychologically beneficial, that the range of possible disease was smaller, the type of food and way of life more healthy, and that apparently unhygienic practices conferred on the primitive some special types of immunity, we have still avoided the most important question to Western eyes. For our own medicine is dedicated not to creating a happy and fulfilling life but to extending its length for the maximum possible period. We have come to believe that life expectancy — the average number of years a new-born baby can expect to live — is the only medical parameter of importance. But while other parameters are clearly of equal or greater importance, it will not do to dodge the question: did primitive man, or Western man, live the longest?

To answer it, we shall have to define our terms more carefully. In the West life expectancy has risen from thirty or forty years a century or so ago to between sixty-five and seventy years of age today. The historical record shows a rapid growth in life expectancy over the centuries and the implication is clearly that in primitive society life expectancy was even smaller than it was, say, in the Middle Ages in Europe. Unfortunately, because the estimation of life expectancy requires many detailed records of birth and death over long periods of time, there is little direct primitive data on which we can draw. We should note, however, that a population with a life expectancy of, say, thirty is not a society without middle-aged or even old people. Thirty is not the age at which the average member of the population dies. Such a statistic reflects the fact that infant mortality — particularly at birth and in the first one or two years of life — was very heavy. But those that survived their traumatic first few years may well have lived as long as we do. In the survey of the :Kung Bushmen of the Kalahari desert reported by Dr R. B. Lee,[1] it was found that 46 out of a population of 466 Bushmen were over sixty years of age and that one individual was estimated to be between seventy-nine and eighty-five years old. This compares well with our society, where the eighty-year-olds are few and far between and where even those over sixty do not comprise more than between 10 and 14 per cent. Surveys among the Australian Aboriginals have shown that the fifty-year-olds made up a relatively large segment of the population. The evidence is quite strong that this was a general phenomenon in primitive populations.

Indeed, there are many popular accounts of primitive or rural communities which habitually live to a ripe old age. The most famous are the Georgian centenarians, but a less well known group in Ecuador is more remarkable still. There, high up in the Andean valley of Vilcabamba, is to be found a certain José David whose birth date is apparently authentically recorded as 1840. At one hundred and forty-five David has a number of almost equally aged colleagues. In fact more than 17 per cent of the rural population there is over sixty; 28 are over eighty-five, 16 over ninety, 9 over a hundred, 4 over a hundred and ten and 3 over a hundred and twenty (out of a total of 819 people).

The locality is warm and peaceful, and its inhabitants largely vegetarian. Dr David Davies who has studied these people writes:

> Indeed, it is this tranquillity that is regarded by doctors who have visited the valley and studied the people, as the cause of their great ages. It is also worth mentioning that few of the inhabitants have been to the capital, Loja, some 52 kilometres away. Hypertension, heart disease, and cancer are comparatively uncommon. Death is usually the result of an accident, or of catching influenza from the few outsiders who visit the place.[2]

The lack of cancer is particularly surprising, for not only do the inhabitants regularly drink from two to four cups of rum each day but they also smoke between forty and sixty cigarettes daily. 'But', adds Dr Davies, 'the rum is unrefined and the cigarettes are home-made, usually from tobacco grown in their gardens, and wrapped in maize leaves (though toilet paper is preferred if available).'

Although the primitive may have lived to a ripe old age far more commonly than we have assumed, this does not mean his population statistics could compare with ours. For a real comparison a graph plotting the percentage of the population surviving in each decade of life is needed. Such 'life curves' are almost unknown for primitive societies, but one has been prepared by a team of anthropologists for the Yanomama tribe living in Venezuela and Brazil. Though the population did not achieve the average longevity of a Western society, the life curve was substantially superior to that of Indians in the year 1900. 'One way to view these curves', writes James V. Neel, 'is that the advent of civilization dealt a blow to man's health from which he is only now recovering.'[3]

Such a conclusion is supported by others. Thus even John Bleakley, Chief Protector of Aborigines in Queensland from 1914 to 1942 and a man to whom the advantages of civilization were quite obvious, was forced to admit:

> Civilization has brought to the [Torres Strait] Islanders many material benefits such as wealth, business prosperity, improved living conditions and standards, but unfortunately, these have been won at the cost of serious health deterioration.[4]

All this leaves us with a puzzle. Surveys from the field show more and more frequently that primitive populations are often found in generally good health and that disease is not the principal factor in keeping the population size in check. How is it then that primitive populations, without exception (or we would see the results today), did not suffer from the explosion of population numbers which threatens contemporary society? There can only be two possible explanations: either that enormous numbers of infants died in all these societies; or that social or biological factors were at work which cut down the average number of children born to each woman. We shall examine these ideas in turn, for they both contributed to the phenomenon of the primitive's population stability.

First, a higher infant mortality was undoubtedly the price the primitive paid for his way of life. Western medicine has since brought infant mortality rates tumbling down; this, and virtually this alone, has been responsible for our own population explosion. But there is a paradox here, for the primitive clearly did not regard high infant mortality as a 'price'. On the contrary, the natural rate of infant mortality was not considered sufficiently high in the primitive world, for almost every tribe practised infanticide. Sometimes, to be sure, new-born babies were killed only during exceptionally hard times or if they were clearly deformed at birth (one of the more admirable and universal primitive customs was to refuse the right of any crippled baby to live). But in other societies 20 or even 30 per cent of new babies were killed at birth, regardless of the prevailing conditions or their state of physical health. The advantage to the primitive is obvious enough; this practice freed him from all the problems of a grow-ing society demanding an ever higher share of the natural resources to be found in the environment.

Yet such a practice demarcates primitive from civilized life more clearly than any other. For us, infanticide is the grossest of crimes. The fact that in most primitive groups the decision to kill a baby was taken directly by the mother or father rather than the society at large, and that often the mother was somehow adapted to recognizing the child as her own, not at the time of the birth but at the time of the decision to let the new arrival live, only compounds the inhumanity of the situation. So in making any attempt at an apologia for infanticide one has to tread warily indeed. What follows is not intended as an argument that we would best solve our population problems by similar methods; but it is intended to stress that the practice of infanticide has had beneficial results and that, as far as the question of humaneness is concerned, we ourselves indulge in far more cruel actions.

The anthropologist Raymond Firth writes:

... just as in a civilized community in time of war (sic), civil disturbance or action against crime, life is taken to preserve life, so in Tikopia infants just born might be allowed to have their faces turned down, and to be debarred from the world they have merely glimpsed, in order that the economic equilibrium might be preserved, and the society maintain its balanced existence.[5]

Nor, of course, is the problem of maintaining equilibrium only an abstract one. In our own efforts to improve the world we have considerably worsened the situation: nearly half of all the deaths that occur in the world today are those of small children in Asia, Africa and Latin America whose resistance to disease has been so undermined by malnutrition that they have never known good health. Their deaths are more agonizing, their departures more deeply mourned, their sacrifice far greater than any of those other new-born babies whose faces were 'turned down' in primitive society.

At the other end of the scale, we should also ask questions about the state of health of some of the aged in our society who are kept alive by modern medicine. Professor Garrett Hardin of the University of California writes:

> There are at this moment quite literally tens of thousands of (legal) human beings in the United States whom the mythical man-from-Mars would probably classify as vegetables if he saw them ... I do not exaggerate. The caretakers who tend these creatures cynically speak of 'watering the vegetables', and so, too, would you if you took care of them. But you don't. You don't tend to them. You don't see them. And, except possibly for a few seconds a year, you don't even know that these vegetables exist ... The present system is tolerated because we shield ourselves from the knowledge of what is being done. We hide the vegetables away from sight, and hire people who can get no better jobs to do what we are unwilling to do; then we hide the costs of paying these people in other budgets so we scarcely know that we've hired them.[6]

Compare the lot of the aged in primitive society. Dr Lee writes of the :Kung Bushmen:

The aged hold a respected position in Bushmen society and are the effective leaders of the camps. Senilicide is extremely rare. Long after their productive years have passed the old people are fed and cared for by their children and grandchildren. The blind, the senile and the crippled are respected for the special ritual and technical skills they possess.[7]

And generally, in all pre-literate societies, the aged are the only ones who have the time to learn the contents of the whole culture by word of mouth. The short cut of books is not available and hence the elders become, not vegetables, but in effect the libraries and librarians of the society.

Fortunately, perhaps, we need not make too literal a comparison of the relative inhumanities of infanticide and our own cultural equivalents. For all the evidence now indicates that infant mortality—whether through infanticide or not—was not the most important means of population control. In one still primitive tribe in Brazil a medical study has shown that 16 per cent of those born healthy fail to survive to the age of fifteen.[8] This, of course, is a high figure compared to ours in the West. But in acculturated Brazilian Indians in general the comparable figure is 41 per cent[9] and their population increases fast in spite of this. Yet a tribe with only a 16 per cent rate—what demographers call an 'intermediate rate' of infant mortality—continues to stabilize its population. Clearly some powerful techniques of population control are at work here.

In this the primitive was considerably more experimental than are we for the techniques he used were far more diverse. Not only did they probably include all the physical methods of contraception known to us but they used a huge variety of social customs as well. But as the very idea of population control is today more or less synonymous with contraception, we should begin with the physical techniques.

A study of primitive custom makes it quite clear that the condom had a much earlier history than is suggested by the fact that Dr Condom, a physician of Charles II's court, is attributed with the invention of this device. The Bush Negroes of Dutch Guiana, for instance, used a five-inch long okra-like seed-pod, with one end cut off, for much the same purpose. The fact that it was the women who inserted this device into the vagina, rather than the men who actually wore it, does not change the mechanical principle of the device. Nearly all primitive societies had magical herbs and rites said to prevent conception but except in a few cases we now have no means of knowing whether they were useless or effective. In some Central African tribes women plugged their vaginas with rags or finely chopped grass. Cherokee Indian women chew and swallow the musquash root for four consecutive days. And some Guianan tribes douche with a solution of lemon juice and juice from the mahogany nut. Doubtless this did have some effect, for the acid has been shown to have a spermicidal action. The Acheh women of Sumatra used a black pill-like object to place in the vagina and this substance has also been shown to have some effect, from the tannic acid it has been found to contain. The literature is full of descriptions of the various other devices which primitive women used to block the entrance to the uterus and doubtless some of those were effective, particularly the ones that depended on the use of sponge-like substances. Coitus interruptus, too, has been widely used in primitive society and the Australian aboriginal invented a rather traumatic if permanent solution to this problem by making a 'sub-incision' in the penis during initiation rites through which the semen escapes without entering the vagina (some of it, at any rate). Finally, at the risk of irrelevancy, one cannot resist quoting Casanova, who was concerned about these matters. In his day condoms were made from animal membranes and he remarks, 'I do not care to shut myself up in a piece of dead skin to prove that I am perfectly alive.' Instead he offered his women the empty half of a lemon to insert in their vaginas as an early forerunner of the diaphragm; the combination of acid and physical obstruction may well have been functional.

Such devices must have greatly helped the primitive in his search for population stability. But when we realize how much more efficient our own devices must be and yet how large is the rate of population growth even in countries where contraception is regularly practised, other forms of population control must have been much more effective. Professor Neel's surveys in South America have shown the average interval between births in a number of primitive tribes to be between four and five years[10] — implying the average woman gave birth to five or at most six children during her reproductive life. If even this seems high in comparison with our society, we have to remember that infant mortality was higher than ours. And in contrast with other societies, the figure is remarkably low. Thus the Hitterites averaged nine births per woman and agricultural economies such as those of East Pakistan and Ghana record figures of 6·5 and 7 respectively.[11] Furthermore, the South American tribes marry young — usually as soon as reproduction is physiologically feasible — and nearly all their women produce children. In the Xavante study, for example, only 1 woman out of 195 over the age of twenty had not borne at least one child. In the United States, by contrast, between 20 and 25 per cent of the female population never produce.[12]

In many primitive societies, a four- or five-year gap between children was common and, for nomads, it was essential, as no mother could carry more than one child. Often, the aim, as among the Tapirapé of Central Brazil, of one woman to have three live children but no more, is not only deducible from the statistics but is part of the philosophy of the tribe.[13] To this end, as in our society, abortion was widely practised and was brought about by both the use of herbal medicines and physical trauma.

Most of the other techniques practised were social rather than physical. Thus the practice of levying a bride price from prospective grooms often had a delaying effect on marriage; modern demographic studies have shown that probably the most effective means of lowering the rate of population growth is to increase the age of marriage. In primitive society, this custom had the additional effect of pairing young girls with older, and therefore richer, men. As a result, the couple's fertility may have decreased if the man died before the woman reached menopause or if the end of his own reproductive ability came sooner.

In primitive cultures, too, women tended to do harder physical labour than today. Modern socio-medical studies have shown a strong connection between the rates of miscarriage, still births and defective births and the stress of the social environment. But so far, women's liberation movements have chosen not to stress this additional 'advantage' of job equality. Another of the more unpleasant population control devices was the practice of circumcision and other mutilations at the time of initiation; while these operations were obviously not intended primarily as devices for ritualized murder, it is clear from the records that they were accompanied by a small but significant mortality rate due to complications setting in after the operation.

A much less gruesome approach may have had to do with the sleeping habits of primitive populations. The idea that a man should sleep in the same bed as his wife all night and every night of the year is Western. The habit has not been universally shared by other societies. In a study made by Dr John W. M. Whiting, it was found that in only 28 out of a total of 136 societies studied did the mother and father sleep together and the children separately. But in 68 mother and child slept together and banished the husband; in 21 the whole family slept together in one bed; and in 19 mother, father and child all slept separately. The immediate reason for this is probably connected with temperature. At least, Dr Whiting found that in societies where the temperature falls below 50 °F in the winter, parents generally slept together but where the climate was warm or mild mother and father slept separately.[14] There are no data to prove it, but it does not need much imagination to see that such a cultural practice would inevitably tend to lower the birth-rate.

It seems doubtful, however, whether any of these devices were as efficient as the customs that surround a woman's life in primitive society for three or four years after birth. First, in nearly all primitive societies babies were breast-fed for between six months and a year. In many of them, this habit extended to the end of the second year. And in some, the child was not properly weaned before the age of four or even five. Now there is an old wives' tale that a woman cannot conceive again while she is still nursing a child. It is untrue—as a great many Western women have found to their cost. But what may be true—and Western medicine has found itself unable to pronounce on the matter—is that there is a statistical effect. In other words, while the individual may well conceive during nursing, a population of nursing women will conceive less often than one which is not nursing. If that is the case, prolonged breast-feeding could go quite some way towards explaining the four- or five-year interval between births that has been recorded for primitive society.

There are certainly other factors. Of these, the most important are the varied forms of taboo on intercourse that surround every ritual and every birth. Men must abstain in many primitive societies before, during and shortly after war, before feasts and always for a period after his wife has given birth. For more purely physiological reasons, we practise a similar taboo for two or three months, but in primitive society the taboo could be for as long as two years. And very often the length of the taboo corresponds exactly to the time during which the mother is still nursing the child. As the Hausa put it:

A mother should not go to her husband while she has a child she is suckling. If she does, the child gets thin, he dries up, he won't be strong, he won't be healthy ... If she only sleeps with her husband and does not become pregnant, it will not hurt the child, it will not spoil her milk. But if another child enters in, her milk will make the first one ill.[15]

Of course, the Hausa may well be quite literally right; our own science has not yet revealed whether pregnancy has an adverse effect on the quality of a mother's milk (and as breast-feeding is limited to six months in the West it is not that likely to be able to reach a verdict). It is therefore of extraordinary interest that Dr Whiting has found that societies with low protein diets are much more likely to have long taboos on intercourse after birth than are societies where protein is abundant. Generally, as protein becomes more available, the length of the taboo shortens.[16]

This is by no means the only example of a social custom which appears to reflect the subtle balance between population size and food supply. In the 1950s Dr J. B. Birdsell made a study of some 400 tribes of Australian Aboriginals. He found that each of these tribes averaged about five hundred people but that some tribes occupied an area of only a square mile or two, while others occupied several hundred square miles. He noticed also that the yearly rainfall varied from 5 inches in the dry areas to more than 150 in the wet ones. The implication was obvious; and when he plotted the area of tribal ground against yearly rainfall on a graph, Dr Birdsell produced the scientist's delight—an almost perfectly smooth curve. The explanation is that the amount of rainfall determines the amount of food that can be gathered from any given area. Hence the Aboriginals varied the size of their tribal sites so that each produced roughly the same quantity of food.[17]

These findings are intriguing. They suggest that the environment in fact determines the population density in each tribe. And the fact that the environment appears to do this with some rigour also means that, by definition as it were, the Aboriginals existed in a stable relationship to their environment. Dr Birdsell also found that the tribes that practised circumcision and sub-incision all came from the driest areas—in the west, from areas where the rainfall was less than 5 inches and in the east where it was less than 8 or 10 inches. Here is confirmatory evidence that these practices helped reduce the population pressure where food was scarcest, either through the contraceptive effect already mentioned or through increased mortality resulting from the operation.[18]

A mechanism of this kind, of course, operates at a subconscious level. The Aboriginals certainly do not calculate the area each tribe should occupy from the recorded rainfall; they merely acquire that knowledge as a result of practical experience. But there are plenty of instances where primitive tribes are decidedly articulate about the relationship between resources and population. Thus the Tapirapé, who have prolonged intercourse taboos, justify these by saying 'We do not want thin children' and 'They would be hungry'.[19] When pressed, they refer specifically to meat —a food which is not the staple diet but which is highly coveted and somewhat rare. Now neighbouring tribes, with much the same food supply, do not have similar taboos. So among the

Tapirapé population size is consciously controlled not through survival pressures as much as the need to provide a food which is deemed culturally very desirable. There is, in other words, just the kind of relationship here between quality of life and population size which is of so much current concern to the civilized world.

It seems likely that primitive as well as contemporary societies often control their own populations not necessarily to optimize the chance of maximum survival but for social and economic reasons connected with less elemental matters. The most coveted product of any primitive society may often be meat, which is regarded as almost a luxury. Mary Douglas has argued convincingly that it is social and economic luxuries of this kind which often determine what a population would consider its optimum level: '... it is the demand for oysters and champagne', she argues, using these Western luxuries as symbols, 'that triggers off social conventions which hold human population down.'[20]

The political message of this idea is far-reaching, for today we exhort the most impoverished groups in global society to stop breeding like rabbits. Our exhortations have little effect. Perhaps if our social and economic systems were more just, and the truly underprivileged could see some chance of gaining their fair share of oysters and champagne, our population problem would solve itself: social conventions would spring into action to optimize population in terms of goods which are now strictly out of reach of those who reproduce the fastest.

Of great relevance in this context were the habits of the Yurok Indians of Northern California, who believed that women and money were incompatible. No man could have intercourse in the house where he kept his shell money. The result, apparently, was that sex was a rarity in the winter months and that all Yurok children were born nine months after the first warm weather when love-making in the open again became possible.[21] This association between sex and wealth is actually almost universal in primitive society. Intercourse is not allowed before hunting, tapping palm wine, planting, fishing, making pottery or even during any great village crisis. Those who have previously tried to interpret this phenomenon have usually relied on deep psychology, Freud and penis envy to buttress a general theory of the type that 'women are bad for men'. Perhaps now we can be permitted to ask whether the primitive in fact recognized the obvious: that his wealth had to be shared and that sex led to more people to share it with. All the evidence suggests that the primitive knew this, that he believed it and that, unlike us, he acted on it. As Professor Neel and his colleagues have put it, there was 'a deep commitment on the part of the primitive peoples to the concept of population regulation and a degree of discipline in reproductive matters which, in proportion to the knowledge available, is notably deficient in civilized man today.'[22]

This is remarkable enough, but we can go further. There have been many definitions as to what distinguishes man from other animals. Some invoke religious creation. Others claim that tool-making or the evolution of language or man's large brain-size are the acid test. Each claim produces conflicting argument, for birds use stones as tools to open eggs, fish have a chemical language uniquely their own and Neanderthal 'man' had a larger brain than we have but is now extinct. Professor Neel suggests that we now have another candidate. Most other primates have to use their natural fertility fully to maintain their numbers. Perhaps the step to man really occurred when social organization and parental care developed so far that the naked ape first produced the ability to raise a population greater than the economy and culture could support in each succeeding generation. Population control, whether by infanticide, sex taboo or condom then became a prerequisite to survival and heralded the emergence of *Homo sapiens*.

This new definition carries a salutary implication. If our very humanity is reflected by our success in population control, we have no choice but to admit that the primitive, by whatever means, aspired to a higher level of humanity than we do today. He succeeded where we are failing

5 Primitive Man and Nature

Because the primitive's relationship with nature is what ultimately separates him from us, we should try to understand the primitive world-view in its own terms. To do so means accepting values which do not exist in any part of Western culture and, in one sense, such an attempt is bound to fail; it leads inevitably to a situation which for historical and geographical reasons is incomprehensible to us.

But however unsatisfactory, the attempt must be made. The basic idea, at least, can be couched in familiar language; it is that the primitive was neither a detached observer nor an exploiter of nature—he was of it, and in it. The system that made up his world was not neatly divided into the living and the dead, the human and the non-human. All that existed in the physical world, as well as in the world of ideas, was integrated into a scheme of things which for the primitive was indivisible.

But in the West man is seen as totally separate from the world of nature. 'Nature Study' is ritually taught to very young children a few hours a week for one or two years. Thereafter, it is a struggle to remember even the difference between an elm and an oak, while the more advanced forms of nature study became known as botany, zoology and ecology, and are confined to specialists. In these Western disciplines, plant and animal life is regarded from the start as an object to be studied without involvement, usually with the hope that the new knowledge acquired will one day prove useful. To this end, the actual animals and plants have been reduced to chemicals, genes and chromosomes which it is believed hold the key to understanding and manipulation. These concerns confirm that, in Western eyes, nature is merely something whose presence must be tolerated until we finally learn to do away with it.

To start with then, let us take a longish walk along the primitive trail, as the anthropologist Harold C. Conklin once did:

At o600 and in a light rain, Langba and I left Parina for Binli ... At Aresaas, Langba told me to cut off several ... strips of bark from an *anapla kilala* tree for protection against leeches. By periodically rubbing the cambium side of the strips ... of bark over our ankles and legs we produced a most effective leech repellent lather of pink suds. At one spot ... Langba stopped suddenly, jabbed his walking stick sharply into the side of the trail and pulled up a small weed which he told me he will use as a lure ... for a spring-spear boar trap. A few minutes later he stopped to dig up a small terrestrial orchid (hardly noticeable beneath the other foliage) ... This herb is useful in the magical control of insect pests which destroy cultivated plants. At Binli, Langba was careful not to damage these herbs when searching through the contents of his palm-leaf shoulder bag for *apug* 'slaked lime' and *tabaku* to offer in exchange for other betel ingredients with the Binli folk. After an evaluative discussion about the local forms of betel pepper Langba got permission to cut sweet potato vines of two vegetatively distinguishable types ... In the camote patch, we cut 25 vine-tip sections of each variety, and carefully wrapped them in the broad fresh leaves of the cultivated *saging saba* so that they would remain moist until we got to Langba's place. Along the way we munched on a few stems of *tuba minuma*, a type of sugar cane, stopped once to gather fallen *bunga* area nuts and another time to pick and eat the wild cherry-like fruits from the *bugnay* shrubs. We arrived at the Mararim by mid-afternoon having spent much of our time on the trail discussing changes in the surrounding vegetation in the last few decades.[1]

In this primitive equivalent of the Sunday afternoon walk, two things stand out: Langba's observational powers and his detailed knowledge of the local flora. Fortunately, recent anthropological studies have made it possible to add a huge amount of new detail to this impressionistic view. For instance, the Hanunóo of the

Philippines classify 93 per cent of their plants as culturally significant and their plant vocabulary involves some two thousand different terms. They recognize 461 animal types including 75 different birds, 12 snakes, more than 60 fish, more than a dozen crustacea, 108 categories of insect, including 13 for ants and termites, and more than 60 salt water molluscs.[2] To add the final flourish, as Dr Conklin writes:

> The Hanunóo classify their local plant world, at the lowest (terminal) level of contrast, into more than 1800 mutually exclusive folk taxa, while botanists divide the same flora — in terms of species — into less than 1300 scientific taxa.[3]

Nor is this one isolated example pulled out at random to make a general point. Primitive classification of the natural world was extremely detailed, showing a specificity that matches our own and an experience of it which is far more direct and involved than our purely theoretical botanical and zoological learning. Thus the Ponapean men, according to Melville J. Herskowitz, had an almost incredible knowledge of the yam:

> Without by any means exhausting their subject, 156 varieties were recorded, together with their shape, size, colour and other characteristics, and in many cases the periods when they were first planted on Ponape, the names of the men who first planted them, and the districts and sections in which this was done.[4]

Such expert classification is not simply academic to the primitive. The Eskimo carvers of Dorset Island, working on ivory pieces no bigger than a match head, are careful to distinguish in their work different varieties of a single species of bird, such as the Common Loon and the Red-throated Loon.[5] This type of knowledge had clearly little in common with the academic objective approach which for three hundred years has enthralled the Western world. It was both more personal and more intimate and served as a language to link primitive man with the environment on which he depended and with which he was always in touch. As we shall see, these differences may be vital; and even in our language knowledge has not yet quite lost its two distinct meanings. Knowledge as the goal of the research laboratory is familiar enough, but the Book of Genesis also tells us that Adam 'knew' Eve—certainly no research programme, as Theodore Roszak has remarked.[6] An Objibwa Indian, in eloquent mood, has expressed the same view neatly and directly:

> We know what the animals do, what are the needs of the beaver, the bear, the salmon, and other creatures, because long ago men married them and acquired this knowledge from their animal wives. Today the priests say we lie, but we know better. The white man has been only a short time in this country and knows very little about the animals; we have lived here thousands of years and were taught long ago by the animals themselves. The white man writes everything down in a book so that it will not be forgotten; but our ancestors married the animals, learned all their ways, and passed on the knowledge from one generation to another.[7]

The primitive, in other words, does not stand alone in the universe but stands, as it were, at one with it. In Australian totemism, for example, we see each clan of each tribe identifying with one particular animal. Thus are all the animals bound together into a unity with all the clans of all the tribes. Nor is there the same sharp division between animate and inanimate, between plant and rock. The heathen, as Christians once thought, bows down to wood and stone, but the point could not be more wrong. In fact he bows not down, nor up, but merely towards: wood and stone are an essential part of the cosmos he sees around him, their presence is to be acknowledged and respected, and their nature to be duly integrated into the world view.

For a primitive, then, nature is clad in 'supernatural' veils. While we 'talk to the trees' only in song or with poetical licence, the primitive does so as a matter of course. As this thought is so different to the Western view, we shall let the primitives give their own account of it. Consider, first, this statement of an old Wintu Indian woman of California:

The White people never cared for land or deer or bear. When we Indians kill meat, we eat it all up. When we dig roots we make little holes. When we build houses, we make little holes. When we burn grass for grasshoppers, we don't ruin things. We shake down acorns and pinenuts. We don't chop down the trees. We use only dead wood. But the White people plough up the ground, pull up the trees, kill everything. The tree says 'Don't. I am sore. Don't hurt me'. But they chop it down and cut it up. The spirit of the land hates them. They blast out trees and stir it up to its depths. They saw up the trees. That hurts them. The Indians never hurt anything, but the White people destroy all. They blast rocks and scatter them on the ground. The rock says, 'Don't. You are hurting me'. But the White people pay no attention. When the Indians use rocks they take little round ones for their cooking ... How can the spirit of the Earth like the White man? ... Everywhere the White man has touched it, it is sore.[8]

In many ways, the primitive view of nature contrasts starkly with even the Christian idea that God created all of nature, and not just man. In the Book of Genesis, the emphasis is clearly on the uniqueness of man, as the Lord of Nature. The birds and beasts were *for* man, and this particularly anthropocentric view, not unique to Christianity, may have profound implications. For the moment, contrast the Christian prayer 'Oh God, who gavest us the Earth and the land and the fields ... ' with the prayer of Black Elk, an Oglala Sioux shaman:

Hear me four quarters of the world, a brother I am, give me the strength to walk the soft Earth, a relative to all that is. Give me the eyes to see and the strength to understand that I may be like you. O, ancient rocks, you are now here with me, the great spirit has made the earth and has placed you next to her. Upon you the generations shall walk and their steps shall not falter. O, rocks, you have neither eyes, nor mouth; you do not move; but by receiving your sacred breath, our people will be long-winded as they walk the path of life.

Your breath is the very breath of life. And, O you people who are always standing, who pierce up through the earth, you tree-people are very many; you trees are the protectors, of the winged people, for upon you they build their lodges and raise their families, and beneath you there are many people whom you shelter. May all these people and all their generations walk together as relatives.[9]

Such a view of the Earth, stressing not merely the brotherhood of man but the brotherhood of man, rocks, trees and birds appears to us to be essentially mystical. It conjures up a vision of man trying to get outside himself in order to communicate with other things which are essentially 'not-man'. But, as Dorothy Lee has argued,[10] this may be merely another of those traps caused by trying to interpret a non-Western situation from a Western background. Primitives did not have any need to seek communion with nature for they found themselves from the start in direct contact with it; as man and nature were never truly separated, man did not have to re-establish a communication that had been previously interrupted. The Arapesh of New Guinea have an apparently peculiar way of describing their relationship to the land and their gardens. It turns out to be difficult to translate the Arapesh word for 'belong' and, according to Margaret Mead, about the nearest equivalent is rendered by the phrase 'We belong to the land'.[11] For a Westerner, the land belongs to him; and once this separation of man and the Earth is made, any attempt to re-establish communication must appear mystical.

The point was vividly made by Smohola, one of the leaders of the Columbia Basin Indian tribes, when the American government tried to change his people's way of life from hunting and gathering to agriculture:

You ask me to plough the ground; shall I take a knife and tear my mother's bosom? Then when I die she will not take me to her bosom to rest. You ask me to dig for stones; shall I dig under her skin for her bones? Then when I die I cannot enter her body to be born again. You ask me to cut grass and make hay and sell it and be rich like White men; but how dare I cut off my mother's hair?[12]

Clearly, no agricultural society could have had exactly this attitude to the land. In fact, it has been suggested that agriculture effected a traumatic divorce between man and nature. Such a view could be reassuring for us in the West. It implies that, because we can never return to a pre-agricultural existence, it is impossible for us to re-establish a mystical view of nature, a view which we now realize was precisely what governed the ecological stability of other societies. However, there is evidence that the world-view of agricultural primitives was hardly different from that of the hunters and gatherers. Robert Redfield and W. Lloyd Warher have put it thus:

> The agriculture of the Maya Indians of south-eastern Yucatan is not simply a way of securing food. It is also a way of worshipping the gods. Before a man plants, he builds an altar in the field and prays there. He must not speak boisterously in the cornfield; it is a sort of temple. The cornfield is planted as an incipient in a perpetual sacred contact between supernatural beings and men. By this agreement, the supernaturals yield part of what is theirs—the riches of the natural environment—to men. In exchange, men are pious and perform the traditional ceremonies in which offerings are made to the supernaturals ... The world is seen as inhabited by the supernaturals; each has his appropriate place in the woods, the sky, or the wells from which the water is drawn.[13]

It is vital that we understand how this view of nature can be reconciled with what we regard as the essentially exploitive nature of agriculture. The Hopi Indian, for instance, does not regard his agriculture as a battle of man against the land. Instead he sees himself as working with the land, the sun and the plants in cooperation with the rain, the pollen and the wind. Just as he benefits from this relationship, so too does the corn which cannot grow so well without his help; the corn enjoys the ceremonies which surround its growth, gladly gives its body for man's food and enjoys living with him in his granary.[14]

Now, if this is agriculture, it is certainly not the Western idea of agriculture. Undoubtedly, we need the produce and it seems superficially reasonable to squeeze every last ton of produce from the Earth regardless of the extra energy, fertilizer and chemicals which have to be used in the process. However, our ecological sciences warn us daily that the techniques we have chosen are far from wise; that we have sacrificed quality for quantity; that the success we have achieved from industrial farming is likely to be short-lived; and that the Earth's fertility is being threatened by our very desire to increase fertility.

That another form of agriculture is possible is now being proved by the New Alchemy Institutes in the United States. There a group of young, ecologically conscious scientists, calling themselves 'stewards of the Earth', are designing new methods of food production which work with nature rather than against her. They eschew all forms of chemical and artificial fertilizer and rely solely on a system in which nothing is wasted and everything returned to the land to enter the cycle again. With research centres already established in California, New Mexico, Massachusetts and Costa Rica, the Institute has already demonstrated the feasibility of an agriculture in which quantity is maintained, quality improved and nature left unraped. The approach bears little resemblance to anything previously known, but is an agriculture based on respect for nature.[15]

The import of this work, of course, is that a respect for nature is in some ways functional—that by learning to work with her, we do ourselves more good than working against her. The same principle should apply to primitive society and many anthropologists now argue that this is indeed the case. Thus Ian McHarg has written of the Iroquois Indians:

... the bear was highly esteemed. When the hunted bear was confronted, the kill was preceded by a long monologue in which the needs of the hunter were fully explained and assurances were given that the killing was motivated by need, not the wish to dishonour. Now if you wish to develop an attitude to prey that would ensure stability in a hunting society, then such views are the guarantee. The hunter who believes that all matter and actions are sacramental and consequential will bring deference and understanding to his relations with the environment; he will achieve a steady state with the environment, he will live in harmony with nature and survive because of it.[16]

Two more detailed investigations make the same general point in a more precise way. The first concerns the practices of the Naskapi Indians of the Labrador Peninsula, which include divination using the shoulder-blade of the caribou. Before the hunt, the bone is cleaned and a handle attached to it. It is then held over some red-hot coals, with the flat surface horizontal and the bone always pointing in the same direction. The flat part then represents a kind of map of the hunting area; and as the heat causes cracks and burnt spots to appear, the Naskapi interpret these signs to be pointing towards the areas where game will be found in the ensuing hunt.

Now the Indians do not use this device when they have other information about where to hunt. They do so when they have nothing else to guide them. Omar Khayyam Moore has argued that the bone in effect acts as a 'random generator', which prevents the Indians over-hunting areas they might follow from instinct or because there were good paths.[17] Human beings are known to be extremely poor random generators — they follow, consciously or even unconsciously, strategies which are conditioned by past successes and failures. The caribou bone thus takes the decision out of fallible human mechanisms and supplants it with a device that sends the Indian off in more or less random directions.

The second example of how such a view of nature can have functional advantages concerns the famous sacred cow of India. Now for years Western biologists have argued that this Hindu belief is the only thing effectively preventing the Indian feeding himself adequately. According to this indictment, there are far too many cows for the resources in India, they are not properly cared for, milked, fed or fenced, and they are not slaughtered at the proper time (if at all). In other words, it is charged, the Indian peasant keeps his cows alive for religious reasons at the expense of his own well-being.

In fact, the cows scavenge for their food during much of the year when they feed off roadside grass. Kept alive on resources not used by humans, they furthermore perform several valuable functions: however undernourished, a cow can be expected eventually to produce some milk and at least two bullocks, essential for traction. Even more important, their dung provides essential fuel – the equivalent of 100 million tons of coal a year – in a land where the grain cannot be metabolized without cooking and where timber and fossil fuels are either scarce or prohibitively expensive. It seems, in fact, that the Hindu belief in the sacredness of the cow may be one of the things that has prevented famine in India becoming much worse than it is.[18] Ghandi evidently thought so. 'We have use for the cow,' he wrote. 'That is why it has become religiously incumbent on us to protect it.'

For that new breed of men called ecological anthropologists, the surprising functionalism of primitive beliefs about the environment has become a novel thesis.[19] Their measurements of energy intake and output, their broad systems analysis of the agricultural system, and their bird's eye view of the total process, tend to confirm one thing: primitive man did not pay any ecological price for his apparently illogical and magical view of nature. On the contrary, the beliefs he had and the practices he observed so meticulously stood him in good biological stead. It was his healthy relationship with nature, in short, which gave him the chance of a healthy life.

The implication of this new finding is quite clear. As our own ecological crisis goes from bad to worse, we will have to re-learn a respect for nature. The medieval historian, Lynn White, goes further for he claims our troubles stem from Judaeo-Christian myth, with its emphasis on fruitfulness, multiplication and an exploitive attitude to nature.[20] St Francis, whose beautiful 'Hymn to the Sun' speaks of Brother Earth in ways reminiscent of the primitive, shall, suggests Professor White, be made the patron saint of ecology, and our own attitudes to nature ruthlessly re-examined if we are not to reduce our once green planet to a stinking and sterile heap.

However, it is not simply a question of re-learning a respect for the natural world. It is a question of *having* that respect. The primitive did not treat his animals and plants 'as though' they were sacred in order that he might get the best out of them. For him, they *were* sacred, they had always been so and they always would be. This distinction, essentially that between merely according respect and actually having it, holds deep significance for us. Reviewed in this light, even our ecological science—which would seem to hold the key to the future—evades the basic issue. For science—even ecology—treats its subject as an object. If there are mysteries, they are there to be ripped away, not worshipped. And here lies the greatest problem facing Western man. His very survival may depend on at least a partial rejection of that system of logical and rational thought which has held sway since the seventeenth century. If we are to survive this crisis, the science of the future will have to be committed and loving, contemplative rather than analytical. This is the ecological message of the primitives; it is profound, hard, deeply philosophical and quite irreconcilable with our present practices. We would do well to heed it, but we should not underestimate the magnitude of its scope.

2

The Social World

6 Man and the Group

For animals, survival may well be a matter of ecology; but to be human is to do more than survive physically. Living is as much to do with social interactions and creative cultural expression as with reproduction and nutrition. 'Man shall not live by bread alone' would be better rewritten as 'Man cannot live by bread alone'; were he ever to try he would cease to be a man—the group is essential to the healthy life of the individual.

The lessons we can learn from the primitive in the ways of social living are in a sense more important than any ecological morals we may draw. Until very recently, the advanced nations of the industrialized world were making determined efforts to show that material comforts were all that really mattered. Today we are mostly all too well aware of the widespread social alienation which the technocracy and exclusive concentration on materialism have produced. However, we are far from solutions, although the importance of small group interactions, a sense of community and the human scale, is becoming accepted. But how to reconcile these things with an advanced technology has posed a monumental problem.

Primitive customs reveal a richness of social interaction fundamental to the way of life they served. The chores of survival were incorporated into socially and spiritually renewing life patterns. The members of the group worked together and lived together in necessary, welcomed co-operation. Any technical process that was adopted in the primitive society also enriched the social milieu. In a way, the primitive counted in the psychological and social factors in his 'cost/benefit' calculations from the word go. The New Guinea tribes who farm out their pigs for friends and relations to look after are well aware that in terms of efficiency of protein production the arrangement is far from ideal. But they count the friends they make through this custom as far more important than a little extra pork.

Part of the secret of the primitive's success as a social being was undoubtedly the absence of a Western respect for specialization, Individuals were never characterized rigidly into one role and one role only. And the fact that many people played many overlapping roles in many activities made society the more closely knit. Consider Dorothy Lee's remarks on Hopi agriculture:

> When a farmer is harvesting a 'successful' corn crop, who has 'succeeded'? Throughout the year, the members of his pueblo, in different organizations, have performed an established series of ceremonies to bring about this harvest. The children have played ball games for days with the children from another pueblo, and thus have helped the corn grow. Men have refrained from intercourse with their wives and sweethearts; eaglets have been captured at considerable risk, women and children have laughed at the antics of ceremonial clowns, priests have gone into retirement and meditation, and much more has been done and wished and thought, to bring about this good harvest. The farmer's achievement in all this may be seen as insignificant; yet it may also be seen as superbly significant.[1]

Contrast this with the stress laid on independent effort in the West. Here families are segregated in separated living units, each equipped with machines that could easily serve the needs of many on a co-operative basis; each has its personal means of transport, and in the richer families each adult member has a car. Parents pride themselves on not prying into the affairs of their children and the ideal is for each individual to live his or her own life without reference to or support from others. In the words of Philip Slater, 'An enormous technology seems to have set itself the task of making it unnecessary for one human being ever to ask anything of another in the course of going about his daily business.'[2]

Yet this is only the grass-roots manifestation of the lofty creed that each should have the right to self-realization and individual independence. It found its most exalted expression in the romantic ideal that a man should follow his destiny no matter what the cost to himself or others, and accounts for the fact that one of the most popular songs of the last decade has been Sinatra's 'My Way'. It is an optimistic and, it seems, a noble ideal, but at its roots lies a dilemma: without this mystical respect for the cult of the individual we would be the poorer by the achievements of Michelangelo and Beethoven—yet, equally, we would have been spared the excesses of Napoleon and Hitler. It is no longer, in our age, quite so easy to be sure that the balance comes out on the credit side. We have given a blank cheque to individualism which may be cashed indifferently in genuine or counterfeit coin; in a not too distant future we may be forced, however unwillingly, to face the dilemma which the dynamic of our civilization poses. We may be forced to recognize that the well-being of the group will demand the imposition of restraint on the ego.

In fact, despite the almost hectoring lip-service that has been paid to the rights of Everyman, those rights have generally been curtly abrogated for the majority of citizens. The factory system and total war teach us that the personalities, even the lives of those individuals with their inalienable rights can be sacrificed to the system by the hundred thousand when rhetoric and occasion seem to demand it.

The tight parameters of primitive life could not afford such prodigality. There is no attitudinizing about inviolable personal rights and so forth, only very practical provisions to look after and conserve the all-important group power that each man and woman, once initiated as a member, represents. The once notorious system of bride wealth, which to European eyes seemed little better than a slave trade, was in fact just such a practical expression of value. A woman, like all members of the kin group, provided labour and skills; but more important of course she was the potential mother of new kin members. To surrender her in marriage to another group was to lose a valuable and valued member. The bride-wealth cattle were a compensation, and they also guaranteed to her husband the rights over any children she might have. People rated human life so highly that they reckoned it in the most practical way they knew how. The importance that the Nuer, for example, attach to people is eloquently shown by the penalty for murder. From their point of view the death penalty for the killer would merely double the loss to the group, so instead he and his kin have to pay a fine equivalent to a woman's bride wealth so that the bereaved kin can raise a new household to replace the one broken up by the murder.

Underlying the way of life of the primitive society was the deep intuitive realization that to live at all men and women had to husband their resources and learn to live together. It may have been merely through the force of necessity, but they found ways of integrating the diverse drives of individuality into a communal direction without destroying it and without producing disruptive rebellion. The force of custom, the sanctions of religion and above all the deep-seated knowledge that all contributed to the well-being of each, helped to make this so. To quote Slater again:

> Most people in most societies have been born into com-
> munities in which the subordination of the individual to the
> welfare of the group was taken for granted, while the ag-
> grandisement of the individual at the expense of his fellows
> was simply a crime.[3]

In return the group conferred protection on the individuals that made it up and their title to humanity. Religion and liberalism in our tradition combine to grant a child full rights of membership of the human race from birth; indeed, the 'sanctity of the individual' operates, in the extremest version of the theory, even before. Theological and humanitarian debate has hotly argued the question at what week in pregnancy the foetus can be reckoned to have a soul or a personality – with the corollary that abortion is termed child-murder by its more rabid opponents. In such a world-view the individual and the group are finally isolated from each other; the individual's standing as a human being takes precedence over his standing as a social being. Even before he or she has given anything to the group, and even though supporting him or her may actually hamper and penalize the group, the individual has an absolute lien on the group's protection from the moment of achieving biological existence. In the primitive experience, while the facts of biology do of course confer existence, it is the facts of society that confer life. The Eskimo mother, whose tribe was pressured by a harsh environment to the practice of infanticide, was conditioned to accept her child only after the decision had been taken to let it live. The Ainu of Japan believed that the soul came into being only during the first twelve days after birth and that not until then was the individual spirit fully formed.[4] Such attitudes were not rare, and everywhere we find underlying the ceremonies of primitive society the idea that becoming a full person went hand in glove with becoming a full member of society. In one of the classic texts of anthropological literature, the French sociologist Van Gennep analysed under the term 'rituals of passage' the ceremonies by which primitive societies marked the individual's transition from one stage of maturity to another.[5] They have been succinctly summarized by Lucy Mair:

> At birth a naming or 'showing' ceremony marks his acceptance as a social being; at puberty he passes from the status of child to adult; at marriage he becomes a potential parent ... and a whole new realignment of relations is created by new ties of affinity; at death he becomes an ancestor and again the alignment of relations between the living is changed when his successor steps into his place.[6]

What interested Van Gennep was the fact that these rituals seemed to take much the same form in very different societies; what interests us here is that in primitive society the transitions of the individual through life were attended by group involvement. Growing up was a process of gradual induction into the dignity, privileges and obligations of being a man or a woman. Final recognition took the form of an often painful, sometimes dangerous, rite of initiation; but once these harsh conditions had been fulfilled the individual's place in society was assured. He did not, like the Westerner, have to make a place for himself, and consequently was spared those neuroses bred in our society by a lifetime's struggle to 'make good'.

Furthermore the primitive can never lose sight of the reality of society nor of his place in it. The social world takes on an objective existence just as real as the external world of nature. Where we have exercised our human ingenuity to the proliferation of material objects—houses, machines, art and all the trappings of civilization—which have taken on such an overbearing life of their own that they sometimes seem to be the 'real' world, the primitive has evolved systems of human social structure far more elaborate and intricate than anything we recognize, which give him a 'real' world of concrete human dimensions. A typical Aboriginal Australian tribe will consist of a hundred divisions and sub-classifications which have to be mastered before an outsider can begin to understand the organization of the whole group.[7] Such societies form a framework in which the personality can extend itself and its dialogue with other men and women, not a battlefield for competitive enterprise. Where we exploit 'contacts', the primitive was involved throughout his waking life in personal relationships. Where we seek to free ourselves as far as possible from all involvements with others, the primitive welcomed them and was committed to them as evidence of his membership of a protective, life-giving group that, while it imposed obligations and demanded allegiance, gave his humanity a context in which it could flourish.

For it is a mistake to suppose that in the primitive way the individual is so oppressed by the social environment that he has no scope nor opportunity to flower. The mistake is certainly easy to make. None of our university courses includes a study of individual primitive psychologies; instead they deal with primitive 'peoples', always in the plural, always in the mass. The vast bulk of the literature concerns itself with group studies and social analysis; there are virtually no biographies and only rarely do the men and women, whose co-operation provides the basis for the anthropologists' work, emerge as vivid, individual personalities. Yet his investigations of North American Indian societies led Paul Radin to conclude that 'the primitive had both sympathetic forbearance and respect for everyman's individuality in all its multiform and kaleidoscopic manifestations'.[8] Despite the most rigorous prohibitions, a young man falls in love with a girl of a kin that may not marry with his and loudly demands that he be allowed to marry her. A Winnebago Indian begins his autobiography with the claim that 'this man's mother was told by the gods that she was going to mother an extraordinary individual'.[9] And another anthropologist received three accounts of the nature of the world and the origins of things, each differing from the others and all wildly at odds with the orthodox myths of the tribe.

The individual is no less important to the dynamism of the primitive group than he is in our system; it is only that primitives hold to a different system of priorities, rating the group's wellbeing higher than the individual's unbridled rights to self-expression. In our world, too, individuality has to learn to curb its dreams. When the adolescent is forced out into the world to earn a living on the shop floor or behind a desk, there is little scope left for those adventures of self-expression and imagination that school encouraged. Indeed, if the majority were to live up to the ideals that the enlightened educationalists preach, the whole industrial process would come to a halt: if all were free to do their own thing, few would choose an eight-hour day as a unit in the industrial or commercial machine.

It is against this background that the youthful counter-culture made its stand. The determination to 'be' rather than to spend a lifetime trying to 'have' is the direct expression of the desire for individuality in the face of a repressive socio-industrial system. Where their elders permitted no noise, no smell and no colour, the young have celebrated all three senses to convince themselves that they are really living.

The result is fascinating. As the counter-culture grows, it tries to organize itself. Human survival under industrialism is far from easy and the first lesson that is always learnt is the survival value of group solidarity. It is quickly discovered that doing your own thing without restraint and living with others are, to put it mildly, incompatible. The inherent conflict between the individual and the group has to be realized from experience. For some the apparent contradiction is too much. Having sought freedom from all social restraint, they drift from commune to commune, wondering how it is that their brave ideals always seem to end in human friction. For others the lesson is learnt. They begin from scratch the laborious business of building a society in tune with their ideals and learn to live with the new restraints that its survival demands. They learn what the primitives had always known, that when social survival is the name of the game the group ranks first and the individual second.

It is the beginning of wisdom, but the full lesson, how to achieve a happy fusion between the needs of the individual and the needs of his society, demands the continuing study and commitment of generations. When the lesson is learned and lived, it produces ways of living that our distracted world should envy. The evolution of integrative social patterns was primitive man's finest achievement just as, some would argue, the failure to maintain them is our worst fault. For the Dakota Indians, the ideal of social harmony and co-operation is so important and pursued with such thoroughness that one man, asked by an anthropologist about the education of his children, said: 'We teach our children that to serve the tribe is to serve oneself. To fail in one's duty to others means to fail in the test of manhood.'[10]

As we explore how the delicate balance between individual and society was achieved we find, at the heart of the matter, the kin group. The study of kinship systems has been one of the largest areas covered by anthropology ever since it came of age in the nineteenth century. Decades of research have produced libraries of information on kin systems recruited through the male line, the female line or both; on the selection of permitted marriage partners with the related theme of incest taboos; and above all on the actual terminology used by tribe members of one another. Words such as 'brother' and 'sister', 'father' and 'mother', which for us have straightforward biological connotations, are applied in other societies to age peers or to seniors so that a person may have many 'fathers', some of his own age group, or many 'sisters', some biologically his cousins.

Even in our society, the terminology of kinship is still used in a wide variety of situations. Trade unionists still call fellow members 'brother'; the Catholic priest receives the courtesy title of 'father'; in hospitals, senior ranking nurses are called 'sister' or 'matron'. The potent symbolism of these familiar words is for the most part dead but they form the attenuated memory of a once deeply unifying habit of mind. In place of the lively and strongly felt principle of kinship which bound primitive society together, we have corporations, trade unions, schools or clubs which, while they may generate an artificial sense of group loyalty, cannot emulate the reality of the primitive kin. The Australian Aboriginals reckoned all persons with whom they had social dealings as in some degree related to them, with prescribed modes of address and behaviour governing their relations.[11] Such a concept of kin has no real counterpart among us, and now even the family itself is strictly circumscribed. In the sections that follow we shall see how primitive society, composed of a network of personally felt ties and connections, built on the principle of the family to con-solidate itself and succour its members. The point of departure is the institution of marriage, which not only links the two in-dividuals involved more closely than any other tie but also brings two kin groups together.

7 Men and Their Wives

It might seem a little perverse to begin a section on the primitive attitude to sex and marriage with a discussion of marriage. After all, almost since their first contact with the primitive world, Europeans have entertained a prurient fascination for the supposedly orgiastic and promiscuous sex life of savages. The nineteenth-century American anthropologist Lewis Morgan traced what he thought was a progressive development from prehistoric, primitive promiscuity to modern, moral monogamy,[1] and we still live in the shadow of such thinking. In fact the primitive societies of the world were a good deal more, and more seriously, concerned with marriage than we are and regarded the sexual commerce between men and women as only one, and by no means the most important, aspect of their dealings with one another.

It was St Paul's view that it was 'better to marry than to burn',[2] and the views of this confirmed celibate, heavily reinforced since the eleventh century by an officially celibate priesthood, have so enmeshed sexuality and the Christian style of monogamous marriage that some of its present-day critics may be forgiven their opinion that it is a licence for sex and little else. In a way that would astonish the Primitive observer, the relations between men and women in modern Western society are dominated by sex to the exclusion of almost everything else. It seems almost as though a right to have it with all or any were a part of some fundamental charter of human liberties, and this is perhaps understandable in our fragmented individualist civilization. Where 'self-fulfilment and the personal exploration of experience' are reckoned the loftiest human goals, it is not surprising that sex, the most intense experience readily available to most people, should be so highly rated. Today, it is more or less de rigeur among the candidates for the self-selecting enlightened bourgeoisie to cultivate an ostentatious super-tolerance for the sexual odysseys of their marriage partners.

To most primitive peoples, such casual permissiveness about marriage would seem absurd. Marriage confers status on men and women alike—the Navaho Indians regard it as the inevitable state for the mature man or woman—and it has vital functions that make it one of the foundation stones of the social fabric. Attitudes to sexuality in general and premarital sex in particular may often be more relaxed than the classic orthodoxies of the West, but infidelity in marriage, and especially infidelity of the wife, is an altogether different matter. For the first, and possibly the most important, function of marriage in these societies is the legitimating of children; it provides the matrix within which the new members of the group can be brought into being.

Nor is this at all surprising in social structures consisting of kin groups. Where the individual's place in society depends on his or her place in such a kin group, that place must be a socially accepted fact and for that the birth must be publicly recognized and sanctioned. From the child's point of view the marriage of its parents can be regarded as the first rite of passage which, even before birth, proclaims his or her right to membership of the network of kin ties and loyalties without which social life is impossible. Naturally, in societies where every step in life requires the participation and authorization of the group, marriage is marked by ceremony. The form this takes is as varied as the whole gamut of Western practices, from the full church wedding to the simple ceremony at the register office. The Trobrianders, for example, reckoned a man and woman married when they had eaten together in the home of the husband.[4] The rituals of the Nuer of the Sudan, as described by Evans-Pritchard, are very much more elaborate and more interesting from our point of view; for they involve the whole kin both past and present and highlight the future role of the partnership as a child-bearing union.[5]

The betrothal of the two people involved has little to do with them, being settled in discussions between their families. Since property and inheritance of property can turn on the marriage, this need not unduly surprise us and was of course a common practice in Europe until quite recently. On the date agreed the first instalments of the bride-wealth cattle are driven to the home of the bride's family. The private negotiations are now proclaimed publicly for the first time and the occasion is marked with an impressive ceremony of sacrifice and feasting which ensures that no one who should know of the new union is not fully informed. The dead too are duly notified and the ancestors are invoked as witnesses. The festivities over, the groom asks formal leave of the bride's mother to take her back to his village; and there the marriage is consummated though not before the young woman has put up a becoming display of maidenly modesty. Like those Western brides who still wear white though its symbolism of chastity has long since generally been overtaken by events, the Nuer girl is rarely a virgin. The pretence, however, is maintained because the sex relationship she is now entering upon is one formally sanctioned by society for the all-important matter of establishing the status of new members to be born into the kin.

The importance attached to the legitimization of children is revealed still more clearly by the procedures of traditional Bemba society in Africa and the Nayar society of India. Among the Bemba, boy and girl committed themselves to each other as children; during the protracted courtship, gifts and labour were exchanged, the boy worked for the girl's father and the girl did household chores in the boy's house. The two slept together from time to time and began their first explorations of sex play. Then when the girl seemed to be approaching her first menstruation she was brought home to prevent her conceiving before she had been initiated by the puberty rites which inaugurated her into womanhood and permitted her to bear children. The groom took part in this ceremony, bringing further gifts to symbolize his contribution to the new joint household and weapons to signal his new role as the protector of his wife and the hunter for the family cookpot. Only then could the full consummation of the marriage follow.[6]

Although unique in the anthropological literature, the customs of the Nayar people of Kerala in India confirm what appears to be man's universal urge to institutionalize in some way or another the relations between men, women and children who are biologically related.[7] In the words of Lévi-Strauss, 'Anthropologists now lean towards the conviction that the family consisting of a more or less durable union, socially approved, of a man, a woman and their children, is a universal phenomenon, present in each and every type of society!'[8]

Now in the Nayar case the union is certainly less rather than more durable, but its function in legitimizing children is unmistakable. Being Hindu, the society was status-structured by caste and, being matri-linear, it determined kinship allegiance by descent through the mother rather than the father. Nayar women lived out their lives in the household of their kinsfolk, supported by the men of the family. Before she reached puberty a girl underwent a ritual marriage. Her ritual husband had to be her caste equal, but sex had no part in the proceedings nor ever need do in the future unless the partners wished it. Although cast in the form of a marriage, this performed the function of an initiation ceremony which, as among the Bemba, inaugurated the Nayar girl into adulthood and permitted her to bear children. These children could be, indeed usually were, born to other men but without the ritual marriage, neither mother nor children would be able to enjoy the status conferred by her caste.

Once the girl became physically mature she took lovers, termed 'visiting husbands' by the anthropologist Kathleen Gough, who in their turn were free to have liaisons with other girls. A man's only necessary qualification was to be at least the caste equal of the woman and his one obligation was to pay the costs of delivering her children as an acknowledgment of paternity. Whether one or more of the visiting husbands discharged this duty for a child was immaterial; what was vital was that the child's caste purity be assured. In fact, the Nayar child absolutely needed his two fathers. His ritual father, by conferring status rights on his mother conferred them also on him (our suggestion that marriage could be viewed as a pre-natal rite of passage could hardly be more neatly supported); the visiting father, by guaranteeing the caste purity of the birth, enabled the child to enjoy those rights. Without his fathers a Nayar child had neither caste nor lineage status, while his progenitors secured for the child his future place in society without enmeshing themselves in emotional commitments to one another that might one day weigh heavily. The child was brought up with his brothers and sisters at his mother's home in an atmosphere of stability and familiarity where the mother was a fixed point and the changing circle of her suitors provided a varied and friendly collection of group fathers. The Nayar system, which disentangled the young child's development from the emotional tensions that the promiscuous urges of parental sexuality can generate, has lessons perhaps for other societies. Yet we notice that even the Nayar conform to the universal social imperative of formalizing the circumstances surrounding birth.

If we set the Nayar permissiveness towards sex in marriage in the context of primitive practice as a whole and the confused debates on the subject that distract our own society, we are led to an interesting conclusion. It seems that tolerance of extra-marital sex is only possible when the marriage tie is very weak indeed. It is now nearly half a century since Margaret Mead published her brilliant and influential book *Coming of Age in Samoa*.[9] In it she described a society whose full-hearted delight in sexuality was matched by an open tolerance and lack of inhibition, and this struck vibrant chords in post-war Western society, boisterously liberating itself from the crabbed moralities of an earlier time. It was the ambition of every Samoan girl to win lovers and of the boys to prove their mastery of the arts of sex. Yet even the happy and easy-going Samoans paid lip-service to a conventional wisdom which held that excessive promiscuity could lead to barrenness, that 'only persistent monogamy was rewarded by conception' and that a girl who was too indiscreet could mar her chances of a good marriage. At the top of the social scale sex was strictly regulated, the chief jealously guarding the virginity of his daughters, who were even expected to sleep with a chaperone, and a chief's wife bringing disgrace on her high position if she was found guilty of adultery.

In fact, attitudes to sex vary widely throughout the primitive world. At the opposite pole from the Samoans stand the Manus, people of New Guinea, also studied by Margaret Mead,[10] for whom sex is a matter of shame almost as intense as it was in high Victorian England. The Hopi Indians warn their children against sex play with the threat that even little girls can have babies and that if they do all the people of the tribe will die; the boys are told that sexual promiscuity stunts growth.[11] Among the Navaho attitudes to sex are complex and ambivalent. Sexual matters are discussed openly and are supposed to be as interesting to women as to men; masturbation among children is regarded as a natural part of growing up; and, like many other societies, the Navaho publicly celebrate their young people's arrival at the age of puberty rather than make it a matter of concealment and embarrassed comment as it has conventionally been in the West. However, there are other conventions which reflect cautious respect for the power of the human sex drive. Even children are warned against unrestrained indulgence; little boys are warned that the vagina may bite off their penis; a boy is reckoned to have come of age when his voice has broken because it is immodest to notice a man's pubic hairs; too much sex, even between married couples, may, it is thought lead to bleeding in the genitals or madness. Men and women are supposed to abstain from intercourse in the first four nights of their marriage as though to signal respect for the power of the sexual act, and the conventions of decency require them to be at least partly clothed when they make love.[12]

The Yao have truly dramatic views on the potency of sex. It is their belief that the sexually active radiate an influence which, if not neutralized by the correct ceremonies and ritual medicines, will infect the sexually inactive—the children and the aged—with a mysterious disease named *ndaka*. Consequently, in Yao society the marriage ceremony has an added dimension, that of rendering harmless the potency of the newly sexually active members of the group. They too, like the Navaho, believe that excessive promiscuity is dangerous, because it may be the cause of protracted labour in childbirth. More seriously, if a woman was a notorious good-time girl before her marriage, her husband's kin may refuse their essential co-operation in enlisting the help of diviners if the child falls ill. Yet among the Yao pre-marital sex was common enough and it is difficult to see why, in the prevailing attitude of tolerance, a girl should be penalized in this way.[13] In fact there are many societies with what we should regard as permissive codes, which retain ideal conventions of modesty. We have seen how the Nuer bride is required to pretend embarrassed modesty on her wedding night though few people really suppose her to be a virgin;[14] in theory a Navaho husband can claim the return of part of the bride wealth if his bride is found to be not a virgin.[15] Nyansongo society is tolerant of sex before marriage, but should a girl let herself become pregnant she faces disgrace. She does everything she can to persuade the father into marriage before her condition becomes obvious for if he should realize the facts he would leave the village rather than marry her. Though wives are ideally expected to be virgins at their marriage they rarely are and no one worries unduly; but a suspiciously early birth of the first child would be too glaring a breach of convention to be overlooked.[16]

It may perhaps come as something of a surprise to the reader to find that many primitive societies hold views on sexuality which are ambivalent and sometimes self-contradictory. Societies like the Samoan might seem to suggest that 'in the primitive state' man enjoyed a simple and wholesome attitude to his sexuality which has been warped by the pressures of civilization. In fact, it appears that in most parts of the world men and women have found it difficult to reconcile the powerful drives of sex with their ideals of social organization and that the most important lesson we can learn from their experience is that a mature attitude to sex involves an intelligent appreciation of its power.

After marriage the whole perspective of sex in primitive societies changed. The pleasures of the chase and the passions of fulfilment were subordinated to a nexus of rights and obligations between husband and wife. When we come to look at the status of women we shall find that the rights and obligations were generally weighted heavily in favour of the man but the woman's ability to bear children, regarded by the more ardent advocates of women's lib as a penalty imposed by a capricious cosmos on the oppressed half of the race, gave women in the primitive world a status and an importance which in general they jealously guarded. The Yao women, for example, held a special ritual to celebrate the first quickening in the womb on a woman's first pregnancy to symbolize her transition from maidenhood to motherhood. Their society rated a woman's right to bear children as so absolute that a husband's impotence or sterility were sufficient grounds for divorce.[17] Among the Nyansongo this is taken a somewhat startling stage further; a husband who becomes impotent before he has been able to impregnate his wife may be obliged to agree to her sleeping with another man to get children by him. It is perhaps understandable that once they have been initiated the girls of the Nyansongo do little else but talk and plan marriage.[18]

Most societies honour the status of motherhood but few accord it the rights described, while in other matters women occupy a secondary position. Even among the Yao all authority is wielded by the men, despite the fact that the society traces descent through the mother and it is usually the man who moves house to go and live in his wife's village. The Yao, in other words, may be matrilineal but they are certainly not matriarchal in their social organization.[19] For the most part women throughout the primitive world are second-class citizens. They contribute heavily to the labour of the group and are generally left in charge of the upbringing of the children, yet they take little part in decision-making and are firmly excluded from the religious mysteries. Even in the mild-mannered world of the Polynesian Tikopia, the men forbade them all access to the rituals and the *tapu* was so strong that a baby girl who toddled by mistake into a ritual site would be shooed firmly off.[20] Among the Australian Aboriginal tribes women occupied an inferior position to the initiated men, being grouped along with the children, and this despite the fact that it was the women who as the gatherers provided most of the food for the group. The prestigious pursuit of the hunt, reserved to the men, brought in only a fraction of the total protein requirements. Women were excluded from the sacred mysteries and were forbidden to see the bull roarer—indeed they were not even supposed to know that it was this instrument which produced the terrifying 'voices' of the spirits during the night ceremonies.[21] Particularly among the desert tribes, 'the men have a full, rich and interesting secret life, while the women have a few scrappy ceremonies of their own.'[22]

Yet in marked contrast to the actual status of women, one finds in many societies a submerged respect and even fear of them. Among the Aboriginals there is a widely held belief that in the distant mythological past of the Dreaming, women were the dominant sex and the bull roarer was then their exclusive property.[23] For others it is the mysteries of the monthly period and the act of birth which surround womanhood with a puzzling and disturbing aura. The Navaho, for example, combining this attitude with what we might regard as a precaution of elementary hygiene, believe that to eat food prepared by a woman with menstrual blood on her hands will make a person a hunchback.[24] Similar superstitions can be quoted from all over the world, while the cult of the mother goddess which seems to have prevailed throughout the prehistoric Mediterranean world is further evidence of the awe in which men have held the female principle. It required a male psychiatrist to coin the notion of 'penis envy' according to which little girls are fated to develop an inferiority complex when they learn of the fancy bit of equipment depending from the male crotch. But others, with perhaps greater force, have proposed the whole elaborate edifice of the arts and sciences and religion to be the fruit of men's desperate endeavour to equal woman's capacity for creating people. 'Womb envy' so to speak. However, in discussing the actual status of women in society, whether civilized or primitive, we can confidently side-track such metaphysical speculations. Their influence in simpler societies is often more apparent and real than in the classic model of Western civilization and, no doubt, men have paid them the tribute of a certain worried uncertainty about their hidden powers; but in the balance of the sexes men do seem generally to have weighted the scales in their own favour. We must now investigate a little how the two work in the context of marriage to continue the species.

8 Kin and Family and Individual

In the primitive world kin is social structure; it is also the grand matrix within which family and individual move. The result contrasts strikingly with what has been termed the nuclear family of Western society. It is something of an oddity in human history, consisting on average of only four members, mother, father, and two children, isolated from kin and society. The adjective 'nuclear' is supposed to imply that the four, parents and children, form the centre of a kin group with all the other relatives revolving around them like electrons round a nucleus. However, new forms of work, almost limitless possibilities of travel, the demands of the state, allegiance away from the family to clubs, professional bodies and schools, have separated these electrons so far that the nucleus is very much a loner. No cloud of relatives is to be seen near the nuclear family except on occasional visits, which easily become more a chore and a duty than a pleasure and a help.

By contrast the primitive family is surrounded at all times by a greater kin grouping into which it imperceptibly merges and which helps it through the crises and irritations of life and celebrates with it the big moments. The kins are actively concerned in the dealings between husband and wife; the Yao is just one society which appoints sponsors of a marriage to act as sureties for the interests of the two partners.[1] It is they who decide when a man should eat his first ceremonial meal in the wife's village and when he should take up residence there; and it is they who are asked to mediate in any major domestic rows or to see to the correct termination of the marriage in the event of death or divorce. Among the Ifugao of the Philippines, as described in 1919 by the anthropologist R. F. Barton, the kin's position in the marriage was almost absolute. Throughout their lives husband and wife remained 'merely allies'; both brought equal economic resources to the 'alliance' and continued to work their separate fields as separate units. In the event of a dispute between the kins, the man and wife separated without more ado.[2] This was extreme even in primitive customs but in most societies the kin were the last refuge and court of appeal for either spouse who felt wronged.

As they were married within the kin structure so did men and women in the primitive world find themselves supported at every turn of life by men and women called 'brother', 'sister', 'father', 'mother', who formed with them a vast family where a sense of shared lineage and communal identity was far more important than the simple biological links that pass for family relationships among us. In this chapter we shall see how the kin group accompanied the individual in all the crucial stages of his early life and we can well imagine the value of such contact in terms of social stability and personal security.

In almost all societies childbirth is a matter of major concern to the kin. Among the Navaho, if the labour is protracted, all the women in the vicinity and the long-haired men untie their hair and let it fall; if the mother continues to have difficulty, all the horses and tethered animals in the vicinity are unleashed. The woman is helped by many others, her female relations and those of her husband, and the most prestigious function at the ceremony is to receive the child as it is delivered and then to bathe it and 'shape' it with the hands so that its limbs shall grow strong and well formed and it shall be a handsome child.[3] The Nyansongo, who rate children very highly and look on a woman's first giving birth as a major event in her life, expect the birth to take place in the house of the mother-in-law, who is in charge of the proceedings which will involve as many as fifteen women. The husband is not allowed near the delivery-room because his wife would be ashamed for him to see her at such a time; but should the birth be difficult other men may be called in to perform specific jobs. The mother is terrified of the ordeal facing her, interestingly enough a common response in the primitive world, and it is doubtful whether her anguish is much eased, during a protracted labour, by her relatives slapping and pinching her (the approved ways of helping a birth) or by their urging her to confess the name of the man whose adultery is supposedly at the back of her difficulties. Nevertheless, all these vexations apart, the birth as an event of public concern is a far more human procedure than clinical delivery in even the best-equipped hospital. The next stage in the child's life occurs a few days later at the naming ceremony. The women who helped at the birth come to name the child, usually after a dead relative. After the name has been chosen the women eat and the paternal grandmother shaves the head of the child and bounces it in her arms saying as she does so: 'We shall call you ... ' The nurture of the child and its preparation for adulthood remains the concern of the kin, and its education is in the charge of a cloud of friendly relations instead of the kind of extra-familial authority represented by our school system.[4]

In his classic work *We, The Tikopia*, Raymond Firth observes that for the primitive 'education is not an imagined preparation for social life but is actually a vital part of it'.[5] Everything he learns in his upbringing adds to the primitive child's knowledge of the world he will actually inhabit—almost exactly the reverse of education as we know it in our society. With us the best years of the child's life are absorbed in schooling which manages to set up a series of values and motivations often at odds with his home and which at the same time has nothing to do with real life. Worse still, in what Robert Irvine Smith of York University's Department of Education has called a 'system of institutionalized failure',[6] the classic educational structure of syllabus and ex- amination ensures that all but a very small percentage of the children it processes leave the system at some stage along the line with certificates that testify either to failure or to inability to continue to the next grade. Probably an ingenious mind could devise a more effective way of discouraging the will to learn and explore the world on one's own account but so far none has done so.

There is a strong and growing body of opinion among forward- thinking educationalists that the whole structure of formalized education as we at present know it should be done away with in favour of one which took children up to the basic level of some agreed minima and left them free either to continue or to leave school at perhaps the age of twelve. The true revolutionists who advocate the complete abolition of all education are largely confined to the research institutes or those whose books earn a healthy royalty. Despite all possible evidence, teachers are not noticeably more stupid than the rest of the population and it has not escaped their alert minds that the abolition of education would significantly affect employment prospects among teachers. Yet for all the good done by the vast investment in education made by the advanced nations of the world, it is at least interesting to speculate what the results of some such abolition might be. The root dilemma for main-stream education today is one of objectives. Should it be vocational, or academic, or designed to heighten awareness and liberate the individual's creativity? And how, if all three are important, are they to be combined? Is it the job of the school to prepare the young for their place in society and if so, what kind of society? As to society itself, it has serious reservations about the value of the whole exercise. With wealth and power being the two most widely admired qualities, it is observable that good schooling alone has brought them to very few people. Whatever the secrets of success, society concludes that they are not taught in schools and as a result is quite content to pay its teachers a pittance. In fact, the important lessons of socialization are taught in the home, the club and the factory or office, for socialization is the process by which the young individual learns what will be expected of an adult and how to discharge the role. Since in our fractured society even that is a matter of uncertainty, books on child-care flood the market and rise to the top of the best-seller lists.

Child-care and training methods in the primitive world are almost as numerous and diverse as the theories put out year after year by Western baby doctors. But in every case mother, family and society are agreed on the adult roles the child will have to fill and that the best way of preparing for them is the way prescribed by tradition. The Yurok Indians, for instance, value the qualities of independence and self-restraint and the mother begins the training of the child in these qualities even before he is born. As she works she leans forward so that the child in the womb cannot 'rest against her backbone' and rubs her abdomen from time to time to keep the child awake. For the first ten days after birth the child is fed with a thin nut gruel from a tiny shell cup, so that the first contact with the world is not with the comfort of the mother's breast and its easy and generous flow of milk. The first lesson in austerity has been taught but, once the breast is offered, feeding is generous and frequent, in typical Indian fashion. However, the training in self-reliance and autonomy is early resumed and the child is forcibly weaned from the sixth to twelfth month. As it grows older the lesson of self-restraint is reinforced: it is taught not to grab for food and never to ask for a second helping.[7]

The Sioux put a high premium on self-will and strong passions. They reckoned that the boy-child's success as a hunter could be gauged from his infantile furies and, while the breast was withheld in the first days, it was for a quite different reason. Sioux mothers believed that the first watery secretion of the milk glands (known as colostrum) might be poisonous and certainly was too weak to be nutritious. It seemed unreasonable that the baby should work hard to be rewarded only with such thin stuff. Accordingly the child's first meal was a cordial pressed from the finest berries and herbs that could be found and prepared in a buffalo bladder like a feeding bottle.[8] A Nyansongo feeds her child on gruel for the first few days for yet another reason—in her view the sooner the child learns to eat ordinary food like everyone else the better it will be for the mother.[9] The women of the Marquesan islands take pragmatic self-interest a stage further. Firm, well-shaped breasts are highly rated for their sex appeal by Marquesan men and so mothers wean their children as quickly as possible because they believe breast-feeding ruins the figure. Interestingly enough, a comparative study of nurture and weaning found that the only group which, like the Marquesans, reckoned to complete weaning by the age of six months was that of middle-class American mothers.[10]

During the first few years of infancy children are almost the exclusive province of the women. A Tikopian father may be allowed to fondle and nurse his baby child but only under strict female supervision and he meekly accepts scoldings and instruction on how to discharge the delicate business. A little later he may be called in as baby-minder while the mother goes out fishing but it is not until the child can crawl or is beginning to walk that father is allowed to take an active part in his training.[11] Nyansongo women believe babies are far too fragile to be looked after by men. They sleep with their infants in their arms so that the child can take the breast at will if it wakes up during the night; and if it falls ill for any reason the family may be expected to pay the diviner/medicine man the large fee of one or two goats to heal even minor ailments.[12]

But after the dangerous early period is past, bringing up the babies becomes a group concern in most societies and while father and uncles come only slowly into the child's picture of the world, he or she is in constant contact with other kin members. In this way involvement with the group begins early and is to continue throughout life. The Kgatla baby is under the care and supervision of a sister or cousin from the age of a few months until it is weaned. The anthropologist Isaac Schapera saw groups of eight- or nine-year-olds playing between the huts, each with a baby strapped to her back; from time to time one of the little nurses would leave the group as the insistent screams of her charge signalled feeding-time.[13] It was a typical picture of group self-help and education in action. The baby is part of the life of the community from the word go, whereas so many babies in advanced societies spend their first months cocooned in pram or carry cot, their view of ceiling or sky interrupted from time to time only by the face of the mother looking down. The Kgatla mother was liberated to get on with her own affairs while the little girls were learning at first hand the vital if not always welcome lessons of responsibility and co-operation.

There are very few primitive societies where baby-care isolates the infant from its human environment in the way it so often does in the West. Even the Navaho baby, which spends the first months of life strapped tightly to a cradle-board,[14] is more in touch than many a Western child. For if the board immobilizes him it also enables the mother to have the baby close at hand without the fear that he will interfere with her work or come to harm. Better still she can prop the child up to watch the world go by and since the mother is usually sitting cross-legged on the floor at her work of weaving or preparing the food, the baby's eyes are almost at a level with hers and it feels neither dwarfed nor intimidated by the adult world.

As the child grows older, the circle of people with an active part in its welfare widens. If a Kgatla child seemed unhappy at home it was sent to stay with an aunt or an uncle. A couple with an already large family might come to an agreement with childless relations that their next child should be 'born for' these relations. After it had been weaned the child was sent from the parental home to be brought up in its new family.[15] In such a social environment each child finds itself surrounded with a group of kinsfolk orientated towards him or her. There are other societies where group concern for the children finds still more explicit expression in foster-care. Among the Gonja of West Africa the families of both parents can claim rights in the children. A boy's maternal uncle, for example, may claim him as a foster-child by paying the barber who shaves the 'ghost hairs' at the naming ceremony seven days after the child's birth. The boy goes to his foster home at the age of six when he 'has sense'.[16] Margaret Mead, in her study of the Arapesh of New Guinea gives us a characteristically vivid insight into the way such social arrangements affect the young personality:

A child learns to think of the world as filled with parents, not merely a place in which all his safety and happiness depend on the continuance of his relationship with his own particular parents. The result is that the child grows up with a sense of security in the care of others ...[17]

In many other societies, while the child is brought up in the parental home, affection and nurture come from many people. Nyansongo children, nursed by mother and aunts indiscriminately after weaning, live in a world populated by mothers.[18] If we compare this with the common situation in the West, where the visit to relations is something of an event and aunts, uncles and grandparents are in consequence often strangers, we can see how impoverished personal relations can become in the context of the industrialized society and the nuclear family.

Yet though the middle-class Western family may be a circumscribed environment with a far smaller range of personal contacts than the extended family of other societies, for the first five years of life the child does belong there and can feel herself to be contributing. A toddler can hold the brushes for daddy while he paints the door; or can be sent off to get the smoothing-brush, which the to her god-like, but essentially amateur, handyman has left in the shed and now, at the top of the ladder, desperately needs if the beautifully positioned first length of wallpaper is not to collapse grimy and creased to the floor. Later, though not for long, she will be found proudly washing the dishes 'all by myself', a fully fledged, indispensable member of the team. Kids love to contribute to the action and want to belong to the work as well as the play. But in our machine-served, time-conscious world, efficiency is at such a premium that it requires an exercise of imagination to accept the help offered in the sure knowledge that the job may be done more slowly and less than perfectly. If their help is accepted, the children do feel themselves vital members of their home and so of the most significant society they know. The beginning of primary school is the first break in the consolidating system of understood obligations. From then on there is a growing division between the loyalties to home and school and uncertainty as to where the important society may be. None of this of course is necessarily traumatic, but it does contrast markedly with the continuing evolution of social involvement which is the life of the child in a primitive society.

But it was hardly an easy life. Everybody was required to contribute and children, too, were soon put to work. In traditional Nyansongo society married men and women herded the cattle; the boys and girls herded the sheep and goats; and the youngest children were at everybody's beck and call—an adult would never fetch anything for himself if there was a child around.[19] In Navaho villages boys and girls of six might be seen looking after the herds,[20] and among the Tikopia children were so important a help with the chores of the house that a childless family was thought to be seriously disadvantaged.[21] The children are expected to be obedient, but conformity to the will of the senior is regarded as a concession to be granted, not as a right to be expected. Since everybody in the villages of the primitive world has work to do, it is hardly surprising that the children should be mobilized; and at first there is little distinction between the chores of the girls and boys, though division of labour by sex is general among adults. The Navaho symbolize the future roles of the children at birth; the umbilical cord is kept until withered and then buried in a propitious place – for a girl under a loom; for a boy in the horse corral. Up to the age of six or seven the children may be seen herding the animals together but from eight on they are separated and begin to emphasize their sex differences. The girls imitate and dress like their mothers, the boys their fathers.[22] A Sioux girl over the age of five who was seen playing boys' games would be teased unmercifully,[23] and among the Nyansongo the girls look forward to their initiation eagerly for then they will be excused cattle herding, which is properly speaking boy's work, and be given the work of women – hoeing, harvesting and cooking.[24]

The climax of growing up and probably the greatest single experience in the lives of many primitives is the initiation, or puberty rite. This celebration by the group that new members have reached the age of maturity and the age of child-bearing, involves every member of the village and takes a multitude of impressive and symbolic forms that have fascinated the Western anthropologist as much as they absorbed the practitioners. They involve severe endurance tests of stamina and courage, often some form of scarification or other ritual mutilation, heavy emphasis on sex differentiations which confirm the acculturation to sex awareness already emphasized in the period of nurture and, for the boys, initiation into some of the religious mysteries that are the preserve of the men.

The ceremony itself often lasts days and preparations for it are still more drawn-out. It is woven into the life of the community so that nobody is unaware of what is in the air and everybody has some part to play. The children may run errands and carry the food which is being prepared for the ceremonial feast. The adults help with the organization of the event and instruct the participants in what is expected of them. No boy or girl may avoid the ceremony and none would want to, since, although it is often painful and terrifying, without it a child would not win the rights of adulthood. However, the child may have the chance to decide when it should submit; Nyansongo girls up to a certain maximum age, are free to choose their time, and to test them their mothers will try to dissuade them from making the decision. But most are eager. Not only does it entitle them to real woman's work but they can expect to win suitors among the grown-up circumcised boys. And of course one of the most compelling considerations is the fear of being left behind by their age mates. Thereafter the girl's only interest is marriage and they become increasingly difficult to control.[25]

The Nyansongo ceremony for the girls is more elaborate than that for the boys. It is organized by the youths and girls who have already been initiated but are not yet married, some acting as sponsors for the novices, others escorting them to and from the circumcision which is the focus of the proceedings. After the operation on the girl she is escorted home by a rowdy and boisterous procession of women shouting obscenities to all and sundry and particularly at any men they may pass, and dancing bawdily, lifting their skirts to flaunt their sex and imitating the act of copulation. It is a day of turmoil when the social order is turned upside down; men avoid the goings-on and the women may run amok, tearing up the crops and destroying property. In comparison, the boy's ceremony is a subdued affair but also more significant. He is led to the operation by sponsors but neither his parents nor his kin fathers may witness this part of the proceedings. The boy is indeed very much on his own—whereas the girl is supported and restrained by women as she faces the knife, the boy stands alone. Afterwards he is taken back to a hut that has been specially built for him by a procession of men singing bawdy songs but not so boisterously as the women. At the feast which concludes the proceedings the boy is expected to face other tests of endurance, pulling tent pegs from the ground surrounding the fire and eating and holding down nauseous foods.[26]

The elements of such ceremonies are repeated in many other societies. The event is deadly serious and is a true ordeal – the novice may find himself taunted and jeered at by other initiates and the courage with which he faces his punishment is an important part of the test. The super-incision ceremony on the foreskin of a Tikopia boy is supposed by the men who administer the operation to be painless; but some of the younger men confirmed to Raymond Firth that this was far from the truth. A gentler introduction to adult life is the Tikopia's first torchlight canoe fishing expedition. He paddles as one of the crew and the next day food is prepared by the boy's parents. He is smeared with turmeric and sent to stay in his uncle's house overnight. The two exchange food in the kind of kin ceremony so common in primitive life.[27]

Social and kin involvement in the life of the individual finds its highest expression in the initiation ceremonies. There is nothing to parallel it in our experience, though parallels have been drawn. In the view of the American academic, Pierre Maranda, the purpose of the initiation rites was 'to demonstrate to oneself and to others that one can fend for oneself in the unknown. An adult is essentially someone who, having proved personal independence, is consequently in a position to contribute positively to social life.' It is a neat idea and as developed by Maranda suggests thought-provoking comparisons with the West. Observing that initiation ceremonies often impose severe tests – 'a physical passage, followed by a return to the native world' which 'signifies the sociological passage from adolescence to adulthood' – Maranda compares this with the urge felt by adolescents in Western society to travel abroad and then 'to come back endowed with new Powers.' 'It is necessary to prove to oneself and to one's peers and to one's elders that maturity has come: that one can master nature and thus give evidence of one's cultural capability.'[28] On this theory drug trips may also be regarded as self-imposed initiation rites by today's young proclaiming their adulthood by a willingness to venture into the unknown realms of inner space.

However, the hypothesis breaks down at a number of significant points. The primitive initiation rite is demanded by society and not chosen spontaneously by the youth. The rites, universally associated with puberty, do not demonstrate inner personal merit so much as proclaim society's cognizance that the individual has reached another landmark in the process of becoming a full social being. As their name for themselves shows, the 'drop-outs' of today, far from proclaiming their readiness to take on the roles which society has allotted them, are flaunting their contemptuous rejection of society and all its works. In fact, though it may ape them with degree ceremonies, coming-of-age parties, the membership ceremonies of the professions or the street gangs, Western society has no initiation rites. Where the primitive world celebrates the stages from birth to puberty by which the human personality is shaped into maturity, and inaugurates its new social members with pomp and friendship, the civilized state simply puts a new name on the voters' register, permits marriage between consenting adults and hands out different types of sentence to the law-breaker. Even the family ceremonies are atrophying in many parts of society with the general reaction against formalities of all kinds. Perhaps it is natural enough in a civilization whose policy is 'separate but equal development' for individuals, but by looking at the primitive experience we can see that both people are the poorer if they draw apart from one another.

9 Rules for the Anti-Social

All societies, it appears, face the problem of anti-social behaviour, ranging from murder to disputes over grazing rights. It is certainly mistaken to suppose that the primitive acts out his life governed by ageless, unquestioned custom as administered by incurious and uncomprehending elders; the balancing of individual interests against the general good requires the recurrent exercise of imagination and intelligence, however well-adapted the pattern inherited from the past may be. In the words of High Forehead the Sioux: 'The Indian on the Prairie, before there was the white man to put him in the guardhouse, had to have something to keep him from doing wrong.'[1] The legal apparatus of the primitive may not be elaborate, it may sometimes be minimal, but it is there. Moreover, it is supported by the consensus of the people; it operates according to fixed procedures and it is motivated by principles that are often radically different from those that appear to govern the dispensations of civilized justice.

Without the 'guardhouse' of a penal system or a prison service, the primitive society disposes of effective sanctions. Among the Cheyenne Indians, the most heinous crime was murder. It was believed that the entrails of the murderer began to rot within him and that his crime stank in the nostrils of nature so that the game animals avoided the territory of the people and the whole tribe suffered from the wrong-doing of one. Yet so strong was the sentiment against the killing of a member of the tribe that not even the tribal council could take the life of the criminal. His penalty instead was exile and the humiliation of his kin.[2]

A Cheyenne murder involved the whole nation in an elaborate ritual process, but elsewhere in the primitive world anti-social behaviour might be controlled in less obvious ways. In his classic study of crime and custom among the Trobriand Islanders, Malinowski observes:

> The free and easy way in which all transactions are conducted, the good manners which pervade all and cover any hitches or maladjustments make it difficult for the superficial to see the keen self-interest and watchful reckoning which runs right through.[3]

The building of a Trobriand canoe is a good example of this apparently amicable co-operation at work. One man is recognized as the master and owner of the vessel but its building is the work of many, each of whom has a share in its operations and each of whom can call on the owner to assist him in his turn. Thus reciprocal obligations take on the aspect of legal sanctions. And the case is even clearer in the ritual trading relationship known as the *kyasa*, between the gardeners of the inland villages and the fishermen on the coast. Neither partner may refuse the gift proffered by the other and neither dare delay repayment when it falls due. An elaborate economic relationship rests apparently on the friendly basis of mutual obligations, yet in former times failure to fulfil them could lead to bloodshed. At times of famine the inlanders driven by hunger to poach fish from the lagoons were hunted down and killed by the coast-dwellers.[4] In primitive as in civilized societies, then, economic hardship and crisis can precipitate a breakdown in the rule of law.

Yet, in general, 'respect for the law' is common enough among primitive peoples. The Eskimo Igsivalitaq, who had killed a man in a fight of honour, fled into exile but not—as he explained to the anthropolgist Knud Rasmussen who tracked him down—because he wished to evade the law. He was prepared to suffer the vengeance of his victim's kinsfolk according to custom but not the humiliation of being dealt with by the white man's police.[5] The Comanche Indians likewise respected their own code. Absconding with the wife of another man was a common form of challenge and bravado, yet the offenders notwithstanding paid the fine required by law rather than resort to force of arms.[6]

What we might call the enforcement agencies behind the Eskimo and Comanche codes are exiguous in the extreme; the physical sanctions that they can command are pitiful when compared with the battery of punishments available to even the most liberal of Western codes. Yet even so they can evoke a response of willing recognition. Everything that we learn from the primitive reinforces the idea that the norms of social behaviour expressed by the laws of any society pre-date the sanctions system that buttress those laws. It is not the penalties that uphold the law but rather the fact that most people, in a healthy society, concur in the law that makes the penalties enforceable. Once the majority in society has lost commitment to the law then no amount of apparatus will be able to enforce it.

There are many institutions in the primitive world that we can easily identify in terms of our legal system – the Ashanti chief sitting in formal council with the elders of the tribe; the tribal council of the Pueblo Indians convened for a judicial sitting; the Anuak headman holding court and arbitrating disputes at the public hearth outside his gates. Here is the apparatus of the law. The very word 'court' as applied to a judicial process is a reminder that in our own distant history justice was dispensed, as among the Anuak, in the palace court – the household of the king. But there are other primitive societies where the trappings of law are not so evident and it is these that interest us.

The Eskimo shaman has some of the functions of a lawman. He conducts the public confession of a taboo-breaker and absolves the contrite offender and punishes the unrepentant. One girl was exiled from her community in the dead of winter at the orders of the shaman, because she persisted in breaking the taboo on the eating of caribou and seal together.[7] But there is no formalized body or legal apparatus. Even murder, which outside the context of a feud is recognized as a major crime, is dealt with in an apparently *ad hoc* fashion. Action against the criminal may depend on some man public-spirited enough, or with some personal interest strong enough, to initiate proceedings. First he interviews all the men of the tribe individually to get a unanimous agreement that the murder must be dealt with; if this is forthcoming, the self-appointed executioner takes the first opportunity of ridding the community of the public menace in the knowledge that he will not be the victim of a revenge killing from the family of the criminal.[8]

The need for a unanimous verdict reflects the reluctance, common to many primitive peoples, to deprive a man of life by calculated cold decision. In some Eskimo groups this aversion to judicial murder is so strong, and the conventions of the feud so stringent, that no family will risk the job of executioner and the sentence is left to be carried out by a member of the criminal's own family. Uvdorliasgussuk, in Western parlance a fratricide but enjoying respect and esteem in his own village, explained to Rasmussen how he had come to take his brother's life. Some years previously the brother had run amok, stabbing his wife on numerous occasions and finally killing a man. The men of the village agreed unanimously that he should be killed and that his elder brother, as head of the family, should carry out the sentence. Uvdorliasgussuk sought out his brother, told him of the sentence and asked him to choose the means of his execution. The young man chose death by shooting and offered no resistance as his brother carried out the sentence. Perhaps not since Socrates accepted the judgment of the citizens of Athens has a legal code enjoyed such acceptance and assent.[9]

Such examples show how, in the primitive context, traditional procedures enable individuals to operate the laws with little or no formal or official structure. Yet at the back of this apparently free-wheeling system lies a fundamental consensus on the common value of the society. We see this consensus at work in the Nuer procedure for settling disputes. The Nuer assume that the individual will assert his interests against all-comers and that the man who does not do so does not deserve to have his rights respected. They are saved from the selfish anarchy that so generally characterizes Western society, first by the power of the kin group, which supports the man when he is in the right, and second by that wide consensus as to rights and obligations which leads the kin to make him moderate his demands when he is in the wrong.

A man whose rights have been infringed is entitled to compensation in cattle, but there is no obligation on the offender to volunteer it. Accordingly, the 'plaintiff', with members of his kin, goes to the byre of the 'defendant' and drives away the number of cows which the injury entitles him to. Everyone knows what is going on and the offender can expect little help even from his kin if he is in the wrong. Without lawyers or law courts the case has already been decided at the bar of public opinion. If, however, the claim is contested and violence seems likely, neighbours intervene and try to bring the parties to agreement. Only if this fails are the mediating services of the leopard-skin chief called upon and as a final resort he may decree a judicial combat. The contestants use clubs not spears so as to avoid a killing which would spark off a feud. In this way the Nuer leave the settlement of disputes, as far as possible, to the contending parties but wisely provide for the limitation of conflict by traditional procedures and a semi-official mediator if one becomes essential.[10]

In other primitive societies such assessors are used more regularly and may even be paid for their services. The Ifugao *monkalun* (advisor or mediator) is a man of high social status with a high reputation; each successful mediation not only enhances that reputation but also brings him additional wealth in the form of the pigs that are paid to him by the parties in dispute.[11] His success depends largely on his personal authority and his experience combined with common sense and imagination. Among the Tiv, neighbours of the Nuer, however, the elders who act as arbitrators must be experts in the full sense of the term. Since the social structure of the tribe is based on kinship, with families owing allegiance to common ancestors looking on others as potential opponents, a dispute between two individuals quickly widens to include many members of the rival families. Points of genealogy bulk large in the settlements and the elders, heirs to a vast aural tradition on tribal history and descent, are called in to advise. The confused and extensive family trees allow scope for interpretation, so the settlement mediated by the elders can be a true compromise based on discretion as well as expertise.

In fact, compromise rather than decision is generally the hallmark of primitive dispute settlements. Naturally, where a society is comparatively small and disputes concern matters of common experience, the kind of consensus judgments we have been discussing and mutual willingness to compromise must be easier than in the highly separatist kind of society that generally characterizes the civilized world. Yet the example of the world's greatest and oldest civilization shows that the will to social harmony can find expression even outside the supposedly simple conditions of the primitive tribe. For the emphasis in much primitive law is on restoring the harmonious pattern of society broken by the criminal act and it is this same emphasis that we find in the civil law of China, both ancient and modern.

Under the Manchus, the last of the imperial dynasties, much of this mediatory law was implemented outside the framework of state law—that, indeed, was deliberately made expensive and humiliating so as to discourage litigants. In the words of the emperor K'ang-hsi:

> ... lawsuits would tend to increase to a frightening extent if people were not afraid of the tribunals and if they felt confident of always finding in them ready and perfect justice. A man is apt to delude himself concerning his own interests, contests would become interminable and the one half of the empire would not suffice to settle lawsuits of the other half. I desire therefore that those who have recourse to the tribunals should be treated without pity and in such a manner that they shall be disgusted with law and tremble to appear before a magistrate.[12]

The emperor then went on to recommend his subjects to settle their disputes within their community 'like brothers', calling in mediators to help them. 'As for those who are troublesome, obstinate and quarrelsome, let them be ruled in the law courts— that is the justice due to them.'

As a formula for reducing the burden on the bureaucracy, K'ang-hsi's directive had no doubt much to recommend it. It was also in tune with the Confucianist ethic which held that litigiousness revealed a shameless obsession with one's own interests and disregard for the well-being of society. Law, considered in the West as one of the finest achievements that a society can boast of, was looked upon by educated Chinese as a regrettable necessity; disputes should be settled not by force, the ultimate sanction of all law, but by moral persuasion and by compromise. Whereas Western society admires the man who 'sticks up for his rights', the Chinese believed that a man of honour would rather suffer a little injustice than disrupt the social fabric and, if in the right, would willingly concede something to his enemy. In the words of the historian Jean Escarra, 'To take advantage of one's position to invoke one's rights has always been looked on askance in China.'[13]

Not that the ancient Chinese system was a model of just dealing and mutual forbearance. Far from it. While the principle of mediation worked well enough between equals it was all too easily bent and corrupted by the powerful in their dealings with the poor. The great revolution of modern China succeeded precisely because of the real oppression and injustice endured by the mass of the population under the old regime. The point to be emphasized is that the concepts underlying traditional Chinese law were both different in principle and more socially cohesive than those behind Western law. The ultimate pressures on the disputants to accept the compromise offered was the sanction of complete social ostracism for those persisting in a quarrel. The village elders, backed up in this way by public opinion could generally settle the dispute in the local teahouse, the party at fault paying the bill for refreshments – compromise was always at the heart of the matter. The system fostered social cohesion by applying the community values that lay at the foundation of village life, and so providing a regular opportunity for the re-education of the group in its own traditions and beliefs.

This ancient Chinese practice is not of merely academic interest since it has been continued and developed in the local courts of modern China. The system of village community 'courts' squares well with the concern of the Communist regime for peasant control and local self-help, while the deep roots of such a system in the past is a further point in its favour in a country where tradition still plays a major role. A judgment imposed according to the dictates of an abstract law divides the disputants, by definition, as winner and loser; mediation, by contrast, aims to win the consent of both parties. It is not therefore surprising to find mediation the preferred mode for dispute settlement in a society that has social integration as its top priority. It should be a matter of urgent interest to Western society, heir to an urban civilization now apparently in the last stages of disintegration, to find from the example of the world's oldest urban civilization a system of justice that shares so much with the harmonious ideals of the primitive world. One estimate suggests that there are more than two hundred thousand peoples' mediation committees at work in China today. There is little sign that this age-old community device for reducing the tensions of dispute is in danger of decay.[14]

When the need arises, primitive man is quite able to evolve formal structures of authority as is demonstrated by the regulation of the bison hunt among the Plains Indians. The introduction of the horse to America in the sixteenth century quickly revolutionized the whole pattern of Indian life and above all the hunt. The horse, soon rated at law as equivalent to a man for the purposes of compensations, not only extended the range of the marauding parties of warriors but also opened up the prairie and its great herds of bison as never before. But the spirited new steeds often tempted the young braves to shows of bravado, dashing ahead of their fellows and stampeding the herd before the line of huntsmen had time to come to grips with it. The patience of the tracker and woodman broke down before the impetuosity of the cavalier and the need for a new kind of discipline became obvious.[15]

For the duration of the hunt this imposed discipline, so alien to the spirit of the Indian, was absolute and was enforced by members of the military associations. This creative use of an existing institution rather than the special formation of a new one shows constitutional sophistication. For the associations, originally formed as social clubs, were well placed to exercise a legal and administrative role. Since their membership comprised all the warriors of the tribe, the authority of their leaders was unquestioned. Soon it came to extend to other matters until, among the Cheyenne for example, it stopped short only at cases of homicide and adultery, traditionally the preserve of the chief.

To the Westerner, suspicious with good cause of the forces of 'law and order' and familiar with the excesses of the police state, it is remarkable that the leaders of the military associations of the Plains Indians never sought to develop their unquestioned power-base into an authoritarian oligarchy. Not only was their rule supreme during the all-important communal activity of the hunt but also they held important responsibilities during the great festivals. No doubt their failure to capitalize on their position is in part a reflection of the fluid conditions of life on the plains; it is also the direct outcome of the fierce individualism of the Plains Indians. Members of a society where the enforcement of law can be one of the prime attributes of state oppression, we can only envy the Indians their practical and relaxed approach to the problem of discipline.

We also have much to learn from their whole approach to the function and administration of law; it is summed up in an example recalled in 1935 by the old Cheyenne, Stump Horn. Two young braves had ridden out ahead of the hunt and were summarily punished—their horses were killed, their rifles broken and they themselves given a beating by the soldiers. These draconian measures were followed up with a lecture, and at the end of it all the two culprits were well and truly repentant, as well they might be. Immediately the whole mood of the proceedings changed.

> One of the soldiers spoke up: 'Well, I have some extra horses, I will give one of them to them.' Then another soldier did the same thing. Bear Standing on a Ridge was the third to speak out: 'Well', he announced; 'We broke those guns they had but I have two guns, I will give them one.' All the others said: '*Ipewa*', good.[16]

The moral is clear enough. The aim of law is not simply to hand out penalties but also to restore social harmony. The law must be upheld and anti-social behaviour corrected; nevertheless, no good purpose is served by giving the offender cause for resentment.

Among the many ideals governing our legal attitudes is the notion that the criminal can 'pay his debt to society', as the saying has it, and then be received back without recrimination or discrimination. It is rarely achieved – a prison sentence usually being enough to mark a man for life. Despite all attempts at reform, Western penal systems and their administrators too often treat the criminal simply as an enemy of society and once he has been cast in that role everything conspires to keep him in it. In primitive systems, by contrast, the aim is, first and foremost, to restore the harmony broken by the crime and to reintegrate the offender as quickly as possible.

The Cheyenne, for example, regard the killing of one of their tribesmen by another as such a heinous offence that not even the tribal council can exact a life for a life; instead the penalty is exile. Nevertheless, after a period of only five years the murderer may, with the consent of the victim's family, be re-admitted to the tribe. Now it must be conceded that his reinstatement is not complete for he is forever barred from sharing the common pipe or eating or drinking from the common bowl at ceremonial feasts. Yet this one-time criminal may work and hunt with his fellows; he re-occupies his place on the council and is restored to his former social status. Clearly the proscription laid on him is no mere gesture of social vindictiveness; rather it is the simple but inexorable consequence of his crime. The pollution a man brings on himself by murder is not a penalty of the law nor is it an act of social retribution; it is just one of the attributes of being a murderer. Society can no more wash away such pollution than it can remove the act of murder from the man's past.[17]

These prohibitions on the Cheyenne murderer are simply the outward expression of a fact about him that is known to everyone and that is self-inflicted. They also have a positive function. By proclaiming the ineradicable nature of the murderer's pollution and at the same time obliging him to bear the consequences on certain public occasions, the ritual penalty isolates the fact from the man. Fear, unease or resentment at his rehabilitation, all natural enough reactions, find a formalized and public focus, and thus relations within the group are freed of unvoiced fears and suspicions. As far as possible the harmony has been restored, even after the dissonance of murder.

Such forthright acceptance of the criminal and his crime, combined with the positive will to reintegrate him into the community, has surely much to teach the West, where popular attitudes to crime are still largely combative and negative. However, restoring the harmony of life after an act of murder was a far more serious business than the reinstatement of the criminal. By his act the whole tribe was polluted, for murder stained the feathers of the Medicine Arrows of the Cheyenne. Only after their renewal could life return to its normal tenor. The act of re-dedication was a great ceremony lasting for several hours; apart from former murderers and their families, every member of the tribe had to be present and complete silence was enforced by the military societies who policed the assembly; the children were forbidden to play and any barking dogs were instantly killed.

> ... by means of this renewal ritual the Cheyennes achieved a social result of tremendous value ... the act which could shatter the tribe—homicide—was made the incident that formally reinforced the integrity of the people as a people. Not vengeance, not further blood-letting, not the cruel punishment of imprisonment, but purification from a sin shared by all and a reinforcement of the social bond were the results achieved by the Cheyenne action.[18]

The notion that a crime can be creatively used in reaffirmation of group solidarity would appear laughable in the Western context. Not least, perhaps, because the whole idea of group solidarity seems to be fracturing beyond repair. In his book *Law Without Sanctions*, Michael Barkun speaks of 'the jural community', defining it as 'an area in which all the actors recognize that a common method exists for resolving the disputes between them'.[19] Intellectually, such a definition seems apt and acceptable; but when we come to apply it to the societies of the West we see that the concept is in jeopardy. The Catholics of Northern Ireland and the

Blacks of America no longer recognize a 'common method of resolving disputes' shared with the other members of the community, and for that very reason those societies are destructively divided. Elsewhere, more and more groups, chief among them the young, are rejecting the very machinery for dispute' settlement.

As revolutionary slogans ring about them politicans appeal to the silent majority, thus betraying, whatever their motives, their conviction that an effective legal system depends not on its sanctions but on a social consensus. Yet even among the silent majority such a consensus in favour of the law does not exist. Quite the contrary. The thriving business of tax evasion shows in one massive area a conspiracy among the bulk of the citizenry to evade the law—an evasion every bit as unsocial as the most angry demonstration, for it entails the withholding of funds legally demanded in the common good. It has been calculated for England alone that the annual sum represented by the evasion of estate duties and other taxes would be sufficient to raise the weekly pension—for many old retired people the sole means of support—by no less than £2. Sharply defined and conflicting interests are the bane of civilizations. They institutionalize and strengthen the conflicts to be found in any human society and thereby make them more intractable. The law and methods of dispute settlement, which in the primitive context are part of an understood and accepted structure for the regulation of anti-social behaviour, come to be regarded as the weapons of the interest group in the ascendant against those less powerful.

It is a feature of urban civilizations that large segments of the population have a strong sense of injustice. In one like the West, which, in theory, vaunts the equality of all men yet in practice is so structured as to ensure their gross and unmistakable inequality, this sense of injustice is bound to be intensified. Appeals to the law have little weight in sections of the community condemned by social deprivation to live their lives as second-class citizens. At times when the forces of 'law and order' feel themselves under pressure, the tendency is to look to higher penalties as the answer to lawlessness. Penalties and sanctions there are in any system of social regulation but, as we have seen, they must be recognized and consented to by the society as a whole. Law depends neither on elaborate machinery nor on meticulous drafting. It rests on a general agreement as to the norms of behaviour that are to be observed in the interests of all and a deep underlying sense that the social structure is indeed ordered in the interests of all. While we know this, the primitives practise it. In such a system compromise is possible and cohesive, punishment is truly corrective and the offender can be fully received back to play his useful part in society.

10 The Problems of the Polis

The more civilized man becomes, it has been said, the greater his need for law and the more of it he creates. Whether this necessarily means that civilizations must therefore be bureaucracies is unclear – but it is obviously true that law-making is one of the most important and time-consuming activities in civilized society. In the time of the Greeks, of course, the art of law-making was raised to a high status and gave birth indirectly to the idea of democratic politics which, it is thought by some, still governs the practice of politics in the West today.

However, between the Greek polis and the contemporary corridors of power something seems to have gone wrong. Today, the vast political edifice which is meant to keep our society moving smoothly along its proper course is dangerously near collapse and has long since lost popular credibility. The cynical belief that politicians are for the most part in the game for their personal advantage; the observed fact that the problems of modern society are too numerous and too complex for solution by traditional means; and the sense of helplessness that citizens feel before the all-pervasive power of the bureaucratic state; all produce bitterness, discontent and alienation. People feel excluded from the very decisions that affect their lives, and many believe that life would be better if there were no politicians at all.

For contrast, we turn again to the Kalahari Desert, and the nomadic :Kung Bushmen. The sparse nature of their environment dictates the division of the small population into little groups of no more than fifty or sixty people; even so they have an embryonic political organization. Each band has rights of gathering the vegetation of a specific territory, and a group studied by Lorna Marshall could not remember a single case of infringement. In fact she had practical experience of this 'territorial imperative'. Photographing the band on one of its gathering expeditions she asked them to move a few hundred yards to a spot where the lighting was better, and was met with a blank refusal. The new site, it was explained, lay in the territory of a neighbouring band.[1]

The rights of each band to the vegetation and water of its territory are embodied in the person of an hereditary headman who is said by some :Kung to 'own' these resources. The other families of the band are entitled to gather in his territory only because of their ties of kinship with the headman.

In a very literal sense, then, the headman is the father of his people, but because he embodies the people's sense of identity and validates their territorial claims, he discharges a true political function analagous to that of a constitutional monarch or the president of a modern state. Nevertheless, he enjoys very few special privileges. He does his own work, carries his own load and gathers his own food. He carries no distinguishing marks of office and is careful to avoid giving himself airs.

He does occasionally have to make decisions—for instance, in which order foods should be gathered if something happens to disturb the seasonal and traditional pattern. He may lead the band when it moves camp, and he has the somewhat more practical advantage of selecting the best site for his personal fireplace. It may also fall to him to perform the ritual lighting of the first fire at a new site, though sometimes this is done by a revered older member of the tribe. The :Kung abominate conflict so that even the dubious honour of leading a war party is denied the headman. Moreover, hunting forays are organized communally and disputes settled between the contending parties without arbitration so that the headman's duties and his opportunities for exercising power are effectively nil.

But the headman may not be the leader of the band. In constitutional theory he might be classed as a king, but the position does not give him the automatic control of decision-making once enjoyed, *ex officio*, by the monarchs of Europe. If he is too young, too old or is not generally respected, the members of the band may simply turn to another for advice. :Kung society has little need of leaders, and those who on occasion discharge the functions enjoy no special respect; yet, as one :Kung observed to Lorna Marshall, they are blamed if anything goes wrong with their plans.

Complaints against leaders are not unknown in our own society where the powerful public figure expatiating on the heavy burdens of office is common. His words might carry more weight if the rewards of office were not quite so obvious and if the sighing altruist did not repeatedly seek the very responsibilities he complains of. The Western politician seeks power by all means available and proudly proclaims his qualifications for leadership, whereas the unfortunate :Kung, with greatness thrust upon him, finds himself criticized even though he made no effort to win prominence. For this reason the members of many primitive societies do all in their power to avoid political responsibility.

When the Nambikuara of Brazil come to choose a new chief, it is common for candidates to refuse the honour.[2] They have good reason. The chief is responsible for the all-important decisions in the life of the tribe; he must select the routes during the nomadic periods of the year; determine when the wanderings shall begin and end; choose the camp site; and ensure that the people can find sufficient food. Although the chief has well-worn traditions to guide him, if anything goes wrong he is held responsible. More onerous yet is the chief's obligation to generosity. Although little better-off than others, he is expected to distribute presents of tools, ornaments and weapons whenever conceivably possible. 'There is little doubt', writes Lévi-Strauss, 'that the chief's ability to give is exploited to the utmost.'[3] Not only that— in distributing his gifts he may well cause offence to the unlucky ones. Chiefs may even return gifts from visitors rather than face the invidious duty of picking out whom to give them to.

If these are the chief's obligations, what are his privileges? According to the philosopher Montaigne, who met a group of Amerindian chiefs brought to Rouen in the 1560s, the privilege of the chief was 'to walk ahead on the warpath'.[7] In four centuries the answer had not changed and Lévi-Strauss got the same reply from his Nambikuara informant. We can easily understand the vehemence with which most candidates refuse office—but why does any Nambikuara ever accept? The Lévi-Strauss answer may seem almost unscientific yet, because it speaks of basic human motivation, it rings true. He writes:

I am imperiously led to this answer: there are chiefs because there are in any human group men who, unlike most of their companions, enjoy prestige for its own sake, feel a strong appeal to responsibility, and to whom the burden of public affairs brings its own reward.[5]

The obligation to generosity lies on every primitive leader if he wishes to hold his position. Unlike the :Kung headman, a chief of the Anuak, one of the Nilotic peoples of the Southern Sudan, does enjoy real prestige as mediator and judge. Disputes are settled and matters of public interest debated at the hearth before his gateway, and his homestead becomes a court which reflects his own status and brings prestige to the village. Since there is great rivalry between Anuak villages, the young men compete to decorate the fence round the headman's compound with ceremonial carvings. But this they do only so long as the headman continues his generosity. If his 'largesse' shows signs of falling off, his following simply melts away and attaches itself to another.'[6]

In fact, generosity buys support almost everywhere. The nobles of medieval Europe made a point of display and liberality, not only because they enjoyed appearing magnanimous but so as to keep their supporters happy. At their feasts whole carcasses of beef, mutton and venison were consumed at a single sitting and any member of the lord's following was entitled to carry away from the kitchens as much meat as he could skewer with a cooking knife or dagger. Such was the pay-off for the 'poor man at the gate'; inside the hall the great could expect to be more elegantly, if no less comprehensively, plundered by their fashionable retainers. At a banquet of the Order of the Golden Fleece, held by Duke Philip the Good of Burgundy, 'the dinner was accompanied by the music of viols and trumpets and the cries of "largesse" from the heralds, who received great gifts of jewellery and money from the knights'.[7] The parallels between the primitive or the medieval leader buying support with generosity and the modern politician with his promise of cuts in taxation, increases in social benefits and a higher standard of living, need hardly be laboured. The differences are less obvious. Among the Anuak, the assumption that a man earns support by what he pays for is neither veiled nor questioned. When the young men of the village find that their services are repaid inadequately, they go and openly look for another headman. In primitive societies, which are small and with a strong sense of cohesion, support is bought from all by distribution of favours to all; in fragmented modern societies, however, a power-base can be built on support from some to the disadvantage of others. To conceal this sort of injustice in our less straightforward world, the materialistic motives of politics are concealed by talk of principle.

The degree to which the political function can be integrated in a primitive society is richly illustrated by the Nyakyusa, a Bantu tribe.[8] One element in the classic political system of the theorists is an elite who share the positions of authority. The very idea is divisive and the Nyakyusa would seem to have avoided the danger by defining the elite in terms of age. Yet in their wise and elaborate traditions the generation gap combined with an elitist type of political structure produced harmony where we would expect only conflict. The ultimate source of authority was an hereditary chief who, as elsewhere, embodied the group's sense of identity. But real decision-making rested with the married warriors, from whose ranks, for example, were drawn the village headman. A man's social rank depended on the number of his wives, and since men married late, the young enjoyed no political status and in fact lived in separate villages. At about the age of ten the boys moved out of their parents' settlement to build a new village which then admitted new recruits until the founders reached the age of sixteen.

The Nyakyusa, who thought it wrong for a youth to witness his parents' sex life and also recognized the dangers of incest in a household composed of young sons and the father's young wives, saw their system in terms of sexual morality. But it also lessened the opportunities of conflict between young and old; for politically deprived though they were, it was the young men, during their long bachelor years, who could most completely fulfil the Nyakyusa ideal of the good life. It was called *ukwangala* and it rested on male sodality—it was a life of wit, urbanity and generosity, lived out in the company of one's age mates. As they brought wives into the village and thereby acquired responsibilities and status, the men approached the time when they should become the elite in their turn.

Once in each generation, at an *ubusoka* or 'coming out' ceremony presided over by the tribal chief, responsibilities for defence and administration passed to the 'junior' villages. The retiring generation took up responsibilities in matters of ritual and the tribal chief gave his functions to his two eldest sons, and appointed new village headmen. As tradition prevented him from instituting his other sons as village headmen, and within the villages themselves a headman's son was debarred from occupying his father's position, the system provided against even the dangers of a self-perpetuating hereditary oligarchy. Down to the 'checks and balances' beloved of Western constitutional theory, the tradition of the Nyakyusa showed itself politically subtle and effective.

The society, it must be admitted, held women in low esteem, but that characteristic it shared with most primitive and civilized societies including, until recently, our own. In other respects it was a system enviable in its completeness. Among the Nyakyusa, the tension between age and youth, a force of disruption in the West, resolved itself and was a means of life enrichment. Among them sexual morality, a social ideal, and political arrangements reinforced and flowed into one another; in contrast we, with our competitive interest groups and our 'individualist' rather than social priorities, still search for the secret of harmony between the world of dreams and the world of 'reality'.

While the Nyakyusa define their political elite in terms of age, and competition has little place, elsewhere different criteria are used. On the island of Kiriwina, in Papua, there is a small group of sub-clans whose members form the political elite permitted to compete for leadership. The story of Daibuna in one of their villages illustrates how one ambitious young man, in a competitive primitive political environment made a career for himself.[9] First he built up his personal wealth and prestige by making gifts to and performing services for the senior members of his elite sub-clan. In return he received plots of land, the exclusive use of coconut palms or other advantages. Daibuna, who took his career very seriously, won control of six plots by his early thirties—about twice the amount of land usual for a man of his age. His skill as a gardener won him a position in the work-force recruited for the garden of the district headman. When bad health forced the headman to delegate some of his duties, Daibuna was chosen. He supervised the building of the canoe for a trading expedition, organized the fencing of new garden sites and led his village's contribution to a major festival. In this way, by seeking responsibilities and discharging them efficiently, Daibuna established his claim as the successor of the village headman. The pattern seems to have much in common with Western systems. But there is a difference: as a member of an elite, Daibuna was entitled to compete for a position of authority. But his success came not from expertise in an arena for political specialists, but by demonstrating competence in the common skills of Kiriwinan life and by serving the community in a practical way.

From the virtually republican system of the :Kung to the competitive world of Kiriwina, primitive cultures exhibit as rich a spectrum of administrative structures as civilization. One aspect, however, is remarkable by its absence: revolution. In his brilliant essay 'The Search for the Primitive', Stanley Diamond comments: 'It is probably safe to say that there has never been a revolution in a primitive society; revolutions are peculiar to political societies.'[10] The point is obvious enough if we accept that primitive society cannot be called 'political' in the Western sense of the term. What does this mean?

The societies discussed in this chapter contain many of the ingredients of our own political system: competition, leadership, the idea of a territorial unity; and the existence of elite groups and rules governing their rivalry are all there. Yet what we see going on has no relation to the operation of pressure groups, struggle for power or the party politics of our own culture. Urban man regards society as a battlefield, the terrain on which he must fight for his survival and his own success; he tends to see himself and the group to which be belongs as embattled against the rest of society; and he aims to modify the system in his own interest by lobbying as a pressure group. Politics is the activity that flows from the competition of the many rival vested interests; under labels of principle the battle is fought out and the innumerable factions that together constitute our fractured society are united only by mutual struggle. Hence politics in a civilized society is the articulation of injustice and the expression of institutionalized rival interests.

A high level of material civilization is, in fact, impossible without injustice, since it depends on an economic surplus generated by large reserves of manpower exploited either in mind or body. Throughout history the latent pressure this causes has exploded from time to time as the depressed groups in society have struggled to win a privileged place in the operations of the political elite. Such revolutions have usually been violent and though they may change the relative standing of the various groups in the civilization, the exploitation of one group by another and of one man by another has continued and the fundamental state of tension remains. The true and deep revolution that must eliminate tension and exploitation from our civilization, and thus bring it nearer to the primitive mode of co-operative living, is still to come. Meanwhile politics, in its strict sense found only in our kind of society, provides a regulator for imbalance and a palliative of injustice. It has been defined by one political theorist as:

> ... a sociological activity which has the anthropological function of preserving a community grown too complicated for either tradition alone or pure arbitrary rule to preserve it without the undue use of coercion.[11]

If all this is true, can we hope to apply the lessons of the primitive experience to our own situation? For although we find among the primitives some of the trappings of our own politicking, what we do not find is ideological disputes about the way in which society should be run; bitter feuds between have and have-not factions; and a sense of alienation between the majority of the people and those in the positions of authority, who make decisions affecting their very lives. Minorities are governed in theory by the rule of the majority, and minorities, whether twenty million blacks in the United States or a few hundred thousand Catholics in Northern Ireland, must fend for themselves. The primitive lives in accordance with familiar, understood and generally accepted patterns laid down by tradition. In such a society one man does not rule others, even though he may be termed chief. The nearest translation of 'the chief rules the people', in the language of the Wintu Indians of California, is: 'the chief stands with the people.'[12] In such a society, to quote the words of Dorothy Lee, 'the authority of the headman or the chief or the leader is in many ways like the authority of the dictionary or of Einstein'.[13] In such a society there is no place and no call for revolution, since 'the basic needs for food, clothing, shelter and personal participation are satisfied in a socially non-exploitative manner'.[14]

From whatever point we approach the society of primitive man we find the gentle laws of harmony and balance at the heart of the matter. In this chapter we have abstracted certain social patterns for study since they seem to conform to the political and governmental functions of our own highly specialized world. In reality such analysis is artificial. Conflict, leadership, decision and corporate action are all integrated into the life of every member of the tribe to form a complete pattern of living. When industrial man wrote the grand principle of balance out of his social constitution, and substituted for it the violent doctrine of dynamic progress, he may have surrendered finally the hope of a stable and a just society. The primitive, constrained by the social and moral code of his people, finds freedom not by overthrowing the system but by living to the full within it. Nostalgically we may envy him his harmony with his society but, as our whole society rests on disharmony, disequilibrium and exploitation, we should not hope that we shall ever enjoy it—unless that system, together with the fundamental values that it embodies, be rewritten.

3

The World of
Economics

11 A Mountain of Blankets

One day in the twelfth century, that golden age of medieval European culture which witnessed the brilliant career of Peter Abelard, the building of Chartres Cathedral and the assembling of the first scholars at Oxford, a somewhat unexpected ceremony was going forward outside the French town of Limoges. The occasion was a great 'court' of chivalry, and the high point in the proceedings was a contest in honour and wealth between three knights. The first of the nobles, had one of his serfs plough up an acre of land and then sow it with silver pieces; meanwhile, the second knight was regaling the company to a feast where not the food but the fuel was the focus of interest, for the whole menu was to be cooked over expensive and highly valued wax candles. By these grotesque insults to the honourable and basic human activities of farming and cooking the knights seemed to intend to emphasize their superiority to the common herd as well as to outdo their rivals in their destruction of wealth. But the third of these jolly cavaliers must be reckoned to have gone several better, for he, 'through mere boastfulness', had thirty of his finest horses burnt alive![1] Who could fail to be impressed?

Such an orgy of destruction may have been something of an oddity in medieval Europe but it would have presented few problems of interpretation to a chief in the Kwakiutl tribes of the north-west coast of America. There, the cluster of ceremonials known as the 'potlatch' provided close parallels to this medieval battle for prestige by the ritual destruction of property.[2]

In the potlatch proper, vast quantities of wealth were disposed of; indeed the word itself means 'to give'. At the opening of the ceremony the host group proudly displayed the hereditary possessions and privileges that it already held. After songs and dances, there followed a recitation of the legendary origins and recent history of the privileges. Then certain members of the host group would be presented as the authentic bearers of those privileges and finally new names and privileges were conferred on them. After this, the lavish distribution of presents, which gave the whole ceremony its name, took place. Complicated and rigid rules governed the order of precedence to be observed among the recipients; a mistake would cause angry scenes and badly damage the reputation of the host chief. A potlatch might last two or three days and the host's skill in organization was as important a factor in his prestige as the display of wealth. In practical terms it was of particular significance in the events leading up to the potlatch proper, since to raise the wherewithal to hold it a chief generally had to organize the sale of one of his Coppers.

These Coppers, used as symbols of wealth, were shield-shaped pieces of sheet copper, about three feet long. They represented values that might run into thousands of dollars, but were not units of currency. Instead, the value of a Copper was determined by the amount paid for it the last time it changed hands (like a rare stamp or a valuable antique in our society); the very ability to buy any given specimen – all were named and their values public knowledge – was an exact measure of the buyer's standing. Because of this a Copper was usually offered for sale to a rival tribe; if no one could raise the purchase price the whole tribe lost face. Conversely, any chief intending to buy could not only call in any loans owing to him personally, but ask additional assistance from his fellow tribesmen, 'to keep our name as high as it is now'.

The actual sale was an involved exchange of ritual barter, even though both sides knew how much would eventually have to be given. At the sale of the Copper named 'All-other-are-ashamed-to-look-at-it', recorded by Franz Boas in 1895, the proceedings opened with the purchaser, Chief Owaxalagilis of the Kwakiutl, having 1,000 blankets placed in piles between the two posts set up on the beach to mark the potlatch site. 'Tribes,' he announced, 'I buy the Copper with these 1,000 blankets. I shall not give more unless the chiefs of all the tribes should ask for more! That is my speech, chiefs of the Kwakiutl.' Thereupon one of the chiefs of the Mameleleqala rose up to ask in astonishment. 'Are those your words, Kwakiutl? Did you say this was all that you were going to give for the Copper? Are there 1,000 blankets?' Being complacently assured that all this was indeed so, he carried on scathingly, 'Thank you, Owaxalagilis, chief. Do you think you have finished? You Chief ... give 200 more.' Nothing could have pleased Owaxalagilis better than this request; unhesitatingly he ordered his young men to bring the 200 blankets from his store. Four hundred blankets later it looked as if Owaxalagilis was unwilling to up his offer any more. 'I say it is enough, Mameleleqala. Now you have seen my name. This mountain of blankets rises through our heaven.' But in reality this is only the beginning. At the end of the day, having eagerly capitulated to demand after demand, Owaxalagilis bore off his Copper in triumph for the princely sum of 4,200 blankets. Honour was satisfied on both sides and the next day the Mameleleqala chiefs had a splendid potlatch at which, among other things, the blankets paid for the Copper were given away.[3]

Such unaccustomed goings on could hardly fail to astonish the first European observers and the sensational elements in the ceremony can still obscure the deep social purpose it served. A recent reassessment describes the potlatch as

> the heart of the Southern Kwakiutl social structure, the system of hereditary rank. An Indian might be entitled by birth to a noble name, a name that defined his position in native society as one entitled to honour and respect. Yet he could never use that name or any of the accompanying privileges unless he gave a potlatch at which he testified publicly to his hereditary right to assume it.[4]

Seen in this light, the potlatch despite its magnificent, not to say mind-boggling rituals, takes on the aspect of a legal deed. In England, at least, the testator to a legal document must even today solemnly place his index finger on a small red disc, specially stuck to the papers for the purpose, and intone the words 'I hereby deliver this as my word and bond'. From this to the Kwakiutl potlatch is a journey from the ridiculous to the sublimely ridiculous—yet in principle the two have something in common; without a distinct physical act the legal fact cannot be made good. The Englishman looks and feels a little foolish, the Kwakiutl Indian throws a massive party and gives away a fortune; but in both instances, and possibly more so in the second, the witnesses do not forget the transaction.

The origins of potlatching are obscure, and explanations inevitably numerous. Some Indian informants themselves favoured the idea that the potlatch had developed as a substitute for the inter-tribal warfare that had been endemic before the coming of the Europeans; they described potlatching as 'fighting with property'. Certainly, in the form of potlatch known as the 'rivalry gesture', sublimation of physical combat does seem to have been a central element. While Indians regarded tribal warfare as a regular part of life, they rarely allowed family feuds within the tribe to degenerate into armed conflict. Here the rivalry gesture, drawing on the conventions of the potlatch, was the ideal mechanism for directing such animosities into less dangerous channels. The feuds, bitter and long-lived, often stemmed from disputes about placings in the potlatch hierarchy of precedence. The fact that the issue had long since been settled by the council of chiefs did not affect matters one jot. The aggrieved party took every suitable opportunity at tribal assemblies to humiliate his rival with huge presentations of blankets, oil, fish or furs, forcing him to redeem his honour by the return of some still more magnificent gift, or bankrupt himself in the attempt. An even more popular manoeuvre was the destruction of property. Like the Limousin knights, a tribesman of the Southern Kwakiutl wishing to vindicate the family honour would destroy some object of great value, accompanying the gesture with a stream of invective, bristling with warlike imagery. At the next ceremony, the man thus challenged had to destroy wealth at least equal in value or lose face.

In a case where an issue of privilege or precedence was still in dispute, however, lobbying of the council of chiefs was intensified by the practice known to anthropologists as the 'rivalry potlatch'. Here the destruction of property was undoubtedly used as a weapon, the object being two-fold: if possible to bankrupt the opponent and, still more important, to demonstrate that the potlatcher controlled the resources to maintain the dignity of the rank claimed. In the campaign to win recognition, a claimant might go to the length of breaking a Copper and giving the pieces to the rival. The only valid response to this was to break a still more valuable Copper and return it, together with the original pieces, to the challenger or, still more tellingly, to have the whole lot sunk out to sea (a less harmful habit than our own sinking of much more expensive chemical weapons!). Even when a man had thus disposed irrevocably of fifteen or twenty thousand dollars' worth of property, his claim remained in doubt until the council had decided in his favour. Success or failure at the pot-latch complex might affect a man's good name but it had no effect on the all-important matter of his social rank unless he received that vital, formal acknowledgment.

Coppers, like the paintings of Rembrandt, had a universally known and admitted value. Like Rembrandts, they represented for the buyers cult objects from the past, of no intrinsic worth but of immense exchange value. As the Rembrandt or the Rubens, the Cézanne or the Van Gogh, makes its way from one bank vault to another, it is for a moment the centre of the dignified and well-dressed potlatch of the sale-room. More rivals take part in the bidding and the ritual is completed at breathtaking speed and with well simulated indifference. Just as the Kwakiutl chief barely deigned to accept the blankets when they were eventually handed over, so the auctioneer and his clients make only passing and decorous mention of the final purchase price. Inside the sale-room that is. For in the civilized Copper sale the crucial part of the ritual takes place outside, in the columns of the press and on the television. With those tense two minutes, bought perhaps at the rate of a million pounds a minute, the Western chief also acquires national coverage. But while the Rembrandt is not only a source of prestige to its owners but also a recognized part of the Western economic system, the Copper was not an economic object; it was not bought as an investment nor as a hedge against inflation but in the pursuit of socially defined values.

The Europeans did their utmost to stamp out such 'savage practices'. For they rightly saw in the potlatch ceremonial a deep contempt for the concept of 'wealth for wealth's sake'. Like so much of today's youthful counter-culture, those who practised the potlatch had a disregard for the value of property for its own sake that struck right to the heart of Victorian ideology.

On occasion, authors are tempted to believe that there is a Special Bureau of Quotations run by their patron saint in the sky. From time to time, it seems, it inspires some otherwise nondescript individual to sum up in one loaded comment the prejudices of an era. Take as an example the following:

> The Indians' idea of the ideal and that of the Whites do not at all correspond. Their chief aim is to go through life as easily as possible and get all the fun and glory they can out of it. The glory comes from the potlatch, the fun in doing nothing as often as possible. The only hope of improvement is through the education of the young.[5]

In passing, we note wrily that the speaker, Mr Haliday the Canadian government agent at Fort Rupert from 1906, really did believe that an attitude to life demanding from it only fun and glory needed improvement. Elsewhere, he notes: 'The Indians get their food so easily that the spur of necessity has never been applied to them', and goes on to say:

> The chief reason for the want of progress is the apathy of the Indians themselves. They do not realize that they have sunk into a rut and only an active effort on their part will pull them out of it.

The rut to which he refers, of course, was the Indians' determination to fulfil duties imposed on them by their own culture and to persist in the satisfying, understood and exciting business of conducting their own lives within the context of an honoured and long-established tradition. The point was put forcibly to Boas by an Indian chief.

> We will dance when our laws command us to dance, we will feast when our hearts desire to feast. It is a strict law that

bids us dance. It is a strict law that bids us distribute our property among our friends and neighbours. It is a good law. Let the white man observe his law, we shall observe ours.[6]

Yet while Haliday's Indians did find glory in the potlatch, by no means did they endeavour 'to do nothing as often as possible'. Quite the reverse. The Kwakiutl were, in the words of the anthropologist Helen Codere, 'a people of marked economic ability' who were in fact to make 'a success in the new economy created by the Europeans'.[7] Indeed, for early administrators and missionaries they presented an exasperating contradiction. They exhibited a gratifying and unusual willingness to work hard and regularly for the pittance thought adequate for native labour, and so thoroughly appreciated the economic foundations of the white man's civilization that they happily followed him to the shady frontier of profiteering—prostituting their daughters and bootlegging liquor to their neighbours with a will. Even these transactions were encouraging as signs that the Indian had become a convert to the Western gospel of cash. But the use to which he put his hard-won gains seemed almost insolent in its perversity. For instead of ploughing his money back into the white man's economy, instead of making the shrewd investment or acquiring the domestic appliance, he merely bought blankets to give away in ever more magnificent potlatches. How were these primitive tribesmen to be led into the paths of progress if they persisted in giving away or even destroying each small fortune as they amassed it? The answer seemed to be force, and laws were passed forbidding the holding of potlatches, laws that successive agents were to try to enforce with varying degrees of failure.

From the early nineteenth century, with the incursion of cheap Europeans goods, potlatches became more frequent and larger. The Kwakiutl economic system which, like that of the West, was geared to the production of a surplus, was now so flooded that the surplus threatened to become unmanageable. Now the potlatch came into its own as the classic answer to the problem of over-production. Where America once destroyed her wheat surpluses, Brazil burnt her coffee harvests and the farmers of the European Economic Community left tons of fruit to rot in fields (sprayed with paint lest someone should think to eat it), the Kwakiutl gave away his blankets and burnt his fish oil. None of us, save certain economic planners, ever fully understood the former; but all the Kwakiutl understood the latter and appreciated the important social function it fulfilled.

Where Western man makes good his claim to status by the acquisition of wealth, the Kwakiutl made good such claims by distributing it. It would be difficult to imagine a more direct affront to Western values. Thanks to his technology, the European can manufacture anything from an electric toothbrush to a supersonic transport on which to expend the wealth of overproduction so that the relentless pursuit of work and riches can be made to appear rational. In a primitive economy the modes of exteriorizing wealth were less varied, and the most effective way of showing you had more was either to put it on show as in the Trobriand yam display, to give it away, as in the Melanesia Kula trading ring or, most sensational of all, to destroy it. In the sections that follow we shall see that the ways in which the primitive economy handled the problems of work, trade, money and surplus gave the concept of wealth a social meaning. For all its apparent fatuity the Kwakiutl potlatch constituted an integrative function in society whereas in the West wealth is only, and is only meant to be, a symbol of difference and a means of social discrimination. By setting a limit to the accumulation of wealth, the potlatch gave meaning to it; whereas in the West there is nothing left but to get richer.

12 To Be or To Have

'The difference between the white man and the black man in Africa is that the white man "has" and the black man "is".' These are the words of an old African hunter and they are too near the truth for comfort. Even at his work the white man is not an actor but a salesman; his skill, his strength, his alertness of mind, are not faculties to be extended and enjoyed, they are commodities for sale to the highest bidder. Through the strength of his purse, the buyer acquires the right to exploit them as efficiently as he can in order to maximize not craftsmanship but profit. As a result, in the industrial process men tend to become 'operatives' or 'experts'. In either case the whole conception of work as a dignified and worthwhile human activity is negated.

Further, both operatives and experts can succeed only to the extent that they can suppress their personality as men. To be efficient, the operator must adapt as closely as possible to the rhythms and requirements of the machine; to be successful the expert must repress his personal opinions and passions and become, in his turn, a detached objective operator. For the work of the industrial society to be done effectively, it must in short be drained of what people now call the 'human element'. The attempt to introduce this strange, lively and unpredictable ingredient into the operations of industry is the basic cause of industrial unrest. The 'labour problem' that so exercises politicians and industrialists refers essentially to the tiresome necessity of having to put up with men and women at all.

The production line and the machine tool are specifically designed to eliminate the taxing problems that confront the craftsman. As little as possible is demanded of the industrial operative in the hope that thereby both incompetence and the time-consuming business of overcoming difficulties and solving problems will be eliminated. Placed in a situation where 'the job in hand' makes minimal demands on him as a human being, the factory worker nevertheless persists in behaving as far as possible as a man. Bending work schedules, cutting corners and 'figuring angles' become not merely the means to making money but challenging exercises in ingenuity. Debating grievances and organizing and participating in strikes provide the format for group action – a vital ingredient of human life.

The contrast with the primitive situation could hardly be more complete. Armed with simple tools the craftsman confronts the material direct. For him the job in hand is part of being alive and involves all his capacity and awareness. The Trobriand islanders were first-rate seamen and shipwrights. Building a sea-going canoe was a co-operative understaking which exercised all the strength, acquired skills, and natural cunning of the men of the village.

Equally, it required the benevolent good will of the spirit world. The Trobriander is no fool! He does not suppose that crops will grow or complicated pieces of equipment mystically construct themselves if he simply casts a spell or intones an incantation. But he does believe that man's life on earth is part of a spirit environment in which non-human powers are active. Common sense requires that he gain their co-operation. Each stage of the work is marked by traditional rites so that in his work, as in every aspect of his life, the primitive acknowledges and reaffirms his membership of a numinous environment.[1]

Even in the West overt ritual is occasionally allowed in the work context. Important building projects are sometimes initiated by a dignitary laying the 'first' stone; bridges are ceremonially opened by mayors or governors; while landscaping projects are dignified with a tree planted by a prince or monarch. In ancient China the first sod of the agricultural year was cut by the emperor himself. He used a paper plough which sailed effortlessly through a prepared furrow where the earth was pulled aside with carefully contrived strings. The artificiality of the emperor's labours did not signify; what mattered was that he and only he could maintain the divine harmony of heaven and earth and thus ensure the fertility of the soil. The primitive world is rich in this kind of symbolic yet essential ritual. In the West, the few ceremonies that remain have little meaning; and industrial man's contempt for all such observance was neatly summed up by Alfred Emanuel Smith, four times governor of New York State, when asked to lay the foundation stone of the New York State Office Building. 'Nothing doing', he replied. 'That's just baloney. Everybody knows I can't lay bricks.' The remark also illustrates a healthy respect for the basic industrial principle of the division of labour.

The concept of the division of labour lies at the root of the industrial 'take-off'. A classic description was made in the mid-eighteenth century by the economist Adam Smith, who observed the operations of a pin factory. He found that the business of making pins by hand had been divided into half a dozen distinct operations each conducted by a separate group of workers. The example pleased Smith because for him it demonstrated a great principle in a humble context. For us it carries a somewhat different significance. The inability of workers, in a modern industrial operation, to identify themselves with the finished product, the object of their labours, is one of the most debilitating features of the industrial process. Naturally, specialization is found in non-industrial societies: the Trobriand canoe, for instance, is built by co-operation among a number of specialists; but each worker is completely involved with the whole production process and can point with pride to his contribution to the finished product.

Co-operative effort is characteristic of all primitive work. In Haiti a farmer needing to clear a large field for planting spread the word and made preparations for a *combite*—a communal work-day. The prime requirement was food; the prosperous man would slaughter a beast, but whether the provisions be rich or humble a feast must follow the day's work. All were welcome to the *combite* but hard work was expected and it was supervised by a single man acting as overseer for the day. The rhythm of the hoeing was reinforced by drummers and by work songs, and, as a result, far more was achieved by the group than would be achieved by each man working separately: in a short day's work, fifty men would expect to clear several acres. There was no co-ercion, and no work norms, but when the time came to distribute the food the best cuts of meat or the largest portions went to the men who had put in the most work and known malingerers subsequently found it difficult to get co-operation when they had to hold a *combite*. In the Pacific Island of Mangaia the food provided at a working bee may be so generous that workers are able to take some home with them. In the kingdom of Tonga co-operative fishing is systematic and thorough; the operation is supervised by as many as forty skilled fishermen and the communal labour force can be anything up to a thousand.[2]

Among the craftsmen of Dahomey the principle of the co-operative has been developed with some sophistication. The comparatively elaborate equipment required by the iron-worker is usually shared among a number of men. But while the equipment is owned by the co-operative, the iron is not, each craftsman buying for himself what he can afford. The stock of each is worked in turn by all members and the implements produced from it are sold by the owner for his personal gain—not for the common profit of the group. When he has disposed of his stock at the market, the craftsman returns to the forge to work the iron of the other members until his turn comes round again.[3] By this means skilled craftsmen who, in the West, would be obliged to work for another if they could not afford the capital to set up on their own, are able to retain their independence. Equally important is the fact that in such a system unemployment is virtually impossible.

In the primitive world men and women do on occasion work for others—but as equals not as employees. Undoubtedly such an arrangement is less economically 'efficient' than the specialized system of the West. The ability to organize others so as to exploit a market to maximum advantage is quite distinct from the craftsman's skill in working materials. Dahomeian iron-workers could doubtless produce more hoes if they developed a managerial class and a sales force; but the point of their work is not to produce more hoes but rather to produce enough and, in the process, to exercise their craft. In short, in the words of Melville J. Herskowitz in his classic book *Economic Anthropology*, 'The data from non-literate societies make it quite clear that considerations other than those of economic best advantage dictate labour.'⁴ In these societies men deal with each other as men.

In primitive society work is a socially cohesive rather than a divisive force. In our world, where types of work receive prestige ratings according to their contribution to the productive process, conflict is an inevitable, perhaps even a necessary, part of the system. Since the objective of the work is the socially and humanly irrelevant concept of profit and the production target, the fact that a man's standing at work and in society at large is governed by how he contributes to that objective necessarily breeds bitterness. The work situation allows no opportunity for men to measure themselves against each other as men, and outside the work situation social and economic factors keep them apart. In the primitive world such conflicts have little chance to develop. A man lives, so to speak, at his place of work amongst his work colleagues and in regular and close contact with his social or religious superiors.

When the industrial age divorced work from life, two broad attitudes developed towards it. For the industrialist, since it brought profit and prestige, work achieved the status of a virtue in its own right; for the labourer it was a necessary evil. For both the idea of work was divided by a great gulf from the idea of leisure. The holiday or vacation is unique to Western society and it is the natural outcome of the alienation of man's creative faculties from the business of living. For more than forty hours a week he must direct himself to irrelevant activity whose only function is to provide him with food and shelter. It demands little of him as a man but rather deadens his imagination and zest for life. Small wonder that he looks for release in hobbies, holidays and entertainment. Legislators and social engineers are now heard speaking of the problem of leisure; but like the 'problem' of labour with which we began this chapter it is only one aspect of the wider 'problem' of living at all.

13 Gifts Were Never Free

In fact, the more one ponders Western society, the more one realizes that its most persistent problem is the need to accommodate people. Without them all the systems of industry and commerce would function effortlessly and always at maximun profit. The streamlining of 'retail outlets' (once called 'shops') to avoid as far as possible the human element indicates the problem and monoculture's way round it. The supermarket is a machine for shifting products and maximizing retail profits. Goods are displayed to urge buying decisions on customers. Personal contact between customer and shopkeeper is positively discouraged since it is liable to provoke thought and conscious decision-making. Soft music and glossy, misleading packaging are the order of the day and the nearest the shopper gets to meeting a person of the other party to the exchange is over a machine, the cash-register. Yet people still enjoy the personal contact in their trading encounters. The 'little shop round the corner' survives not only because it is convenient but also because people like the occasional opportunity of that personal contact; while the rich are pleased to pay excessively for the luxury of personal service, which gives them the prestige of being able to pay so much and the cachet of being on personal terms with the manager. In a tourist city the market street, the kasbah or the bazaar is always a prime attraction. Traders here habitually add a percentage to their intended sale price simply to give the buyer a sense of triumph in the cutthroat business of bargaining. But person-to-person confrontation is the essence of primitive trading and sometimes in fact its whole *raison d'être*.

A basic principle underlying the whole concept of exchange is undoubtedly the principle of reciprocity, that a gift demands a return gift and that honour dictates the discharge of this obligation. The Maori believed that a gift is possessed by a spirit or *hau* which forces on the recipient the obligation to repay the gift so that the *hau* may return to its original home.[1] This kind of intervention from the supernatural is not general in the primitive world, but the triple obligation to give, to receive and to repay is very widespread. A gift once given can be neither refused nor ignored.

The French anthropologist Marcel Mauss, who gave the first and still classic analysis of this triple obligation of giving, receiving and repaying, coined the phrase 'prestation' to describe the relationship of reciprocal exchange.[2] Indeed, the assumption of reciprocity is deeply embodied in the concept of the gift. The modern advertising man, astonished at his own generosity in presenting to the customers a plastic daffodil with their washing-powder, finds words quite literally failing him. Attempting to express the notion of giving without expectation of reward, he has coined the vibrant tautology of 'free gift'. Yet if we think for a moment we are bound to confess that some such phrase is needed to cover a gesture so alien to the normal run of human behaviour.

The conventions of polite society, as it was once termed, were bound up with the etiquette of reciprocity. Dinner invitations were expected to be returned and social calls repaid. Even now, presents at birthday and Christmas tend to be made only to those expected to be making presents in return. Christenings and weddings can bring presents from unexpected quarters and the donor family may be noted down for a gift at the next suitable 'festival of prestation' as we might term it, whether birthday or Christmas. Generosity is a noble sentiment, but a sense of mutual obligation is a socially cohesive one. 'It is more blessed to give than to receive' is, regrettably perhaps, a statement of fact rather than a laudable admonition. When we find examples of apparently selfless generosity, the experience is so unsettling that we usually try to explain it away as a case of conscience money.

Such altruistic generosity is as rare in primitive society.

An Indian never gives away anything without an expectation of return ... If one observes another in possession of a fine horse he would like to have he will take an occasion of some feast or dance and publicly present him with a gun or something of value, flattering his bravery, praising his liberality and throwing out several hints as to his object ... He will then let the matter rest for some days, and, if the other does not present him with the horse, will demand his gift returned, which is done.[3]

In primitive trade and exchange the principle of reciprocity links men with mutual and honourable bonds and makes of society a self-reinforcing organism, obliging those temporarily well placed to help those in difficulties in the confident knowledge that they will be helped in their turn. Because it meant contact with strangers, trade between tribes might well lead to tension, suspicion and conflict. Among the Yanomamo of Bolivia, a population where warfare is in any case endemic, the ceremonies leading to an alliance between two villages exteriorize the suspicions to be expected in such a situation in ritual combat and also in trading. They are two distinct episodes in the preliminary negotiations, but the actual bartering may also lead to blows if one party feels he is being cheated.[4]

In the primitive world, trade among people of the same culture or tribe is more frequently a vehicle of social co-operation. Among the Pangwe of West Africa (as reported by Richard Thurnwald), social visits, reciprocal gift-giving and trade are all linked together. The slightest degree of acquaintanceship is enough reason for an unannounced visit, and the younger members of the community in particular are continually calling on one another. Sometimes such visits involve journeys of as much as a week's march and take on the appearance of a full-scale trading expedition. On arrival the visitors are greeted with warmth at the meeting-house of the village. When they have taken their seats all the members of the host family, men and women, sit on their guests' knees and embrace them. This is followed by a ceremonial meal over which news is exchanged and stories are told and the guests are then taken to their lodgings. Their stay may last a month or more and during this time they live as members of the host's family, working in his fields and gardens and taking their meals with him. As the end of the visit draws near, men of the host's party leave the village to get the presents that must be given to the guests on their departure.

When the guests leave the host will very probably accompany them, to pay a visit in his turn and to receive presents in due course, usually more valuable than the ones he gave. Such exchanges of visits can continue over long periods and such trade enriches mutual dependence rather than competition and rivalry.[5]

In the integrated primitive experience trade even becomes a part of ritual. The *kula* trading ring that linked the island communities of the Solomon Sea off the eastern tip of New Guinea is an example. Expeditions might travel up to one hundred miles across the open sea. The focus of the *kula* was two articles—a necklace of red shells called *soulava* and an armband of bone called *mwali*. They travelled round the ring in opposite directions and could be traded only for each other. Strictly speaking they were body ornaments but were rarely if ever worn; indeed some were so small that only a child could get them on. They had, in fact, about as much practical relevance to the life of the traders as the crown jewels have to the queen of England. But like the crown jewels they were priceless—rich in history and tradition. In his classic account of the *kula*[6], Bronislaw Malinowski described the awed pride of an important villager briefly in possession of one of the great pieces. 'With reverence he would name them, and tell their history and by whom and when they were worn and how they changed hands and how their temporary possession was a great sign of importance and glory to the village.' The holder of such a piece would soon be courted by others for the honour of trading for it and would be offered handsome presents of pigs, large axe-blades or whale-bone lime spoons as preliminary inducements.

Kula trading at this level was the preserve of a privileged minority who entered into formal partnerships—a man could trade only with his partners and, however much he wanted a piece, had to wait until it came into the hands of one of them. These partnerships were for life and a man might have few or many, local or distant, depending on his rank and social position;

as a result the whole archipelago was linked by a network of personal ties. And even though the actual exchange was confined to certain villagers, the mounting of a large overseas expedition involved the whole community.

If the visitor is lucky enough to pass at the time of feasts, trading expeditions or any other big tribal gathering, many a fine sea-going canoe may be seen approaching the village with the sound of the conch shells blowing melodiously.

The canoes, like virtually every aspect of the islanders' life, were bound into the *kula* complex and their building surrounded with important rituals.

The *kula* occupies much of the time in the life of a successful man in the Trobriand world. To the outsider the whole elaborate and delicate mechanism may seem meaningless. What is it all *for?* he may feel tempted to ask. Exactly the same kind of question could be asked with equal if not more force about almost any of the institutions that occupy the central position in our own society. What, for example, is the Stock Exchange *for?* The answer seems fairly simple and rational; the control of money markets is a way of making money. If the questioner persisted and asked why stock-brokers wished to make money he would get a number of answers ranging from the pitying smile to the explanation that money is the means to power, or some such. In fact, of course, in our civilization his question is meaningless. With us the making of money is a self-justifying activity; it is the one thing that no one need explain because it is, by and large, the focus of our social arrangements. In the same way in the Solomon Sea, the ritual exchange of the *kula* is self-justifying, it is the correct way for any mature, intelligent and responsible man to organize his social contacts. It gives him standing in society but unlike the Stock Exchange it also binds him into the social fabric.

14 A Proper Place for Money

In virtually every instance, primitive economic arrangements tend to buttress the social structure and this is true even of the notorious institution of bride-price, sometimes called bride-wealth. The primitive practice of exchanging cows on the occasion of a marriage is widely known about in the West and is the subject alternately of ribald merriment or moralizings on the depravity of peoples that buy and sell women like cattle. Yet this point of view, which looks on the practice of bride-wealth as the most degraded form of personal exploitation, derives from a simple misunderstanding of what is going on.

All over the primitive world, marriage provided the focus of important economic function. In the Bantu institution of the *bogadi*, the handing over of bride-wealth had strong legal and symbolic overtones.[1] Among these herdsmen cattle were the measure of wealth and, in theory, the bride-price or *bogadi* should be paid in multiples of two — each animal with its mate — to symbolize the union of two people. The new union was legitimated by the transaction and, still more important, the payment of bride-price established a man's right to the children his wife might bear. *Bogadi* could be delayed, in case of hardship for example, but if it were still unpaid when children were born, the wife's family were entitled to claim the offspring. In some tribes, such as the Kgatla, *bogadi* did not have to be paid at all if the wife proved barren.

The practice of the Kgatla illustrates quite clearly that bride price is not the systemized purchase of women that some early European accounts claimed it to be. In the first place, the amount is almost entirely at the discretion of the man's family. If the woman's kin were literally 'selling' her, it would of course be for them to set the price. And in fact, far from reducing her to the level of a commodity, *bogadi* was an important guarantee of a wife's status. Where it was not paid she enjoyed little honour among the husband's kin; she had no redress if he should ill-treat her and was to all intents and purposes a concubine. On the other hand a *bogadi* wife could claim protection from the authorities in her husband's village. The central place that this apparently economic transaction held in Kgatla society was amply demonstrated when it was suspended for a time by a chief converted to Christianity. Marriages became unstable, spouses separated on the flimsiest of pretexts and the chief decided to re-introduce the custom for those of his subjects who did not accept the Christian marriage service.

The idea of transferring rights in a woman and her children from one family to another is found in many primitive societies. In medieval Europe a serf marrying out of one lordship into another had to pay a levy, called *merchet*, to her native lord. In losing the woman the lord lost also the future labour of her children. In a primitive social context, whether European or not, such things were vitally important. Women themselves were fully active contributors to the work of the kin and compensation for their loss to another was reasonable enough.

Related to this is the peculiar Indo-European institution of what an African anthropologist might term groom wealth. Readers of Jane Austen's novels will be well versed in the fascinating problems of dowry. In *Pride and Prejudice* Mr Bennet— the father of five strapping girls—recognizes, when he bothers to think on the matter, that marrying them all off will stretch his slender purse. The assumption was that no man would marry a girl without a decent dowry. Possibly the institution of the dowry is the economic expression of the European traditional convention that women of the upper classes were not expected to work. In this sense, by disposing of his daughters, a father was conferring an economic burden on the husband, not a benefit, and it was only fitting that he provide something towards the girl's upkeep. In fact, in its high noon the European institution of marriage conferred on a man rights over his wife and her property that were more absolute, more arbitrary and more exploitative than anything found in the primitive world.

Perhaps Europeans found the notion of bride-price so repugnant because for them the point of marrying was often not to pay out but to collect. The racier advertisement pages of English newspapers in the eighteenth century ring with offers from 'young men of parts', but no means, to liven the declining days of wealthy widows. It is, perhaps, a trifle smug for a society where for centuries the law transferred a woman's wealth to outright control by her husband to castigate the primitive as he offers gifts to the family of his bride.

The essence of the primitive marriage transaction was not mercenary. Among the Yurok Indians, the status of a man and his family was strictly measured by the goods handed over to the bride's father at the time of the marriage. If a man could not afford the full price of the woman he wished to marry, he worked for her father in payment of the balance.[2] The practice is familiar to us from the Bible; Jacob worked in just this manner for Laban the priest of Midian. In this sort of way marriages became the centre of the primitive social complex which always bound work and economic exchange and personal relationships into a coherent unity where exploitation of people was curbed or excluded.

In other societies the same effect of social stability was achieved by different means. A favourite device was that of separate and mutually exclusive patterns of exchange, each conducted with different kinds of 'money' or conventions of barter; one being used for day-to-day transactions, another for marriage settlements, another for compensation in the case of murder, another for the presentation of gifts at a feast, another perhaps for the settlement of debts of honour. An example of the last of these comes from the Yurok Indians.[3] Conventions of hospitality and of mutual assistance protected all members of the group from outright poverty and want. But these everyday transactions had no connection with the economic superstructure which might bring some men considerable riches. Here the medium used was a shell money which acted as a currency for the compensation of insults to a man's honour. Yurok were trained from childhood to be sensitive to offence and to pursue compensation with all vigour.

As in so many aspects of primitive life, we find a parallel with the attitudes of the aristocracy of pre-industrial Europe for whom honour was also of focal importance. But in Europe, as a money economy took over, the idea of personal honour was relegated to second place in favour of profit. Again we see a separation of those aspects of human life which in the primitive society are part of an interconnecting unity.

The separation of spheres of exchange is more elaborately worked out in Tiv society in Africa than it is among the Yurok. At the level of household transactions, chickens, baskets and food were interchangeable; above this came the sphere of trade and war where guns, metal rods, trade cloth and slaves were exchanged. Finally, the competition for wives, depending for success on the manipulation of ritual and law and on a knowledge of geneaology, can be treated as a third sphere of exchange. In the normal course of events the goods circulating in one area could not be exchanged for those in another. Among the Tiv a man's status was defined by the number of his wives, so that this discontinuity in the trade in goods from the lineage interchange of women ensured the continuing ascendance of the old men, through their expertise in matters of law and ritual.[4]

Similar systems of discontinuous spheres of exchange are to be found among various New Guinean and Papuan tribes. On Rossel Island the system was expressed in the use of the shell money.[5] The lower denominations were kept exclusively for everyday business, the higher for ritual and ceremonial transactions. Demands were varied and numerous so that credit was an essential feature of life for a Rossel Islander. Repayment was at a higher rate than the original loan, but although the elders sometimes debated what was a suitable return over a given length of time, indicating some concept of interest, no exact equivalent existed between the various units. Clearly this was not money in our sense. A network of mutual indebtedness, linked to understood and accepted social obligation rather than to a divisive profit motive, cemented communal solidarity. The system's economic function was less important than was its social one.

As a final example, we take a mixed barter/money economy

which illustrates just how effectively a community can insulate itself against the destructive effects of the exploitative profit system that rules in civilized societies. The Fur people of Central Africa, studied by Fredrik Barth in the 1960s, are a community of Muslim farmers with a wide system of markets and an economic system in which cash plays a part and links the community, through Arab traders, to the outside world.[6] The most valuable commodity that a man will buy with cash is a donkey which has status value as well as use; cattle are also bought. However, they are neither milked nor bred and are tended by a man's children until ready for slaughter. Cattle herding could well have opened the way to capital accumulation, but it was made to fit the limited possibilities of the subsistence economics that underlay the Fur society. In this way the society wisely protected itself from a potentially disruptive economic force. Each man and woman cultivated their own fields, growing millet for their own consumption and, if they wished, tomatoes and wheat for the market. The millet was used for making a kind of porridge that was the staple food and for the brewing of beer. The food was taken to communal feasts while the beer was offered in hospitality to repay neighbours who came to help on the land or in the building of a house. Thus the basic requirements of existence were met from a person's own land and labour, and these were guaranteed to him by the Fur belief that it was right of everyone to have enough land for subsistence. Land was held not by individuals but by kin groups who ensured that all their members had sufficient at least for the basic needs of life.

Unusually among primitive peoples, the Fur were familiar with the operations of an advanced cash economy, thanks to their long contacts with the Arabs; in fact cash has a place, and quite an important one, in their marriage customs. However, because it was confined to a separate economic sub-system it never threatened to dissolve the ties that bound the society together. In contrast, the characteristic of money in the capitalist system is its fluidity, so that eventually every aspect of human life comes to have a money rating. Even the labour and talents of men and women come to be regarded as market commodities, and the lack of money can quickly rob them of their self-respect, sometimes even of life itself. Arrangements like those of the Fur are based on the human rather than economic principle that men have a right to live. Economics are a function of life and not the other way about. In the primitive world, money, where it exists, is denied fluidity; its dangerous solvent power is kept out of the society's foundations; and it is treated as but one aspect among many of an integrated pattern of living.

It would of course be absurd to deny that the impregnation of Western society by an adaptable and versatile money economy has brought about huge changes in that society, often regarded as beneficial. But, comparing our own with the societies evolved by other peoples, we can see what a heavy price we have paid. The erosion of traditional values and the collapse of any socially agreed criterion of priorities is commonly lamented by the official guardians of Western morals; the all pervasive presence of money and cost-benefit thinking is a large part of the cause.

15 Wealth for Whose Sake?

'The artificial wants of mankind', wrote a contributor to the *Family Almanac* of 1850, 'are becoming more numerous than the natural ones in the present age.' His was a familiar cry, even as long ago as Victorian England. At that time the old idea of life depending on necessities and thriving on overcoming the challenges of a limited environment was giving rise to a new concept: that, with sufficient ingenuity, all challenge could be eliminated and all desires fulfilled at the drop of a coin or the turn of a handle. But as this happened, new needs appeared as though manufactured by an ability to satisfy old ones. The same syndrome was described more than a century later by that august body of *savants*, The Organization for Economic Co-Operation and Development. In their 1971 report *Science, Growth and Society* they issued a pungent warning: 'Economic growth tends to generate perceived needs faster than it can satisfy them.'

In our own society, as the bread of life takes its place beside the supersonic transport as just another consumer product, the point is not too obscure. Yet it does not require the wonders of modern technology or the blandishments of the advertising man to indicate the need for food if it is being signalled by the sharp pangs of hunger. The Bengali refugee, shivering in the monsoon rains, perceives the need for shelter, so sophisticated is he, without the prompting of a single television jingle. The Trobriand Islander knows the need for the appropriate rituals at each stage of his gardening work, without the urgings of a late-night religious broadcast. In the primitive experience some things are quite obviously necessary—physiology or tradition reminding men, if by chance they forget or by circumstances they are unable to fulfil them.

For us however the perception of unexpected needs has to be artificially assisted. The factories may even overtake the population's capacity to consume. That day was reached in America in the 1950s and was heralded by Ernest Dale of the Graduate School of Business and Public Administration in Cornell University. He had this to say: 'Marketing men across America are facing a fact that is hard to swallow. America's capacity to produce may have outstripped its capacity to consume.'[1]

In fairness to the devoted work put in by American consumers one must record that, in the decade under review, they had used up and disposed of, on average, two cars per head; that although representing only 6 per cent of the world's population they had annually processed 50 per cent of world industry's raw materials into garbage. But these sterling achievements were not enough. In tones bordering on panic, marketing consultant Victor Lebow implored his countrymen to do better. 'We need', he urged, 'things consumed, burned up, worn out, replaced and discarded at an ever increasing rate.'[2]

In his book *The Waste Makers*, Vance Packard had a compelling vision of the future consumer society.

> One fourth of the factories of Cornucopia city will be located on the edge of a cliff and the ends of their assembly lines can be swung out to the front or rear doors depending on the public demand for the product being produced.[3]

The future was closer than he knew. The metaphor of the cliff edge has been used before on the conflict in South-East Asia — but the edge of this particular cliff? A moment's consideration shows how apt the comparison is. During the 1960s the Vietnam war functioned as American industry's ideal consumer. Demand was insatiable; the product was instantly disposable; the consumer was wasteful without prompting; and there was little quibbling over price (the navy had long been accustomed to paying $2.10 the piece for lamps selling for 25 c. in retail stores). The requirement that mass production be followed by mass consumption could hardly be more completely fulfilled than it is in armament production, the destructible product par excellence.

Similar implications were also apparent in the 1950s, when recession seemed to threaten the United States. At that time, one television propaganda jingle wooed the consumer with this provocative thought: 'Buy now—the job you save may be your own.' The President himself, when asked what the ordinary patriotic citizen could do to avert the threat, replied simply, 'Buy.' Asked exactly what should be bought, he said, 'Anything.' This disarmingly blunt comment nut-shells our talent for the mass-production of meaningless material wealth. It assumes almost mystical import, however, in the mouth of one marketing consultant.

Our enormously productive economy demands that we make consumption our way of life, that we convert the buying and use of goods into rituals, that we seek our spiritual satisfactions, our ego satisfactions in consumption.[4]

But after more than a century of effort there is little evidence that the buying of goods has been converted into a ritual. The festival of Christmas has been appropriated by commerce, it is true; Mother's Day and even, so help us, Father's Day have been introduced to the calendar to increase the opportunities for ritual consumption; while as early as 1960 one Miami supermarket had installed a chapel on its premises. But these are gawky contrivances. If we compare them with the natural integration of economic and social aspects of life found in the primitive world we can see just how mechanical they are.

There, 'the market' is part of the social complex; in the industrial state the situation has been almost entirely reversed. 'It is the modern idea that the pursuit of wealth can be carried out without direct or conscious reference to the other sides of human or social life,' wrote William Cunningham in his *History of English Commerce* of 1882. A generation later the view was given point and emphasis by the anthropologist Marcel Mauss when he observed: 'It is only our Western societies that quite recently turned man into an economic animal.'[5] This does not mean that the concepts of wealth and surplus are unknown in primitive society; on the contrary, they are extremely common, but to quote Mauss again they operate 'in ways and for reasons other than those with which we are familiar from our own societies'. Prestige and acquisition are prominent for instance in the activities of the Trobriand Islanders, the Tolai people and the North American Indian tribes.

But what we can learn is not that industrial man has lost a primal innocence, but rather that he has built a world designed to produce and foster material greed.

In the hunter-gatherer society of the Australian Aboriginal, the yam is collected with great care, part of the tuber being left in the ground to ensure that the plant will yield more fruit the following year. For the Aboriginal, food is an almost constant preoccupation. Even a funeral procession, wending its way with due solemnity along a sea-shore, will detach one of its members to spear a fish lurking in the shallows.

The Trobrianders have no such problem. Yams are grown in profusion. Yet the staple vegetable item in their diet is the banana. Successful cultivation of the yam brings primarily prestige and to no one more than to the breeder of a new variety. He has the honour of naming it; he is remembered as the one who introduced it; and he is careful to guard his secret until there are enough cuttings available to distribute among his friends and neighbours.[6] Size as well as variety is a matter of competitive breeding and, for the ritual display that is the focus for all this activity, quantity is of prime importance. Although yams are considered a delicacy, the people practise special magic to restrain their appetite for them; the more yams that are left to rot in the store-houses, the greater the prestige of the gardener.

In contrast to this is the cultivation of the humble banana. Only three varieties are recognized and when or by whom these were introduced is forgotten. The picture of the economically unimportant product attracting prestige which does not attach to the necessities of life is not unique to Trobriand society. It is found in our own society and, for example, in the potlatch ceremony of the Indian tribes of the north-west coast of America.

Primitive practices differ crucially from our own in the expectation that the man of wealth will distribute his largesse to those less well off. The very act of distribution generally brings public acclaim, so that the economy is provided with a socially respected feed-back system. It can be argued, of course, that the primitive virtue of ostentatious generosity is the child of necessity. A limited technology offers little opportunity for converting units of practical exchange into objects of what we might call ceremonial or prestigious value. Yet even this has been tried. In the potlatch the mere possession of a Copper confers immense prestige; while the Yap Indians exchange wealth for large, flat, circular stones which, even if lost at sea while in transit, are considered part of the assets of the owner.[7] The fame from possessing one of these ritual stones is every bit as great in Yap society as that which accrues to America or the Soviet Union through having their plaques and flags on the moon and assorted planets, and the comparison fits at every point. Both cost the proprietor a fortune; no one can actually see them; nor will they ever be returned to circulation. Nevertheless, they are thought to earn their owners a great deal of respect.

A European who lived among the Tolai tribe of New Britain for nearly eight years felt that 'the stimulus of most of their activities beyond meeting their requirements was the desire to acquire and accumulate shell money'.[8] This shell money, or *tambu*, discharged most of the functions of money as understood by Western economists. It was used as a store of value; it was used in day-to-day trading; and it could be used to make deferred payments. Prices were calculated in fixed lengths of shells threaded on thongs, and in the case of basic food-stuffs such as taro and yams, the laws of supply and demand operated to produce characteristically fluctuating prices. In fact, the Tolai economic system offered so many similarities to that of the West that it has sometimes been described as a primitive capitalist society.

Even skills and traditional specialist services were to be had in exchange for *tambu*. The magician, the wood-carver and the composer of new ceremonial songs charged fees for their work, fees which varied according to the importance of the occasion and the excellence of the work. Enterprise and thrift were highly rated long before the coming of the Europeans in the 1880s. Still more important was the ability to dispose of large quantities of wealth. When the German colonial authorities introduced two rates of poll tax, the Tolai competed to pay the higher rate. But they insisted on receiving payment for copra and coconuts, the staple raw materials of the territory, in *tambu*. Scarlett Epstein, the anthropologist who studied the Tolai, 'observed vendors in Rabaul market allowing prospective customers to pass by rather than accept cash for their produce.'9

Attempts to introduce artificial factory-made *tambu* failed, since the Tolai refused to accept this counterfeit currency. *Tambu* was integrated into the pattern of social prestige and remained vitally important even into the 1960s.

Even profit and investment found a place in the Tolai economy. Young men of the kin lodged their accumulating wealth in the house of the 'big man' who came to perform something of the function of a banker. To discharge his obligations of financing family marriages or sponsoring ritual feasts he might draw on the reserves of *tambu* he was holding in trust for others. The man whose marriage was financed in this way could pay off the debt in terms of labour so that in this sense the big man could put his *tambu* to work for him.

The Tolai have a saying that a woman would rather forsake her child to an enemy than her *tambu*, and even their religion reflects the prevailing attitude to wealth. In fact it provides a model of consistency for the materialistic West. There was no truck with such awkward doctrines as apostolic poverty; the rich not only inherited the earth but held a monopolistic position in heaven too, the poor being dispatched to *jakupia*, a region where they spent eternity living like animals and feeding on dirt and rotten leaves.

However, appearances can be deceptive. The Tolai pursuit of wealth was nevertheless integrative rather than divisive. In the first place the possession of *tambu* not only brought prestige to the individual but also reflected honour on his kin. Nowadays the joint ownership of a copra drying machine, or a truck, confers similar status on the group. Secondly, the 'big man' was expected to advance the finance for the marriages of the junior members of his family and kin and also to sponsor the ceremonies of the *duk duk* secret society of which he was a senior member. Thirdly, he enjoyed his power and prestige only so long as he remained rich, and this, given the prevailing social pressures to extravagant liberality, was at best a fifty–fifty probability. If he had over-extended his resources and was caught out of funds at the time of a major feast he would be displaced by an ambitious rival. Finally, even if he got through life without the humiliation of bankruptcy, his family could not expect to build a position of privilege on his fortune.

On arrival at *tingenatabaran*, the land of the blessed, the soul of the departed was submitted to a rigorous cross-examination with the object of determining how much *tambu* had been distributed at his funeral. Even after death the test of generosity was applied as the proof of wealth. Half the point of being rich was to ensure that 'many people would cry for one, speak of one with respect and arrange many feasts' – and this meant cash. To be sure of treasure in heaven one was obliged to dispense it with a liberal hand on earth. During the wake the dead man's fortune would be almost entirely disposed of while his closer kinsmen might bankrupt themselves to ensure an impressive display. Thus the political stage was cleared for the ambitions of new men and the danger of an entrenched privileged class, resting on inherited wealth, averted. Even the most ingenious system of death duties could never confer on us the egalitarian benefits guaranteed to the Tolai by social convention.

One of the most refreshing lessons to be learnt from anthropology is the capacity for tradition, operating unhampered in a vigorous primitive environment, to throw up satisfying life-styles. We have a perfect example of this in the balance achieved by the Tolai between ambition and equality. Theirs is a tradition of which we should be envious. In our own culture, the conflict between the two themes is rooted in history and now seems irreconcilable. Extreme egalitarians are accused of deploring the very idea of excellence, while from the right of the political spectrum come emotional jeremiads on the dire consequences of checking the mettlesome spirits of ambition and on the grey landscape of uniformity that would result. Flattering themselves on their hard-headed realism, these disingenuous champions of the present system alternate crisp no-nonsense advocacy of 'self-help' with impassioned justifications of inherited wealth. But the argument is threadbare. As the American economist Frank W. Taussig wrote:

No stretch of psychological analysis concerning the spur of ambition, the spice of constant emulation, the staleness and flatness of uniformity, can prevail against the universal conviction that the maximum of human happiness is not promoted by great, glaring, permanent inequality.[10]

Our own system makes possible for some the accumulation of surplus on a scale unheard of in the annals of man while it denies to others the basic necessities of living, no matter how willing or able they may be to work. In the primitive world riches may be keenly pursued, but no man goes hungry while others overeat, and no man is out of work.

The reason is not far to seek. It is that the means of production are open to all but it is left to the individual to decide how much work he shall do towards the upkeep of himself and his family. The idea of the idle savage sitting beneath his coconut tree waiting for the fruit to drop, and exerting himself only to ensure that it does not drop on his head, is a fabrication. In the words of Melville J. Herskowitz, 'Even those folk who inhabit that romantic area, the South Sea Islands, work and work hard, despite the fact that here, almost uniquely in the world, man is furnished by nature with practically all his needs.'[11]

In this context, the West's faculty for rational analysis has proved fatal. Peter Pan told Wendy that fairies can think only one thing at a time and that is the mentality of our efficiency-conscious generation. *Homo economicus* is the roughest diamond of the lot, cutting through subtleties with ease and profit. The primitives' concept of the pursuit of riches as part and parcel of a coherent social structure is lost to us. And today a social system in which prestige can be registered with wealth but in which unemployment is unknown, where human ambitions can be satisfied though not at the cost of human suffering, seems so remote as to be Utopian. Those who criticize enlightened plans for social innovation as unattainable would do well to remember that such systems have existed, and worked, on most of the Earth throughout most of history.

4

The World of the Spirits

16 Oracles Ancient and Modern

Few things are more characteristic of the primitive than his attitude towards the world of the spirits—the vast structure which he has invented to make life in an alien environment if not easier then at least psychologically more tolerable. Primitive life is marked at every turn by ritual, by ancestor worship, by appeal to totems, by sacrifice, black magic, sorcery and witchcraft, and by forms of animism in which even the rocks of the Earth are raised to supernatural status. These things are the essence of primitive religion. And in our conventional approach to the way other societies live, or have lived, we rational men of the West have with few exceptions dismissed them as representative of an early and crude stage in the evolution of human thought. It used to be commonly thought that man's preoccupation with superstition was but the previous stage to a concern for religion, which in its turn was only the forerunner of science.

Today, as technocratic society falters on the brink of the cliff of its own making, many members of our society—and not only its younger ones—are reshuffling the Tarot pack, consulting the astrologers and searching their souls for spiritual and mystical guidance in the wasteland of materialism. It is too easy to dismiss this new concern with the occult as yet another fad, equalled only by the rise to fame of the health-food shop. Something mysterious is in the air, and its presence makes the re-examination of the mystical world of the primitive much overdue. The record needs setting straight.

In our society, the idea of the sacred is all but dead. Indeed, it is the boast of rational and scientific men that nothing is any longer sacred, that we should dispense with all taboos concerning human behaviour and that every subject—from orgasm to genetic engineering—should be brought into the open, displayed for all to see, assessed objectively and assigned a known and finite value.

Even Christianity, the one area where it might be thought the sacred could be given a chance to linger a little longer, is not excused: ritual is gutted from the church service, to be replaced by trendy churchmen with pop music and guitars, while the Roman Catholic Church abandons the ancient ritual language of Latin.

For once, a broad and sweeping generalization about the primitive can be made which is strictly true: the primitive encounters the sacred many times during the course of his ordinary day. For him the sacred is in the fabric of his life, and instead of being set apart for brief display once a week its presence is felt during just those occasions which are most important and occur most frequently in daily routine. What results we disparagingly call 'mumbo-jumbo', thereby degrading the name of a deity worshipped in West Africa to a synonym for nonsense as hocus-pocus. Indeed, we see primitive life in general as marked by the presence of hocus-pocus, in contrast to our own society which has passed through the superstitious phase and emerged triumphant into the realm of purely rational behaviour. It is this myth which we will first put to the test, for a more detailed examination of our behaviour reveals that it is distressingly full of hocus-pocus; worse, that many of those practices in our society have long since lost either the ritual significance or the practical function which they possess in primitive society.

In primitive culture every aspect of man's life, from agriculture to craftsmanship, from childbirth to death, is linked to the supernatural environment of which he believes himself to be a part. The co-operation of the spirit world is enlisted and the humdrum activities of life validated and given a cosmic significance by the formal procedures prescribed by religion and belief. In his classic study of the rituals attending the crises of life, birth, coming of age, marriage and death, Arnold van Gennep emphasizes that these 'rites of passage' from one state of life to another impose a periodicity on the life of man comparable with the periodicity of the natural world.[1] Primitive man emphasizes at every turn the coherence between his own life and that of the universal environment. Such ritual activity is also a valuable cohesive force in society. The communal expression and re-affirmation of shared beliefs and traditions strengthen the confidence of the group, assert its continuity with the past and reinforce its competence in dealing with the present. Yet apart from the ceremonies of religion and the occasions of state pageantry, such as the opening of Parliament in England or the May Day parades in Red Square, the Europeanized world would seem to have eliminated the ritual part of human life.

The first exception is to be found in the most typical activity of our society—preparation for the waging of war. When a central Australian Aborigine rubs an arrow against a certain stone, he 'charges it with a magic power called *arungquiltha* ... as the arrow falls the *arungquiltha* will follow its course and strike down the enemy'.[2] What the Christian bishop or priest imagines he is doing when he officiates at the launching of a nuclear submarine is, to the untutored lay mind, unclear, but presumably we can take a line through the Australian Aborigine.

Modern ritual also shows an unexpected vigour in the semisecret friendly societies, such as the Freemasons, which cultivate their arcane initiation rites with what seems to the outside world to be an almost childish enthusiasm. The service of the church is also still called on, at the traditional life crises of birth, marriage and death, by people of no religious persuasion. There is nothing hypocritical about this, only the confused but deeply felt need to punctuate the rhythm of life with occasional solemnity. Even the register office wedding is usually followed by a party, while setting up house is still marked by the celebration of housewarming. Indeed, perhaps because it is a pleasant enough activity in its own right, the ritual meal has proved the most enduring type of ritual in modern society. The Old Boys' reunion, the miners' annual gala and the family Christmas are all celebrated with more or less excessive eating and drinking, and group solidarity is reaffirmed and drunkenness is *de rigeur*. Until the tax laws were changed a few years back, British businessmen were unable to negotiate a deal without the consumption of the ritual feast known as the business lunch, while in England candidates for the legal profession are still required to eat a specified number of dinners before being permitted to practise as barristers. Nor is it fanciful to see in the annual office party a fossilization of the old Feast of Fools; in this anarchic parody of high ritual, the role of the bishop was discharged by a choir boy and the roles of authority and subordinates were reversed for a short ritual moment. In both cases, by allowing the submerged conflicts and hidden tensions of the routine world to emerge, the ritual provided a socially acceptable safety-valve.

Of all the concealed ritual situations in our modern society, the most interesting is the political party conference or convention. The point is made often enough by cynical or bored commentators in the way of a joke— yet it is perfectly valid. Public postures or policies are rarely changed by the events of the conference, and delegates may know that their votes and speeches will have little practical result. Nevertheless, the conference has a function. By allowing the members of the tribe to participate with the leadership in traditional and understood patterns of resolutions, speeches and votes it reaffirms the common purpose, and confirms and expresses the solidarity of the group. To outsiders it may appear as essentially a waste of time, to opponents as some form of potentially dangerous black magic. But to the faithful the exercise is meaningful and regenerating. For one more year the gods of discord have been appeased, the authority of the elders reaffirmed and the place of the common man in the congregation acknowledged.

In primitive society the activities of the diviner, like ritual, have a practical social value by indicating a course of action which has the sanction of the supernatural. The diviner may relieve the client of the burden of decision and thus perform a valuable psychological function. But his service can have social as well as personal benefits. Among the Yoruba of west central Nigeria the choice of a house site is often fraught with personal and social problems. As family lineages grow, tensions and conflicts lead to the setting up of new households and secessions split off from the main family. Consequently, when a young man comes to set up on his own, the actual location of the house must indicate either a rejection of the nuclear kin of which he was a member or of the other groups. Although no offence may be intended, it may easily be taken. By turning to the diviner, in accordance with custom, the new householder looks for advice that is both personally and socially acceptable because it is mandatory. In the words of the American anthropologist, George K. Park, the diviner is able 'to remove the agency and responsibility for a decision from the actor himself, casting it upon the heavens where it lies beyond cavil and beyond reproach'.[3]

In much the same way, the modern board of directors, having decided on some revolutionary and inevitably unpopular restructuring of the company, calls in a team of business consultants. Explaining precisely what advice they wish to receive, they are soon presented with a report which, in unintelligible jargon and with a numbing display of expertise, sets forth the unavoidable necessity, say, of sacking half the executives. Armed with this the directors move in. In the words of Professor C. Northcote Parkinson, 'The efficiency expert has done something which they could not do for themselves ... they took the blame for a purge which would have been impossible for those who had to live afterwards in the same neighbourhood.'[4] More than this, they removed the 'agency and responsibility for the decision' from the directors themselves to the heavenly realms of pseudo-science and statistics mediated to common mortals by the computer programmer.

Special scorn is reserved for the primitive because of his alleged inability to spot that the magic in which he dabbles rarely leads to the desired effect. The Western rationalist is hard put to understand how any people could continue to sacrifice to the gods, for example, when this activity clearly amounts only to economic waste – if the process actually worked, the primitive would long ago have reconstructed his version of the Garden of Eden. But of course, the primitive is not so simple. Pleas to the gods are not made lightly, nor are they usually made for a favour which natural events are never likely to fulfil. Magic is usually used to bring about happenings which are, in any case, within the bounds of possibility if not probability. Through sacrifice, for example, primitive man communicates with the gods, propitiating them or enlisting their help. Illness that will not respond to the available simple herbal remedies is thought to be the work of an angry spirit. If the sacrifice in its turn fails, the people assume that either the god is too angry to be propitiated or, more simply, that the professional diviner has got his diagnosis wrong. The occasional ineffective sacrifice is not considered a strong enough ground for surrendering a whole system of belief. Nor if it comes to that are our convictions easily shaken. Like the African diviner, the Western economist exercises an art incomprehensible to the mass of the population; like the diviner, he has, on occasion, been known to be wrong. Yet doubts about the validity of economics as a science are confined to sturdy pioneer sceptics. When the times are out of joint, primitive man checks his pantheon for a disgruntled deity—civilized man his records for a misinterpreted statistic.

A somewhat similar mechanism appears to operate in witch-craft. In many cultures, the idea of 'death from natural causes' is unknown. If a man is not killed in battle, has not been poisoned, has not deliberately taken his own life and is not the victim of a known sorcerer, it is assumed that his death, whether from old age, disease or accident, is the work of a witch. From death the evil works of the witch descend through a gamut that embraces the failure of magical or religious rituals, blight on the crops, plague among cattle, down even to marital disharmony. Witch-craft provides causation for the inexplicable and leaves no room for the idea of coincidence. Not that the primitive believes that the witch creates the murrain that decimates his herds; it is fully understood that cattle plague is a natural phenomenon. The point of interest is why did the plague attack *my* cattle.

The question need not surprise us; it is, after all, heard often enough in our own society. Why should a quirk of the market forces destroy the livelihood of *this* man, who has always worked hard and intelligently? Why is *this* girl killed by a road accident? Why should cancer strike in *this* family? In former days men placed their faith in the workings of an inscrutable providence and the ultimate benevolence of the divine plan. Nowadays we fall back on the cold concepts of statistical probability, chance or coincidence. The primitive still looks for a cause in human terms. And if the apparently chance happenings of the world are the work of human beings, they can in theory be controlled. The witches have only to be identified and neutralized for disaster to cease and mishaps to be averted. Events that otherwise would be inexplicable and therefore disturbing are set in a familiar frame of reference, and human efficacy is firmly located in a world all too obviously alien to man.

In more practical terms the fact of witchcraft saves men the awkward and unsettling business of rethinking still more fundamental beliefs. If the rituals of religion or the curing ceremonies of the shaman/doctor fail, even after the most meticulous discharge of all the prescribed rites, how much better to explain events in terms of unsuspected malignant forces and devote oneself to finding the witch and dealing with him or her, than to question the efficacy of the rituals and the ceremonies themselves. When the malfunction of the economic system throws thousands out of work or misguided military adventures lead to demoralization and defeat, how much more convenient to lay the blame on 'communists' or a 'degenerate hippy generation', than to question the values of society.

For these desirable ends to be achieved, the witches must be exposed. In Europe we are only too well acquainted with the techniques of the unsupported accusation, the forced confession and the show trial. From the heresy trials of the Catholic Middle Ages to the Stalinist purges of the 1930s and the processes of the Committee for Un-American Activities under the able chairmanship of Senator Joe McCarthy, Western civilization has witnessed the elimination or humiliation of millions of innocent people, destroyed by the hate of their fellows and, such is the force of shared convictions, often believing in their own guilt.

The final area in which the primitive is often roundly condemned concerns not a practice but a practitioner—the priest or shaman. The excessive worldly power once the privilege of the Christian priest in Europe certainly has its parallels among primitive peoples—indeed the combination of alleged holiness with considerable political power is found in a number of societies. It mirrors the alliance which church and state have cemented in the West, with considerable success, for centuries. 'God', as Napoleon once said, 'is on the side of the big battalions.' That the same is true in many forms of primitive society is often held to be evidence of the continued existence of barbaric social forms, particularly now that in our society the power of the priest—both worldly and spiritually—is fast on the decline. But it would be a mistake to think that because of this religion is finally a spent force.

In primitive society, the priest's power stems either from the mystical virtues of his office or from close association with the political authorities. Furthermore, he lays claim to special knowledge and access to super-human powers. He is thus in a position purposefully to confuse the obvious so as to impress the mob and buttress his own reputation. In explaining his involved and 'magical' treatment of a throat abscess to a European anthropologist, a Tahitian medicine man had this to say: 'It should be clear enough to you. In order to treat my compatriots, it is necessary to represent the simplest things as though they were the most complicated.'[5]

Until recently doctors in England wrote out their prescriptions in Latin, only reluctantly explaining the treatment to their patients in their native tongue, while the expert in every field cultivates a professional jargon and is happy to blind the populace with science. In short, the priest is a member of a closed group, united by mutual self-interest in maintaining its privileges, and by a long and often arduous professional training.

The kind of authority once accorded unquestioningly to priests has now been assumed in our society by experts of every kind and by none more completely than the computer guru. Meaningful access to the magic circuitry that we believe holds the answers to our problems is confined to a small elite who, thanks to a rigorous professional training, can work the oracle. Like the diviner or the priest, the computer programmer presides over an expertise and equipment that are beyond the average citizen; like the diviner, the computer's advice is thought to absolve the actor from any further responsibility, either in human or social terms. But, like the diviner, the computer responds to problems that are put to it and works only with the information presented to it.

The power mania of our civilization does not prompt consideration of what kind of life we should lead; the priests of our technocracy are not, even notionally, concerned with the deep problems of life – with good and evil, with selfishness, with the ideas of virtue or of purpose. Taken as read are the objectives of material well-being, comfort and ease, and questions of values are ruled out of court as irrelevant and unanswerable. And in the terms of mechanistic technology they are both. The privilege and authority of our technocratic priesthood rest on the mastery of a knowledge which yields nothing in response to the questions of men in a human society, and which derides the idea of a supernatural world outside itself.

17 A Proper Place for Man

How to fit people into the scheme of the world is a secret we have lost but which the primitive, in his religious practice, understood. Of the many theories advanced by anthropologists to interpret primitive religion, one of the most fruitful was 'functionalism'. In essence, this idea ignored both the meaning of primitive ritual and superstition, in a literal sense, and the effects such practices might have on the individual. Instead, the functionalists analysed primitive custom from the sociological point of view, examining each ritual and belief for the integrating effects it exerted on the smooth running of the whole society. Today, it is clear that this is a partial view, and we shall see in later sections that there is much more to primitive religious practice than its mere social function. However, newer ideas in this area in no way discredit the concept of functionalism – they merely add further significance and meaning to what is clearly an operational fact in societies throughout the world: ritual and religious practice have social value.

This school of thought is primarily associated with an Oxford Professor of Anthropology, A. R. Radcliffe-Brown, who summarized it neatly:

> The primary basis of ritual ... is the attribution of ritual value to objects and occasions which are either themselves objects of important common interests linking together the persons of a community or are symbolically representative of such objects.[1]

This insight helps us to identify the difference between ritual in our societies and that in the primitive world: the primitives ritualized what was important for them, we tend to ritualize what is trivial. In Western society important things are held 'too important' for ritual, and the two great concerns of Western man, technology and the economy, are stripped of all but their literal significance. Ritual is reserved for events which no longer have central significance for the majority of citizens and as a result its social value is dissipated.

Not so in primitive society, or indeed in ancient Chinese civilization. There even the idea of anthropological functionalism was well known. In the third century B.C. the Chinese 'Book of Rites' states that 'Ceremonies are the bonds that hold the multitudes together, and if the bonds be removed, those multitudes fall into confusion.'[2] A good example comes from the field known as ancestor worship, a somewhat misleading term for it implies that the practice raises ancestors to the status of divinity, which is rarely the case. However, in very many primitive societies ancestors are treated as powers for good and evil who demand veneration and remembrance. Radcliffe-Brown describes the relation between the living and the dead in a South African tribe thus:

> ... a man feels that he is dependent on his ancestors. From them he has received his life and the cattle that are his inheritance. To them he looks to send him children and to multiply his cattle and in other ways to care for his well-being. This is one side of the matter; on his ancestors he *can* depend. The other side is the belief that the ancestors watch over his conduct, and that if he fails in his duties they will not only cease to send him blessings, but will visit him with sickness or some other misfortune. He cannot stand alone and depend only on his own efforts; on his ancestors he *must* depend.[3]

In such beliefs there are clearly powerful social forces at work. Although death is constantly occurring in any society, and hence threatening to break all the social arrangements by which that society is made to function, the practice of ancestor worship adds a link over time and lessens the severity of the shock to the system. Death is admitted as a fact, not simply ignored or defined away, but its effects are held to be not quite as final as might otherwise be the case. Societies are often careful to define the role and the status of ancestors. Confucius said:

> In dealing with the dead, if we treat them as if they were entirely dead, that would show a want of affection, and

should not be done; or, if we treat them as if they were entirely alive, that would show a want of wisdom, and should not be done. On this account the vessels of bamboo [used in connection with the burial of the dead] are not fit for actual use; those of earthenware cannot be used to wash in; those of wood are incapable of being carved; the lutes are strung but not evenly; the pandean pipes are complete, but not in tune; the bells and musical stones are there, but they have no stands. They are called vessels to the eye of fancy; that is [the dead] are thus treated as if they were spiritual intelligencies.[4]

A similar attitude infuses many primitive societies in which ancestor worship plays an important role. This attitude does not make nonsense of the clearly visible fact of death; but no more does it make possible the spectacle of a successful man ashamed of his parentage, a common enough figure in the West. Such an attitude would have been disgusting to a primitive society; armed with Western language and thought patterns, they would probably have termed it 'primitive'.

To illustrate the reassuring ways in which primitive ritual binds together a society by choosing one example here and another there can be confusing. In the primitive world, ritual, sacrifice, the gods and everyday activity were not separate items to be placed in different boxes and acted on at different times— they were integrated activities which continued without cease. And the way in which the affairs of men were thus bound together, by ritual, religion, sacrifice and myth, are well illustrated by the Dinka, an African tribe of the Southern Sudan. We start with their Myth of Genesis.[5]

In the beginning, according to the Dinka, heaven and earth were joined by a rope so that men and women could climb up to Divinity for its help and advice. In this primitive paradise man did not have to work for his bread, receiving a daily ration of a single millet seed. This somewhat meagre diet was quite sufficient to support him in the state of innocence to which he was then accustomed and, moreover, so long as he was content to submit to Divinity he rested secure in its protection. Came the day, however, when discontent began to rear its head. A woman, who else, decided that the earth could be made to yield more than one millet grain per head per day. Accordingly she set about cultivating the soil, using the long-handled hoe still characteristic of Dinka agriculture. But as she wielded the unfamiliar implement she inadvertently fetched Divinity a nasty blow on the head. Deeply mortified, it sent a bird to peck through the rope and withdrew to the sky far above the Earth, where it is today.

Yet despite this break in their free and easy communion, Divinity is still actively concerned in the world of men. In a direct sense it is seen as father and creator, for the very act of birth is possible only with its active intervention. The Dinka know that conception results from sexual intercourse, but the development of the foetus in the womb is seen as the work of Divinity in a continuing act of creation.

The relations between the people and Divinity compare with those between father and son closely and, according to Godfrey Lienhardt, who studied Dinka religion for many years, such comparisons 'appear spontaneously in the context of Dinka religious thought itself'. Parallels with the Christian view are obvious. A son who has offended his father must try and make amends: someone who has offended Divinity, or one of the lesser spirits, must offer a propitiatory sacrifice. The tensions common between the son looking for independence from the irksome control and protection of the father are seen in the cosmic context of man's break with the deity. In Dinka society the eldest son enjoys the kind of privileged position that he does in the West, and Awiel Longar, the heroic ancestor of the hereditary priesthood, is considered to have been the eldest son of Divinity.

After creativity and fatherhood comes justice. Divinity is thought to see injustice and to reveal its judgment in the accidental misfortunes of life. A man convinced of his case will call upon Divinity to judge in a dispute but, so strong is the belief, few will dare to do so if they know themselves to be in the wrong. Consequently, the mere appeal is usually sufficient to decide the case.

The classic dilemma of Jewish thought between God's justice

and the need for divine mercy, or the conflict that Christians often see between the idea of a loving Creator and the facts of a world hostile to men, find no place in the Dinka view of things. Divinity is the ultimate matrix of the world and man's experience in it. As a kindly father, Divinity gives life, the greatest gift of all; in the incomprehensible violence of the natural world, it reveals only another aspect of its nature. The offence that broke the friendly intimacy of paradise seems trivial, even funny, to the Dinka themselves. But they see no need of explanations. The moral order evidently rests on principles that are obscure to man. Experience may bring some enlightenment but it also shows that men can do nothing to change things. They are as they are, and the Dinka rest content that if they cannot fathom the ultimate nature of the world they have a system of belief and ritual that enables them to keep their appointed place in it.

Ritual sacrifice has a central role to play in keeping this balance, modifying the experience of the people and rectifying the past so that both shall conform as far as possible to the cosmic order. The disruption of this order by homicide, for example, must be repaired by the prescribed sacrifice; in the case of incest the sacrificial animal is divided lengthways through the sexual organs, thus symbolically severing the illicit union. Where the discordant passions of a quarrel have to be allayed, the priest makes a solemn denial of the very quarrel itself; not with any thought of deceiving the god but rather that, in the words of the anthropologist Mary Douglas, 'By ritual and speech what is past is restated and what ought to have been prevails over what was.'[6]

The film *Tora! Tora!* is an apt example, somewhat nearer home, of such restatement of the past by incantation. In this widescreen ritual, American and Japanese film-makers collaborated to present the attack on Pearl Harbour as a mutually heroic action; by ignoring the vicious racist and nationalist responses of the 1940s the film neatly reformulates the past in terms of a present where the two powers come to share an unexpected identity of interests. And this is a common feature of much primitive ritual, nowhere more evident than in the ancestor worship described by Radcliffe-Brown: there are the two powers, the living and the dead, and their identity of interest is their close mutual dependency which continues after death.

The need of the Amba gods of East Africa for sacrifice is sometimes so insistent that they waylay people, usually women, so as to gain through them access to a household. Here they make their presence felt by causing sickness and are soon luxuriating in the scent of propitiatory sacrifices. The attitude of the Amba people is pragmatic. *Balimbu*, the world of the spirit, is dealt with when it cannot be ignored, as in the case above, or when help is needed. Any man who takes his hunting seriously will have a tutelary spirit to whom he sacrifices before an expedition and — if he has been successful — on his return. But most of a man's ritual activities are directed towards the ancestors of various degrees and potency, the more important having a sacred place some way from the village. These are visited only occasionally. From time to time, when things seem to have been going wrong for long enough, the feeling grows that someone's father or grandfather is displeased about something. A diviner is consulted and when he has confirmed the general opinion, the male kin of the ancestor in question set off, accompanied by horns and drums, to make the sacrifice. The first requirement is to clear the holy ground, overgrown, like the average Western graveyard, through years of neglect. Next a shrine is built, the sacrificial animal slaughtered and its blood sprinkled on the ground. A succulent dish is prepared from the meat, with bananas and mushrooms, beer is poured out and the meal offered to the ancestor at the door of the little shrine. Since in every known case he declines to partake, being obliged, no doubt by his disembodied state, to be satisfied with a spiritual simulacrum, a thoroughly enjoyable feast is had by all.[7]

Other religions believe, thriftily as it may appear, that the gods expect only a sort of spiritual essence as their portion. Whatever the origin of this belief its economic benefits are obvious. Charles Doughty, the explorer who spent many years among the Arabian Bedouin, observed that they unashamedly offered to God the least valuable camel that they could come by. Too poor to slaughter a cow camel, 'the womb of the stock', they instead purchased an old and decrepit beast and left it to fatten up for three or four months. At the end of this time they were able not only to discharge their obligation to Allah, but also to enjoy a good meal.[8] The Swazi, who also go in for low-grade offerings, seek to raise the sacrificial virtue of third-rate beasts by tethering next to them the pride of the herd—a kind of super-cow, called a *licabi*, which can be used time and time again.[9]

But the gods are not always deceived. The Ibo, for example, interpreted injuries from a snake bite or a fall as the spirits' punishment for the sacrifice of a chicken when a goat could have been afforded. While the Lugbara of the Southern Sudan, when they heard that their neighbours the Nuer would on occasion substitute a wild cucumber for the required sacrifice of an ox, were frankly incredulous. They themselves did use such vegetable surrogates if times were really hard and the slaughter of a beast impossible; but only with the firm commitment to make the proper sacrifice as soon as circumstance allowed. The idea that there could be a people so mean as to rob the gods of their due in this brazen way appalled them. Nor can one help sharing their astonishment.[10]

Religious practice and belief is such a common feature of the primitive world—indeed a universal one—that one might reinterpret Aristotle's dictum 'Man is a political animal' to read 'Man is a religious animal'. The pinpointing of any single explanation of this fact has defied both those who practise religion and those who study it. Yet clearly some of the vital functions that religion performs can be identified. By postulating a spirit world immanent in nature and approachable by men, it gives human life a place in an otherwise hostile and inscrutable universe. To quote the American philosopher Suzanne Langer: 'Man can adapt himself to anything his imagination can cope with; but he cannot deal with Chaos.'[11] Religion is one way of dealing with Chaos. Through myth, it offers comprehensible and satisfying explanations of problems of meaning which are essentially insoluble yet which, if left unanswered, can work disruptively on man's self-confidence and hence his ability to survive. Ritual gives man the opportunity and even an obligation to play a participatory role in the universe—it places him in his environment. And finally, the fulfilment of ritual obligations and the knowledge of shared beliefs are powerful binding forces for society.

If it be thought that today our technology has removed us from this cosmic uncertainty, we deceive ourselves. Technology does not touch on the questions which disturb men intellectually. Modern man may be able to build a nuclear power station but he certainly understands no more about his place in the universe, or his role on the Earth, than the Australian Aborigine. In fact, it can be argued that he knows less, for his relationship with his external environment is no longer governed by shared beliefs and rituals. We shall see now how the latter integrate men, not only with their internal social environment, but also with their external, physical environment. For the anthropological theory of functionalism has in the past few years been extended to reveal previously hidden relationships between ritual and belief and the closed ecological system constituted by men, the Earth and the Sun.

18 The Ancestors, War and Ecology

Right in the heart of the mountainous and densely forested central areas of New Guinea are found a group of twenty or so tribes who speak the Maring language. During 1962–3 Professor Roy Rappaport of the University of Michigan carried out a field study of one of them, the Tsembaga, which is proving of historic anthropological importance. Rappaport's field data were perhaps the first to open up a new field in anthropology which promises to increase substantially our understanding of primitive ritual and religion by relating them to the physical environment in which primitives live. The story is a complicated one and, as a piece of field work, it still stands almost unique in its significance. For these reasons, the ideas that follow are concerned almost solely with the Tsembaga, and Rappaport's study of them.[1]

The Tsembaga are a small tribe of only two hundred people, living in an area of forest covering just over three square miles and ranging in height from 2,400 to 7,200 ft. They have a good deal of contact—and warfare—with neighbouring Maring-speaking tribes, and their rituals and religious observances are particularly rich. They are slash-and-burn agriculturalists,[2] and have a very egalitarian social structure with no formal chiefs or authorities. Their spirit world is populated by two sets of spirits, one for the high ground and one for the low ground.

The first of the high-ground spirits are called the Red Spirits, who are the souls of the Maring who have been killed in warfare. As they inhabit the high ground, they are concerned with the uppermost parts of the human body and with warfare. These spirits are said to be hot like fires and dry, qualities associated with such martial virtues as strength, anger and hardness. The Maring themselves raise pigs, and so the marsupials which inhabit the higher regions of this area are called the Red Spirits' pigs. The high-ground spirit is Smoke Woman, a supernatural spirit who was never a human being but who enters the heads of the shamans when they smoke the local tobacco and who mediates between the living and the dead.

Her equivalent in the low-ground regions is Koipa Mangiang, associated with death and with fertility. The low-ground equivalent of the Red Spirits are the Spirits of Rot, who are cold, soft and wet, and are associated with the fertility of gardens, women and pigs. These spirits have little to do with warfare but are closely related to cycles of growth, to natural decay and to fertility. They contrast with the spirits of the high ground.

This evocative spirit world clearly reflects all the things that the Maring hold most dear or most important; they are the supernatural beings on whom success in war, in love and in gardening are dependent. As we should expect, the practical, day-to-day life of the Maring is richly reflected in the supernatural world. But in this case—as in many others—'day-to-day' is hardly the apposite term, for few people actually live the tedious and monotonous life of boredom and repetition usually associated with daily routine. On the contrary, the life style of the Maring in general, and the Tsembaga in particular, operates not over a 24-hour period but over a complicated and lengthy 20-year cycle. The Maring spirits are the very essence of this cycle.

The cycle starts with warfare, undertaken against a neighbouring tribe to avenge a death suffered but unavenged in an earlier bout of warfare. During the war, neighbouring groups join one of the two sides, and the war itself is highly ritualized. The two sides stand some way off and loose arrows and shake spears at one another, very rarely securing a hit and even more rarely effecting a mortal injury. Death itself usually results only when one of the two sides charges to finish off a wounded man lying on the ground. This they never do when the two sides are evenly balanced, waiting until the friends and helpers of the opposing side have begun to get bored, and have wandered back to their own territory to continue their more routine activities of gardening. The war ends by common agreement that enough deaths have been suffered on each side. The pressures to end the war are strong because during warfare the gardens are not worked and, as we shall see, sex is taboo. The number involved is never very high, typically about five or ten, or at most 10 per cent of the population of one side.

But if the war is, by the obnoxious standards of the West, trivial and equivalent to little more than one of the multiple killings that are so notable a feature of contemporary life in the United States, the rituals that accompany it are far from trivial. When war starts, the two sets of spirits are segregated from each other and the assistance of the Red Spirits invoked. Fighting stones are hung up from a post in a ritual house, and henceforth the other side become 'axe men' or the enemy. The Red Spirits begin to burn like fire within the heads of the Tsembaga warriors who are forbidden any contact with the soft, wet and cold world – in other words, sex is out of the question, food cooked by women is not eaten and no liquids are drunk. Foods which belong to either the Red Spirits or the Spirits of Rot may not be eaten together. Cold and wet eels are taboo as food.

When the war ends, a truce is called and a shrub known as the rumbim is planted, each man holding it as it is planted to symbolize his connection with the land and with the other members of the group. There is then a slaughter and feast of the pigs, which are offered to the ancestors, the Red Spirits, as partial payment for their help in the war, and a partial lifting of taboo. But a debt to the ancestors still remains, and many of the food and territorial taboos also remain. Furthermore, the pig population is then constantly increased so that the full debt can later be repaid to the Red Spirits. A long period then ensues during which taboos are gradually lifted and the spirits of the high and low ground progressively brought together again. When the pigs are in sufficient supply the boundaries of the new ground are planted out with stakes and taboos about entering any land won during the war are lifted. A taboo on trapping marsupials is lifted and the rumbim uprooted. More pigs are offered, partly in repayment for martial assistance and partly for the marsupials eaten (which are of course the pigs of the Red Spirits). The Red Spirits are asked to leave the bodies of the warriors. The foods of the high and low ground are then cooked and eaten together and a year-long festival begins, in which many local groups are invited to join in the dancing and feasting. The fighting stones are lowered and the taboo on eels is lifted. Eels and pigs are then cooked together in a ritual house in which both Koipa Mangiang and Smoke Woman have been summoned the night before. At this point the world is almost reunited again.

There is a massive slaughter of some 85 per cent (by live weight) of the pigs, and pork is distributed through a special window in a ceremonial fence. Finally, the hosts crash through this fence to join their neighbours: debts to the living and the dead have now been discharged. And the twenty-year cycle begins again, marked as before by first the warfare and separation of the spirits of high and low ground, by a truce, by pig slaughter, and then by gradual lifting of taboos together with innumerable symbolic acts which serve to bring together again the separated parties of both men and spirits. It should be noted that though this description sounds rich enough symbolically, it is only a pale condensation of what actually occurs for the taboos, particularly on foods, are extremely complex and they are lifted only during certain also highly complex rituals. For instance, the cassowary, a fierce and large bird, inhabits the high ground and the soft pandanus fruit grows on the low ground. Eating these foods together is taboo at certain periods, and the taboo is only lifted during a ceremony in which a man dancing on hot stones pierces a pandanus fruit with a cassowary bone.

It is not difficult to interpret this long sequence of complicated ritual activity in functionalist terms: the ways in which ritual reinforces the turning-points of the Maring life-cycle are easy to spot, and the unification of the society—towards which the rituals themselves are constantly directed—that must result from them is easy to visualize. However, Rappaport's analysis of the ritual cycle followed a somewhat different line, for his interests lay in the total ecology of the region of New Guinea involved, and how all the living species on it formed an inter-connected web which seemed ecologically very stable.

Each year the Maring fell a small area of forest for their gardens. They harvest it for a year or two until its natural fertility begins to fall off, and then they leave the garden to return to jungle, and prepare new ones. This form of agriculture has already been discussed in Chapter 2, and it is usually recognised as a rather expensive way to use land. Yet the Tsembaga live on a territory which provides them with only about five acres of arable land a head, and of which most of the land lies fallow for most of the time while it is reverting to natural jungle. In fact, each garden is used on average for one year, and then takes fifteen years to regain its fertility before it can be used again. Clearly, then, the Tsembaga and their pigs would approach the natural 'carrying capacity' of their terrain if their population continued to grow. But it doesn't. Although the natural growth-rate is about 1·6 per cent a year, it seems that the wars every fifteen or twenty years marginally increase the death-rate over a limited time to keep the population in balance.

Furthermore, the pig population is strictly controlled through the ritual cycle. When war ends, and the pigs become more numerous, their tending becomes an increasingly arduous job. At the same time more and more of the gardens have to be devoted solely to growing food for the pigs, and Rappaport found that when the pig population is at its highest no less than one-third of the gardens were producing food for pigs and for pigs alone. At the same time the pigs make more and more trouble for the men, breaking into the gardens intended for human consumption. Fencing becomes a more and more time-consuming job, and the complaints of the women become fiercer and fiercer as they find their job progressively more difficult. This delicate situation is complicated by the fact that nobody keeps their own pigs—they look after the pigs of their friends (in another context, this is the way the Tsembaga achieve social flexibility: when it is pointed out to them that it would be more efficient to mind their own pigs, rather than carry them long distances so that others can tend them, they point out that if this strange advice were to be followed, the Tsembaga women would have no friends).

At some point, then, competition between pigs and humans

becomes so great that the rumbim is pulled up, and the great pig slaughter and feast takes place; at the same time the debt to the ancestors is fully discharged. This growth of the pig population has taken between six and twenty years. Thus the ritual cycle operates in response to signals from the ecosystem which claim that the number of pigs is getting too large, the ancestors are paid and the ecological balance corrected. The ritual is ecologically highly adaptive, and similar principles can be seen to operate in the way taboos on eating and trapping other plants and animals are brought into effect at other times. Our own system of shooting seasons achieves much the same effect ecologically – although it does little to repay our ancestors. Rappaport concludes:

> The operation of these [ritual] cycles helps to maintain an undegraded biotic and physical environment, distributes local surpluses of pig throughout a region in the form of pork and assures people of high quality protein when they are most in need of it. The ritual cycles also limit warfare to frequencies that do not endanger the survival of the regional population but which allow occasional redispersion of people over land and land among people, thus, perhaps tending to correct discrepancies between the population densities of different local groups.[3]

Further light has been shed on all this by two systems analysts working at the Massachusetts Institute of Technology in 1971. There they constructed a computer model of how the Tsembaga human and pig populations interacted with the fertility of their land, and of how the various rituals associated with the Tsembaga cycle affected the long-term survival of the group.

Because each Tsembaga garden is used only for one year in sixteen, the total agricultural area available to the Tsembaga is only sixty-one acres (it is, incidentally, no mean agricultural feat to feed two hundred people and nearly as many pigs off such a small area). Obviously, if the population continued to grow, the area available for food would have to be increased and the interval between successive plantings decreased. Each time, the soil would become less fertile as it would not have fully recovered from the effects of previous cultivation, and the population would soon exceed the carrying capacity of the land. The computer model showed, according to its two programmers, Steven B. Shantzis and William W. Behrens III, that after ninety years

> food shortages can no longer be met by increasing intensity since the land is already being used at a level close to its limit. The population collapses as famine drastically decreases the average lifetime. Even so, the land fertility continues to fall until it is virtually zero and even subsistence is impossible for more than a few tribesmen.[4]

But, as we have seen, the Tsembaga population is not allowed to grow in this way but is controlled through ritual warfare once every twenty years or so. When the systems analysts added to the model the details of deaths from warfare of the human population, and of the pig feasts and slaughters, a very different picture emerged from the computer. Both the human and the pig populations oscillate up and down, and the carrying capacity of the land is never exceeded. Instead, the complaints of the women tending the pigs and the pigs' increasingly frequent incursions into the gardens act as a warning signal that the system needs correction. The pigs are slaughtered and a new round of warfare begins. As the authors put it, 'the Tsembaga unconsciously use the pig herd as both an information monitor and a homeostate in a complex, automatic population control system.'[5]

How effective that system is was learnt from the computer programme which showed that the twenty-year cycle of the Tsembaga could continue for at least five hundred years without any instability setting in. In real life it would probably continue much longer, for computer models always incorporate an inflexibility which probably has no equivalent in the real world.

This model serves to illustrate all the dangers of trying to 'civilize' primitive life. For instance, if a Western public-health programme were to be brought to the Tsembaga which allowed them to increase their population growth-rate to 2 per cent, festivals would become more and more common and would be initiated at lower and lower levels of pigs. The computer predicted that after one hundred years the tribes

can no longer afford to support the pig herd, so the herd declines to zero. The human population grows for 20 years unchecked by wars, until it has so exceeded the carrying capacity that the land can no longer support such large numbers of people. Between years 120 and 135 about 80 per cent of the population starves.[6]

Similarly, an enlightened Western power which succeeds in convincing the Tsembaga to abandon warfare has a disastrous effect. Each festival produces a decline in the pig population but the human population continues to grow, with the same result as in the model which describes the effect of a public health programme. 'Again,' the authors conclude, 'a policy which saved lives in the short run served only to drastically decrease the population size through starvation in the long run.'[7]

This study of the Tsembaga shows clearly how rituals lead to a sophisticated control system in which men are closely adapted to the physical environment in which they live. But knowing as much as we do now about ecology, one may well ask: why ritual? Surely similar effects could be achieved with a scientific approach to the problem, without recourse to what we earlier on called mumbo-jumbo? Professor Rappaport went on from his field studies in New Guinea to answer exactly this question. To do so he had to construct a theory of the significance of ritual in terms of its communication value.

Throughout the animal kingdom, individuals communicate with one another through signs—they signal their anger, their readiness to make love or to fight by displays which are signs of their intention. Thus the cat's back will arch and his fur stand on end when he is about to attack. Humans make recourse to similar techniques but have one added trick up their sleeve. This is known as the symbol and though it is similar enough to a sign there is one essential difference. A sign reflects the actual physical state of the animal concerned and therefore signals something about his intentions. A symbol, of course, merely symbolizes the intention of the human concerned and it may have nothing to do with the physiological state of the man or woman at the time; it may reflect merely an intellectual intention. Thus, for instance, when a man turns the lights low in his sitting-room he is suggesting to the girl in front of him that he wants to make love to her. But he only actually signals this, in the way that other animals do, when the familiar signals of physiological arousal are displayed to the girl directly.

Now symbols are the essence of human culture, and the distinguishing feature between men and animals. Almost all our communication is based on their use, and they have enormous power, enabling us to communicate not only about the present, but about the past and future as well. But they also have tremendous disadvantages for they introduce a new concept, that of lying, into the business of communication. A signal cannot lie because it reflects a physiological state. A symbol can be used to lie, as a wrestler uses a variety of facial gestures to symbolize his ferocity to his opponent when in fact he may have nothing but amicable feelings for him. Man is thus not only the greatest liar in the animal kingdom — he is probably the only one.

In human society symbolic actions, such as bowing and curtseying, are called rituals. But we should be careful to note that there are apparently two kinds of rituals — secular (such as bowing) and religious (such as all the Tsembaga ritual). And clearly religious rituals communicate something more than a mere secular ritual. That something, according to Professor Rappaport, is affirmation of religious belief. When men attend to detail in ritual procedures, they are in effect saying to each other that they believe in the myths and cosmology of their spirit world. They are, in other words, sanctifying their symbolic communications to one another, asserting that in this case they are using their symbols to speak the truth and not to lie. When President Kennedy was assassinated, Vice-President Johnson according to the constitution immediately became president. But before this could happen, or at least be seen to happen, he had to take the oath of presidency, something which he did within hours of the death of

Kennedy. While this ritual is in effect a secular one, the message is clear: religious ritual is used to sanctify, and hence certify, religious belief.

In most primitive societies, there are no authoritarian social forces which could be used to enforce belief—as may happen in a totalitarian or free market economy where such credos as 'What is good for General Motors is good for the country' or 'You have never had it so good' may need constant reinforcement if they are to be believed. To the observer these are unverifiable propositions. In a primitive society similarly unverifiable propositions are sanctified and hence given the status of unquestionable truth by those who partake in the rituals which surround them. It then becomes easy to understand why ritual is as closely related to the physical environment as we saw in the case of the Tsembaga in this chapter and in some other examples in Chapter 5. As long as the society finds that performance of its rituals in high levels of agricultural productivity, or in a proper balance between man and his domestic beasts, his religious beliefs are bolstered. But if a ritual does not achieve this effect, the whole system of unverifiable beliefs on which the religion and cosmology are based falls into disrepute. Men no longer find it possible to participate in their traditional rituals. 'The multitudes', to quote 'The Book of Rites' once again, 'fall into confusion'.[8]

The dilemma of contemporary civilization can also be approached in this way. Unverifiable beliefs about what is good for us and for our countries were once bolstered by religious ritual ('God save the Queen') but are now largely the property of the authorities. Religious belief may be encouraged but generally this happens outside the political arena, and our faith in how society ought to function hangs by a thread from the five-minute party political broadcasts occurring at peak viewing-hours on television. As these are clearly a sham, and are demonstrably false (as shown by deteriorating conditions in spite of whoever promises what), they are maladaptive rituals, poorly enforced by appeal not to ritual itself but to political authority. Such devices, indeed, can easily become pathological, as they always do when the ideas involved lead not to a better adaptation of men to each other and to their environment, but to a worse one. Professor Rappaport concludes:

> It is by no means certain that the representations of nature provided us by science are more adaptive or more functional than those images of the world, inhabited by spirits whom men respect, that guide the actions of the Maring and other 'primitives'. Indeed, they may be less so, for to drape nature in supernatural veils is perhaps to provide her with some protection against human parochialism and destructiveness, a parochialism and destructiveness that may be encouraged by a natural view of nature. It may also be suggested that ... it is not yet clear whether civilization, the state, science and mechanized technology are, in the long run, adaptive. And since civilization, state organization, science and mechanized technology are recent developments in the evolution of culture, we may ask to what ends evolution might be leading us.[9]

We have now taken the idea of functionalism just as far as it can go. In the next chapter we turn to yet more weighty matters surrounding the spirit world of the primitive. This will lead us to philosophical questions concerned not with how adaptive primitive ritual may be, but to what extent the primitive's view of his world is a richer or a better approximation to reality than our own. For even the liberal idea that primitive religion is 'misguided but functional' seems to be a belittlement of primitive philosophy, based on Western arrogance.

19 Reality and Experience

The first thing to notice about the primitive thought world is that it is different from ours. Some points of difference are obvious enough, though they may be no less thought-provoking for that. The Maori believe, for instance, that the first human being was a woman. If mythology requires a unique ancestor a woman certainly seems logically—even biologically—as good a candidate as a man. A somewhat deeper level of difference is revealed in the spiritual autobiography of a wise old Indian:

> When I was ten years old I looked at the land and the rivers, the sky above, and the animals around me and I was so anxious to understand this power that I questioned the trees and the bushes ... Then I had a dream and in my dream one of the small round stones appeared to me and told me that the maker of all was Wakan Tanka.

This was not poetic licence or just a boyish fancy which maturity dispelled. Throughout the old man's intellectual and spiritual life the stones, which appeared to him in that first vision, were to be his mediators with the eternal principle. 'I know that I am not worthy to speak to Wakan Tanka. I make my request of the stones and they are my intercessors.'[1]

St Francis, who saw poverty and death, the birds and the stones and all the phenomena of life as his brothers, offers the Westerner some point of reference here, but it is only a help, nothing more. When the Dakota Indians, for example, speak of a man being possessed by a Bear spirit it is neither metaphor nor poetic hyperbole, but an observed fact of Dakota life. Being thinking men, they require a theory to explain it. The possession, they say, is the work of a *nagiya*, described in Western terms as 'an immaterial essence whose substance may appear in any form it chooses'.[2] Such instances, and there are hundreds of them, illustrate the fact that the primitive thinker simply does not live in the same world as we do. He has different experiences to account for and provides answers to questions that we do not even ask. If we would understand his thought world, we must attempt to sense these different experiences and to face the fact of difference.

The record of one man's voyage into just such a world of difference exists. The writer, Carlos Castaneda, is a trained anthropologist and his book describes a piece of research that developed into an odyssey of experience, alien and, at the end, terrifying. His teacher was a Yaqui Indian sorcerer with the Spanish name of Don Juan and even outsiders to the 'Yaqui way of knowledge' can learn some profound lessons.[3]

At the first encounter Don Juan asked his would-be disciple:

'Why would you like to undertake such learning?'
'I really would like to know about it. Is not just to want to know a good reason?'
'No! You must search in your heart and find out why a young man like you wants to undertake such a task of learning.'

Castaneda's reply is the clear, spontaneous response of Western man faced with the unknown. If any of the classic assumptions of our culture are still left unquestioned it is that the 'want to know' is self-justifying. Yet he discovered that the first great boundary of difference could only be crossed when he had surrendered his fundamental assumption.

The initiation into the Yaqui way centred upon the use of the drug peyote and the discipline and ritual needed to win the favour of the god Mescalito who inhabits it. But drugs were only part of a long course of experience and learning. The way is hard and the mystic experiences that Castaneda describes are vivid, real and haunting. In a vision he communicates in deep mystic sympathy with Mescalito, who manifests himself as a playful dog; but on returning to consciousness Castaneda wept with sadness for: 'I had forgotten that I was a man.' Yet, with his scientific training and Western habit of mind, he attempts to question even this great moment of harmony with the universe.

'Then Mescalito is real? I mean he is something you can see?'
Don Juan seemed baffled by my question. He looked at me
with a sort of blank expression.
'Didn't you see him last night?'
I wanted to say that I saw only a dog, but I noticed his
bewildered look.
'Then you think that what I saw last night was him?'
He looked at me with contempt.

It was the only response possible to the stubborn Western
refusal to acknowledge and accept the truth of inner experience.
As the book progresses we see that Castaneda begins to understand
the Yaqui way and through him we are able to appreciate something of it too. Beyond doubt he experienced things 'impossible'
by the standards of Western man, and, as a climax to his novitiate,
he lived through an eerie and deeply unnerving night of struggle
with unknown spirit forces that were seeking to rob him of his
soul. Don Juan gave no indication as to who the enemy would be,
but:

> He gave me precise instructions about a 'fighting form'
> that had to be used if I was attacked. It consisted of clapping
> the calf and thigh of my right leg and stomping my left foot
> in a kind of dance that I had to do while facing my attacker.

The Western scientist passed the hours of darkness in mortal
terror. More than once he adopted the 'fighting form' against an
enemy which took the form of Don Juan yet invaded his mind
with a sense of black malignity.

Correctly primed by the hygienic traditions of Western thought,
some might interpret this in terms of auto-suggestion and hallucin-
ation. But such an explanation is too glib. The account has authen-
ticity and if anything can open the Western mind to accept that
there are worlds of experience and reality that are unknown to it, a
reading of this book will. For a time Carlos Castaneda lived, quite
literally, in another world.

Perhaps no single concept more completely embodies the
difference between the civilized and the primitive world view
than the attitude to time. The Western view of it as a linear

track, with measured distances and fixed landmarks, along which life moves from a known past to a foreseeable future, is certainly not universal. It has been plausibly argued that the first crucial step towards this mechanistic view of time, indeed towards the modern machine-orientated society, was taken with the development of geared clock mechanisms in the fourteenth century. Every major town in Europe acquired its great clock and some of these elaborate and beautiful mechanisms survive, to remind us of Western man's first blush of pride in the 'marvels of modern science'.

Before this, the ringing of the monastery bells to mark the hours of work and worship was for most men the only indication that regularity could be imposed on time. For the peasant, time existed only in the necessary sequence of tasks imposed by the daily exercise of forcing a livelihood from the land. For the gentry, too, it was ill-defined. In the year 1188, a judicial duel was to be held in the meadows outside Mons, the contestants being required to present themselves before the ninth hour of the day. The only one to turn up arrived at dawn and, after a long wait, claimed to have won the case by default. The point of law was clear enough but the court nevertheless went into a lengthy recess. The position of the sun was checked and clerics present consulted to confirm that the time for the service of nones had indeed passed. Only then was judgment given in favour of the claimant, for even trained legal minds had to take advice before committing themselves to a statement as to the time of day.[4] Night and day were each divided into twelve hours, irrespective of the season of the year so that the length of these 'hours' naturally varied.

Medieval man's 'vast indifference to time' was by no means confined to the hours of the day. Charters, drawn, one would assume, specifically to serve as records, are often undated. Themselves unable to read, lay rulers tended to accept documents as evidence only when they were validated by the memories of eye-witnesses. For the vast majority in the Middle Ages, time was defined by the rhythm of the seasons and the past existed in an oral tradition which, while often remarkably detailed, lacked the graduated scale of dates that we assume. Before the mechanical clock, the European experience of time had much in common with the world of the primitive.

The Ankore of Uganda reckon their day according to the needs of their cattle. It starts with the first milking and the driving to pasture. The morning is a time of rest until about midday, when water is drawn for the villagers before the cattle muddy the water-holes. After the cattle have been watered they are driven back to pasture again, at about three in the afternoon; two hours later they are brought back to the settlement, at six put into their kraals and the day ends about seven with the final milking.[5] A medieval peasant would have been perfectly at home with such arrangements.

In such a time-system, activities rather than abstract concepts of duration are the measure. In some years the 'hunting month' may last twenty-five days, in others thirty-five days but the matter is irrelevant – the month of hunting lasts just so long as the hunters are having success. Among the Latuka people, December is called 'give your kinsmen water', because it is the period of drought; February is called 'let them dig'; June is 'dirty mouth' because the new grain is ready and eating it makes the children's mouths dirty.[6]

It can be readily admitted that a diary based on the time divisions of the Ankore and the Latuka would present a Western businessman with problems, while Western physicists, who recently added a tenth of a second between 1971 and 1972 to satisfy the vibrations of the caesium atom, would no doubt be ill at ease in a world where the months may vary by ten days or so. The Western formulation of time is, of course, an indispensable adjunct of the current mode of Western life; but it is certainly not the only possible formulation or necessarily the richest. On the contrary, it strengthens that divorce from his environment which characterizes the whole outlook of Western man.

Discussing the attitudes to time in his book on African philosophies, John S. Mbiti remarks: 'The rising of the sun is an event recognized by the community as a whole.'[7] A seemingly basic statement, yet one that can hardly be applied to Western society, so far has it drifted from the rhythms of the world. The great facts of sunrise and sunset have for most people lost their deep significance, and are noticed only on a relatively superficial level. In fact Western attitudes to time, as to everything else, are mechanistic and economic.

Time is money, as the saying goes, and our language speaks of spending time and above all of saving it, like money. There is no more contemptuously dismissive description of anything than that it is a 'waste' of time and when the ideal, endlessly active Western man really has nothing better to do with time, he passes it. We have aimed to fill each day with productive activity; to exploit time like any natural resource; we have quarried efficiency out of the sunlight.

Even Westerners occasionally stand back to ask what all the hurry and bustle is for. Why does one save time if only to do something else with it? But the point has never been more neatly made than by a Polynesian Islander, interrupted one afternoon at his siesta by an investigator from an international agency. The conversation reported by the investigator, went along these lines.

'Why are you lazing on the beach like this when you might be fishing?'

'Oh! I took a big enough catch this morning to last me at least three days.'

'But if you went out fishing again you could catch more fish.'

'And why should I do that?'

'So you could sell the surplus.'

'And what would be the point of that?'

'Well then you could buy more up-to-date equipment and catch still more fish.'

'And what would be the point of *that*?'

'So that you could build a fine house for yourself and your family.'

'Why?'

'Well, for one thing you would be able to afford a swimming pool and relax in the sun and swim when you felt like it.'

'And what do you think I'm doing at this very moment?'[8]
As an African might observe; time is how you make it, not how you use it.

But Western man is obsessed by the image of the fleeting moment. 'Time flies' — past us like a plummeting eagle that we try hopelessly to ensnare. Wedged between the future and the past on the narrow ledge of the present, in a continual state of becoming and forgetting, of planning and projecting, civilized man finds all too little time for actually living. One answer to the problem has been to carve out special annual periods devoted to 'really living'; these periods we call 'holidays' and they are unique to our civilization.

The primitive inhabits another world. His life does not alternate between periods of repressed emotional frustration and periods of febrile activity, between 'work' and 'play'. He does not use today's time as a resource for building tomorrow's fantasy. With its eyes fixed eternally ahead, the ideology of the industrial state looks to a distant future when life will be better. We are beginning perhaps to sense that the attitude is destructive of the best in life. Among the primitives where more immediate experiences seem more desirable, it may be literally impossible to envisage a future more remote than a couple of years ahead. Quite apart from anything else the tense structure of language may not permit it.

In place of our clear divisions of a past stretching back to infinity, the present and the future stretching ahead to infinity, the tenses in Swahili are either of Sasa or Zamani, concepts that shape an attitude to life unknown to the West. A man lives in Sasa which embraces his recent past and the 'remote' future up to two years ahead. The older a man grows the longer is his Sasa period, while the Sasa of the community is longer still. Zamani is unlike Sasa in being a completed time dimension into which the Sasa flows, but it is not a dead zone of extinct events. It is full of activity and happenings that surround the 'now'. Life is a process of moving through Sasa towards the realm of Zamani and the process does not stop with a man's death. While there are still people living who have personal memories of him, for whom he is part of the Sasa, a man enjoys an individual, personal immortality. He only passes into the anonymity of Zamani when such immediate remembrances have passed away. Only then is he truly dead.[9]

If such ideas help us to prise loose a little from our vision of time, they will also prepare us for some understanding of the profound and vibrant concepts surrounding the Australian Aborigine's world of The Dreaming. In this, the view of the world, the view of man and society and the view of time become part of a mutually reinforcing pattern of belief which commands respect and requires attention.

The legends of The Dreaming talk of a past which, like Zamani, is also in some mystical way part of the present. As to most primitives, the idea of time as a linear continuum is completely alien to the Aborigines whose numerous languages do not have a single word for the concept of abstract 'time'. It seems that the nearest they approach to it is in an idea of 'social' time, a notion of cyclical generations through which families are enmeshed with the continuing reality of society. Just as the families of the tribe are linked by ties of blood or social obligation, so are the men of the past and the present part of one another.

In some such way too is the world of everyday connected with the world of The Dreaming: time of heroic ancestors; time when the world took shape; time when men and animals, descendants of a common stock, divided their species and their tribes. In this great body of tales and legends, marvels of the natural creation mingle with explanations of social traditions and institutions, and from some of the tales it appears that the social conventions ruling now were also in force during The Dreaming. The heroic age is gone, yet Aborigine thinkers clearly believe that they have the key to the mystery that links the The Dreaming with the here and now. It was the Aborigine who chose the English word 'dreaming' as the nearest description of his legendary moral philosophy—perhaps because in the dream we actually experience time, past and present, on an equal footing.[10]

In fundamental matters primitive thought is clearly different from ours—is it also inferior? Indeed, can primitive man be said to think at all? Only a generation ago, Levy Bruhl, one of the great names in French anthropology, laboured to make a distinction between logical and prelogical thought with the implication that the one was a progressive development of the other. But unless we are to take the arrogant and negative stance of ethnocentrism and judge other cultures by how nearly they approach to our way of thinking, it is apparent that such debates are not only misleading but also irrelevant. To explore the issues that this raises our investigation must open out, but it rests for the moment with the Aborigines.

Unquestionably they hold a special interest. Firstly, they have inhabited the vast sub-continent for some thirty thousand years – a period about five times as long as the whole of recorded history. Secondly, for all but two centuries of that huge era they lived in almost complete isolation. Thirdly, the physical environment has been basically the same. Fourthly, their technology has been on the simplest plane. Fifthly, and most important, they have discovered that a people of few wants, an other-worldly cast of a mind and a simple way of life can attain a unique joy of life. Certainly our society is sadly short of 'joy in life'; is there a key to be found in the thought of the Aborigines?

We shall not find answers aimed at the classic questions of Western philosophy; questions such as 'What is reality?', 'In what sense do we know anything?', 'How is matter constituted?'. We shall not find answers because the questions were not of interest. The Aborigine is capable of abstract thought of a high order, but over the centuries he has directed his attention to a subject that we hardly consider at all – the organization of kins within a social group. Within a single representative tribe there are about a hundred divisions and sub-classifications to be analysed and understood before an outsider can begin to describe the organization of the group.[11] The system is intricate, it rests on ancient custom and depends on a huge body of accumulated knowledge as to the practical workings of that custom; it is a complex body of real knowledge. Whether, of course, we choose to rate the evolution of a subtle and effective social structure as an intellectual achievement, is a matter of taste. Some might think, however, that the West could have devoted more of its energies to the problem with advantage.

Of course there are also primitives that have perfectly 'respectable', 'philosophic' thoughts on the Western pattern. The Winnebago Indians and the Maori and many others have theories that seek to explain the relationship between 'form' and substance. A missionary who objected to Maori religion on the grounds that it endowed things with 'souls' was brought to task for his philosophical naivety, for to the Maori philosophers everything in the phenomenal world derived its form by virtue of being possessed by the soul of a god. The parallels between this idea and Plato's notion of an eternal world of 'ideal forms' that embodied the essence of earthly forms are suggestive.[12] Again, Maori views on the Ego principle in human personality are both subtle and in tune with psychological theories; while the Oglala Indian theory of the circle as the perfect form echoes themes that were once the classic concerns of Western aesthetics and philosophy.[13] Such similarities indicate that 'primitive' man is every bit as capable of abstract speculation as we; but the objects of his attention are different and so are his objectives.

To us it may be a matter of indifference whether the rock and earth are to be regarded as married or not. For the Dakota religious thinker it is important and gives as much scope for refined theorizing as the question of whether the bread of the communion service becomes the body of Christ or not.

One test proposed for the defining of a society as primitive is the presence or absence of writing. Undoubtedly writing affects a society's world view for it gives durability to ideas far beyond the lives of their originators. It makes possible records, so that the past is packed more or less densely with the notifications of events and time is given body by bundles of paper. A society with writings from the past sees the passage of time very differently from one which has none; the rich and numinous world of the Aboriginal Dreaming, for example, could hardly have evolved in an environment of literature and account books, philosophical tracts and biographies. Moreover, writing gives a seeming concreteness to notions, which while it may be deceptive is certainly persuasive. It makes the manipulation of ideas, as a result, more easy and tempts the thinker to confer undue importance on ideas often remote from the practicalities of living or the emotions of the heart.

It is no coincidence that with the arrival of almost universal literacy, poetry retreated into slim volumes and minority reviews, for poetry, as is now being rediscovered, is the art of the spoken word and belongs most fittingly in the worlds of oral tradition. Although neglected by literate societies, human memory is a faculty of immense power. Poems of vast dimensions are transmitted from generation to generation, by word of mouth; it is thought that even the Homeric epics were originally part of a long oral tradition. In such a tradition the poems do not remain utterly unchanged. Tradition prescribes the outline and the episodes, but the story-teller is expected to provide the vital ingredient of imagination that brings the tale home to the hearts of his hearers.

Researchers into the work of Balkan epic-singers or *histrions* showed that the epics varied not only from bard to bard, but even from one telling to another by the same bard.[14] The anthropologist Paul Radin found the same phenomenon in his work with the Winnebago tribe.

> In one instance when I obtained a very markedly divergent version of the most sacred myth of the tribe, the informant, in reply to my question as to why his version differed so much from the others, answered rather irritatingly: 'That is my way of telling the story. Others have different ways.' That was all. No judgment was passed.[15]

'Irritating' indeed to a mind from a literate background, accustomed to the conventions of the 'established text'; doubly irritating no doubt to a scientist searching for the definitive statement of an important article of faith. Radin himself recognizes that what is at issue is not an incapacity on the part of the primitive mind for consistency, but rather a fundamental difference of cultural outlook.

The difference rests on the conventions of an oral tradition as opposed to those of a written one. Some anthropologists, in the dilemma described by Radin, collate as many variants as they can find in the vain attempt to establish a 'correct' version. The classic instance of this misunderstanding between the world of speech and the world of writing comes from the academies of Alexandria in the third century B.C. which worked to compile an agreed text of the great Homeric poems from the numerous versions recorded in different parts of the Greek world. The poet, on the other hand, like the Winnebago Indian, may well have accepted the variant versions of others as different ways of telling the stories.

Scholars of the written word, however, could have no such equanimity and evolved the science of textual criticism to solve their problems. It is surely significant that the West was applying scientific analysis to the scrutiny of the artist's inspiration at such an early date. It is doubly significant that it was applied to texts of religious status; for the Homeric poems, which after all dealt with the doings of the gods, had long been given ceremonial recitations at the great religious festivals of Greece. The tradition of textual criticism survived and flourished in the Christian era and the sacred texts have been subject to analytical treatment for so long that it is difficult, even for the religious, to realize the implications. Obviously, for all 'religions of the Book' the exact words of that book must be assured, a doctrine of divine inspiration being an ideal formula to avert questions. But once the questioning begins the meaning of the text comes to be obscured and the issues of faith and belief, paramount in the religious life and unshaken in the primitive context, come to be eroded by devotion to the written word.

However, the whole of Western culture is wreathed about with writing and its mode of thinking is deeply influenced as a result. For writing captures thought; it sometimes shackles it; it pins it down for reference and refutation in a way that the spoken word cannot. Records not only reinforce memory; they also establish, sometimes artificially, fixed reference points that can be reflected on, improved on. Thus writing can be seen as essential for a progress-orientated society. By fixing the moment, it revolutionizes society's attitude to time; it breeds a sense of history and shapes a world view irremediably different from that of illiterate man.

Perhaps nowhere is the contrast between these two world views more apparent than in the field of myth which was for long the vehicle for transmitting the society's received wisdom on the great questions of life. Man is by nature an asker of questions, and, perversely enough, has shown the most enduring interest in the very questions that cannot be fully answered. These fall into two broad categories. How did things come to be as they are? How does man fit into the scheme? They have exercised and disturbed thinking men in all the times for which we have records and in virtually every society that the anthropologists have discovered. In our own society, in fact, they have been pushed towards one side and a generation or so ago the logical positivist school of philosophers sought, rather cleverly, to dispose of the questions altogether by announcing that they were logically meaningless. Yet since they have seemed meaningful to the bulk of mankind, the answers proposed and the techniques for solving them are a central theme of this book.

Successful myth provides explanations to the profound questions in terms of the experience of its hearers. Eskimo myth, for example, describes a great sea-goddess, a fingerless, woman-like monster that dwells deep in the waters under the ice. As a child she had been thrown out of the family's boat in a storm by her father who cut off her fingers as she struggled to hang on to the gunwale. Her fingers became fish while she sank to the bottom of the sea where she became the ruler of the deeps and the terror of the world above. The imagery of the myth was potent in meaning for a society where a cruel environment enforced the practice of infanticide. The suppressed anguish of such killings was partly assuaged by a tale that rooted the practices at the beginning of time and elevated the innocent girl-victim into the most powerful of the supernatural beings demanding propitiation from society at large.[16]

In a similar way, as we have seen, the tales of The Dreaming from Aboriginal Australia root society's attitudes firmly in the cosmic process and talk of the beginning of things in terms of the accepted moral and social code. A still more direct example of a myth that sanctioned social attitudes comes from the Biblical account of creation in the Book of Genesis. In six days God created the world and on the seventh He rested; Adam the first man was created in the image of God on the sixth day and Eve, the first woman, was shaped from one of his ribs; God brought the animals to Adam for him to name them and placed him and his companion in the paradise of Eden. For centuries the myth served because it reflected the assumptions and practices of Jewish and Christian society. The Sabbath was sanctified as a day of rest by the story; the pre-eminence of man in the animal creation was asserted; and the subordination to woman to him dramatically sanctioned.

A successful myth is a powerful factor in stabilizing a society and is a strong conservative force against change. The security it provides, by giving man a sense of belonging in an alien non-sentient environment and by integrating the human organization with the world of nature, is too valuable to be lightly surrendered. By relieving men of the traumatic fears of isolation in a hostile universe, it frees them for effective and confident living. In this sense the conservative tendencies of society's mythology have a profoundly important function and should rather be described as 'conservatory'. If, however, beliefs become impervious to changing circumstances, they foster tensions in society between belief and practice, tensions that can be ultimately destructive not simply to the myth but also to the social structure itself. It is the advantage of an oral culture resting on a tradition that each generation may modify on the principles described earlier in this chapter, that such rigidities of belief are far less likely than in a society where the myths are embodied in writing. While it fosters change in every other department of thought, the written word ensures that the sacred texts remain immutable and increasingly become out of touch with the intellectual currents of the times.

In its written form a myth has impressive and apparently permanent authority, but its weakness is its inflexibility which makes it highly vulnerable to new ideas. Where the Winnebago is content to account for variations of the tradition simply in terms of the conventions of different story-tellers, the priest of the book has no such escape route. The story must be either right or wrong. The long-drawn-out battle between the scientists and the theologians over the 'accuracy', 'truth' and hence the credibility of the religious account is a classic instance of the fate awaiting the wisdom of an oral tradition once it enters the domain of the written word. It is attacked with weapons it cannot turn and on grounds it never meant to occupy, it is pressed for 'proof' where it only sought to offer assurance. No amount of metaphorical or allegorical 'explanation' can fit it for a function it was never designed to perform.

Myth rests on belief. While it is believed, it can serve a society well. It deals after all in questions that, by their nature, are un-answerable but questions that men nevertheless ask. By providing answers consistent with society's aims and assumptions, myth liberates men for the full pursuit of practical life-related activities. Once it is analysed and questioned it retreats and leaves the field to rationalism and scepticism. It has been the proud boast of science to have 'de-mythologized' Western thought, and in a profound sense the claim is unanswerable. In place of a divine creator we have molecular biology, the Heisenberg 'uncertainty' principle and behaviourism. Instead of seeing mankind related to the principle of the universe as a child is related to its father, we see him once again, as in the dawn of human history before the ages of myth, a lonely, critical faculty in a world indifferent to him. The logical conclusion is bleakly put in the notorious words of Jacques Monod:

> Man knows at last that he is alone in the indifferent immensity of the universe. His duty, like his fate, is written nowhere. It is for him to choose between the kingdom and the dark-ness.[17]

It is not the view of the primitive, nor is it any more 'provable' than the mythological view. Living in a society that has been stripped of its great myths we are well placed to decide which state is better. There are many voices today suggesting that its lack of myth lies at the root of our society's sickness.

20 The Search for Vision

Zeus, Poseidon and Jupiter ... for us, the military technology paradoxically held to be both the means of burning to death several hundred million human beings and the means by which the slender peace will be upheld and the man-made apocalypse avoided. We almost forget the words are gods, the symbols of a culture so strong that we proudly claim to follow directly in its lineage. They were the myth that gave Greek culture the base from which to invent democracy, the city-state, geometry, philosophy—a culture we believe held a prerogative on wisdom little more than two thousand years ago. How conveniently we forget that our intellectual forbears held to a polytheism as rich and varied as any invented by the primitive world. How conveniently we gloss over the awkward fact of Greek divinity, ritual, taboo and sacrifice. How ignorant we remain of the mutually sustaining relationship between Greek philosophy and religious practice. And how easily we assume that primitive 'mumbo-jumbo' was what prevented the primitive ever from moving out of his harsh lot, of inventing tools and techniques, of aspiring to rational thought, of treating his fellows compassionately and as human beings.

Yet enough has been said to see that in cultures other than our own the sacred cannot be parcelled off from the profane. To use a contemporary concept, the two were symbiotic, each mingling with the other, each depending on the other for its continued existence. The attempt to separate them out, the philosophy of reductionism, is the blight of our culture; yet it is this approach that we, men of our own culture, have, perforce, used throughout most of this book. To seek to understand, we have analysed, split up, dissected, detailed and reduced the primitive life to gobbets of experience which seem to have meaning in our context. But, for the final chapter, we have to go further. To see that the primitive philosophy of time or causation is different from ours is one thing; to understand the primitive experience quite another. Even to assume, as Carlos Castaneda did, that such an experience can be couched in the reassuring phrases of everyday language may be a delusion. Men are not that good at communicating with one another at the best of times; to communicate experience, as distinct from thoughts or beliefs, may be beyond us.

The fundamental difficulty, of course, is that we live in two worlds. The first, and on our own judgment by far the more important, is the world of objective fact. This is the world of 'real' things which can be numbered, weighed, measured and relied on to be the same at all times and at all places. The world of objective fact exists quite apart from human beings – although some aspects of people are included in it, such as their numbers and their group behaviour *en masse* – and would continue to do so if human beings disappeared. The second world is the one of subjective experience. It is not greatly heeded by the West, for what people feel about things is held unreliable. Their emotions are known to change from day to day, and hence their experience of the world bears only an oscillating relationship with what we call 'reality'. In fact, for us subjective behaviour is normally regarded as tiresome, human emotions intervening as frequently as they do between a plan and its execution. It is only the presence of people, we sometimes quip, that prevents us from organizing the world as we would really like to see it. Without strikes, greed or anger, without ambitions or sentimentality for the past, the citadel of technical expertise would long since have realized its Utopia on Earth. For the West, people are a problem – particularly when they increase in numbers at an exponential rate and within a social system designed to do away with the need for them.

But because the world of subjective experience so clearly exists, we have not sought to deny it – merely to separate it, fastidiously, from the more hygienic world of objective fact. The task of reconciling these two areas has not yet been attempted and hence we live in a state of permanent schizophrenia, explaining things alternately by reference to one world and then the other, working by day in the world of objective fact but allowing ourselves occasionally to slip into subjective behaviour when confronted by art, by love, or very exceptionally by naked raw experience.

Imagine, then, a situation where this philosophical split never occurred. Where imagination was the mother of invention, where the meanings of things as symbolic truth were as important as their literal truth; where the gods of fertility were as vital to the garden as a spade and fertilizer, and where both classes of things were indivisible. Where the sacred mingled with the profane, and experience rubbed shoulders with reality. Of course, we can imagine no such thing. So deeply rooted is our conviction that the subjective must be separated from the objective, a world where this was not so makes little sense to us even in intellectual terms; to imagine the experience of living in it is quite beyond our grasp. Yet such was the world of the primitive.

What we cannot understand, we should not judge. Yet within us all lurks that sneaking suspicion that our brilliant success as the masters of this plant was in fact *due* to the division we created between fact and experience. Were it not for that, Rand Corporation would be out of a job, and even more of the world's population would be cold, miserable and hungry than they are now. Science would never have flourished, the rights of the individual would never have been championed, and all but a tiny elite would still be primitive peasants toiling to wrest a living from the ground.

But this view leaves much to explain. How can we then account for the fact that most of the technical processes which have transformed human society were invented, if not necessarily in a primitive culture, then at least in one where the numinous was real. Think of agriculture, the city, transport, trade and metal-working—the very stuff of which our civilization is made. Yet these were not our inventions but those of pre-literate and primitive peoples who bowed down to wood and stone thousands of years ago. How could their primitive mentality have wrestled with such concepts?

Of course, we have manufactured our own myths. Fire came

about when man accidentally rubbed two sticks together and produced a spark. Later he dropped some clay by mistake into the fire and invented the pot. He dropped food in and invented cooking. He dropped his excrement where plants grew and invented fertilizer. He failed to tidy up all his wild grain, found that plants grew from it, and invented agriculture. These ridiculous stories we choose to believe in preference to what for us seems the only alternative: that primitive man had his own version of Rand Corporation and ran his own research programmes.

But that is not the only alternative. While we may not be able to reconstruct the past, there is no cause to ridicule it. The primitive's involvement in nature was so intense that for him such inventions were possibly easier and more natural than they would be for us. And undoubtedly the cosmic relationships which were the essence of his myth were not the things which restrained him — they were the very things which inspired him, which enabled him to see the fertilizing rain as the sperm of the divine and the Spirits of Rot as a natural explanation of the cycle of growth and decay.

To be sure, we may today do things more efficiently, although we have yet to count the final cost. And of all the hidden costs, probably none is greater than the psychological cost of stripping the universe bare, of unveiling her secrets and severing the bond between man and his world. We can now explain (or think we can) how it is that an acorn can turn into a majestic oak and take a hundred years to do it. For us there is no mystery. The same process is going on in a billion places on the Earth's surface at the same time. It is a perfectly ordinary event. Yet, in a real sense, it is a quite *extra*-ordinary event — a real miracle which the fine-sounding theories of cellular biology and information theory in fact do nothing to dispel. But we cannot tolerate something which is simultaneously ordinary and extraordinary, so we pigeon-hole it in the first category, reserving the right to wonder only for the credulous.

It is here that the primitive enjoyed an experience unknown to us. For him there was no problem in identifying the ordinary with the extraordinary, of mixing the sacred with the profane in a way which only sounds to us like confusion. We have seen that this practice was functional; but it was more than that. The primitive view of nature was, in fact, correct in regarding the growth of an acorn as an extraordinary, even a sacred, event. If we believe it to be anything else, we may well deceive ourselves — and we certainly deprive ourselves of a rich range of experience and deny our own obvious though deeply hidden capacity for wonder.

Blame for all this, of course, can be laid convincingly at the feet of reductionism, which insists on seeing the acorn as only a set of chemicals and coded instructions. Similarly, it is fashionable to assert not only that the dead are living but also that they have common constituents. Life is *nothing but* a collection of chemicals, each individually no different from those we may find in rock or earth. There is no hidden vital spark which differentiates the quick from the dead. Yet if we stop to think about it, this modern and fashionable theory is clearly nonsense. In almost all cases the distinction between the dead and the living is clear for all to see, and the categories are different. Yet it seems we are quite happy to degrade life from the miracle which it is — a very ordinary miracle, and all the more miraculous for that — to a chemical formula. We reduce the living to the dead.

Not so the primitive. His error, if it was one, was to promote the dead to the living, ascribing to the rocks and the clouds and the rain a quality which we would deny they possess. Structurally, there is a strange symmetry about this. But even if both ideas were wrong, who ended up the richer? Those who see the living in terms of the dead, or those who saw the dead in the terms of the living? Surely there is something deeply characteristic of primitive and Western society in these two attitudes.

What we are talking about here is not perfectly described by the word 'religious'. The difference was not that between a religious primitive community and a modern agnostic society. And though it has become a platitude to lament the passing of our own religious era, even to admit that without it we shall always be searching for something lost, the moral lies elsewhere. For the primitive religious experience is better summarized by words such as magical, mystical, transcendent; their world view was less concerned with faith than with experience and if we search for a modern alternative we soon find that a Christian revival is unlikely to fill the bill. Indeed, it can be well argued that the rise of Christian religion was in fact part and parcel of the slip from visionary experience which characterized men's view of the cosmos for nearly all their history.

It is perhaps surprising that religion in the West lasted as long as it did, rather than that it is at last succumbing. At bottom the only true creed of Western man has been that of dissociated intellect, of faith in the observable world. It is his firm conviction, becoming ever more articulate, that man faces the universe armed only with his reasoning faculty and that with this weapon he can cut back the last veils of the mystery of life on earth. Less than two centuries from the death of Jesus Christ, the cry of the theologian Tertullian—'It is certain because it is impossible'[1]—lodged the paradox of faith and reason firmly in the foundations of Christian thinking where it was to tick away like some kind of theological time bomb. In his steady application of reasoned analysis to the problems of his universe, the medieval theologian was the ancestor of the modern scientist.

Thus Western religion has shaped our approach to the world in a most profound way, introducing intellectual procedure and curious inquiry into the temple of the sacred from the word go. The fact that this intellectual inquiry may be thought to have broken its shackles at the time of the Renaissance is nothing like so important as the fact that it had, by that time, become a habit of mind. Even in his theology, Western man has been an active inquiry agent rather than a contemplative sage.

The Christian faith has also contributed to the development of Western technological society by its insistence, unusual among religions, on the unique significance of the individual, symbolized by the belief that 'eternal salvation' is the purpose of divinity for each separate human being. This Western obsession with the merits and rights of the individual, which for centuries had been little more than a credo of hope for the toiling masses, became, at the time of the Reformation and the Renaissance, a credo of independence for the pioneer in secular or religious fields of thought.

And, finally, among these religious antecedents to the attitudes of today's society we must give a high place to the related ideas of man's obligation to seek to improve himself in the image of the deity seen as Jesus Christ, and of the coming of the Kingdom of God upon Earth. Debased into the idea of progress, both individual and technological, the Christian philosophy can be seen not as a solution to our problems but as a cause.

These bold generalizations should not be taken to imply that Christianity alone shaped the science-based technology of the modern era. What is clear, however, is that it provided the impulse for some of its characteristic directions and proved fertile soil for the growth of some of its basic concepts. In a word, religion played a formative role in our society as it did in that of the primitive. It was formal Christianity, after all, that made it its business to chase out the old gnosis once and for all: idolatry and witchcraft were high on the list of sins, and, interestingly, not so much because they were held to be plain wrong but because they meant dabbling with the mystical powers of evil.

We are thus not only a people without religion but a people without a vision. And while we might yet recapture that religion, we would have to retrace our steps more than a thousand years if we were ever to regain the vision as well. In anthropological terms, that at least makes us unique. The numinous is to us a forgotten environment, and what we know of it is largely denied us by the only religion we have practised in a thousand years.

But there are certainly those who are intent on making a rediscovery. Without articulating their need, the radical young have for more than a decade now been deep in its search for visionary experience. The Tarot pack and astrology are taken seriously; Yoga is practised in middle-class homes throughout the land; Zen and other Eastern religions, of the contemplative rather than the analytical type, flourish in the West for the first time in their long history. And all this is no accident, even though it becomes difficult to distinguish the cult from the search. With an unerring instinct, the young have gone straight to those very forms of religious renewal which alone could satisfy their critique of the society they despise. Their action counts for more than the words that could ever be put into books, for it implies all the criticism pouring from the pens of our professional social critics. They may not have said it, may never perhaps have consciously understood it, but talk to them about it and you soon find they understood it well enough without having to articulate it. This may well be the most significant of the many signs of the times.

> The religious renewal we see happening about us—especially among disaffiliated young people, but by no means only among them—seems to me neither trivial nor irresponsible, neither uncivil nor indecent. On the contrary, I accept it as a profoundly serious sign of the times, a necessary phase of our cultural evolution, and, potentially, a life-enhancing influence of incalculable value. I believe it means we have arrived, after long journeying, at an historical vantage point from which we can at last see where the wasteland ends and where a culture of human wholeness and fulfillment begins.[2]

Thus writes Theodore Roszak in his introduction to *Where the Wasteland Ends*. And there perhaps we might leave it, were it not for the fact that this religious renewal will not on its own suffice.

To be sure, the contemporary movement towards the occult and related matters is not something which should be lightly criticized: it symbolizes a whole new attitude in the West towards forms of philosophy which surely are likely to serve us better than the poorly conceived rag-bag of positivism and reductionism which have led us to the present impasse. But, if we seek to draw some morals from early human history, from what was characteristically primitive, it will not do merely to revive experience, mysticism and a magical world view. That the concept of the sacred must once again well up to the surface of life is clear enough. But that is no object in itself. The primitive did not live in a world which was the antithesis of ours, rejecting the world of objective fact and believing only in subjective experience. He lived the two things at one and the same time, mingling sacred and profane as though they were part of a long, continuous spectrum—which for him indeed they were.

So the religious renewal we see happening has as yet far to go. While it rightly emphasizes that aspect of existence which we have for too long negated, it thus far chooses to ignore that other world which has been so clearly defined by recent Western experience. To reject, out of hand, the learning of several hundred million men and women over more than three centuries can hardly be called wise. Of course, so much is wrong in what we have done, invented and exploited that to turn one's back on what may well have been the ghastliest mistake in human history is understandable enough.

So, in the long run, what may well be a more significant pointer to the future comes not from the young (particularly) and nor from religious renewal (exclusively): it comes instead from the alienation and disenchantment which spreads like fire through the scientific citadel itself. It comes from intellectuals (where else in the West?) who now seek to rescue their sciences from irrelevance, exploitation, objectivity, specialism and empty neutrality.

It is now many years since the psychologist Abraham Maslow pointed out the dilemma of his science: that the detached objective stance of the observer could hardly be expected to produce maximum knowledge about the object when he or she was a person. People do not respond to that kind of approach but tend instead to shy away from it. Yet, Maslow argued, a compassionate science could be achieved in which involvement with the patient was admitted and encouraged—in which objectivity and subjectivity were intermingled to provide the best of both worlds.[3]

In the past few years, his lead has been followed and expanded on by many scientists. First, they would like to recognize that there are areas where some form of science is appropriate and areas where no form is useful. Second, they would like to see that science bounded by ethical and moral concepts, and not left stranded in an impossible neutrality. And, third, they would like the new sciences to be human ones, recognizing the human nature of both the observer and the observed. In this way, they argue, there may yet remain some value in our scientific obsessions which will point the way to a new Renaissance of learning.

Some claim that ecology – once labelled the 'subversive science' on account of its revolutionary social implications – may already be the forerunner of a new breed of science in which nature is not subjected to a reductionist glare but is regarded in a holistic way, even perhaps with reverence. The group of young scientists who call themselves the New Alchemy Institute are reflecting just such an attitude, for alchemy was the ethical ancestor of modern science – ethical in that it was committed to the 'celebration of a cosmic mass' with nature. In 1973 one of the most remarkable sights on British television was that of a group of high-level, middle-class, middle-aged scientists from the Massachusetts Institute of Technology sitting cross-legged round a log fire in the open, attempting to communicate and experience the true nature of energy through trance and meditation.[4] Their ordinary experience was in the laboratory where they are attempting to harness the energy of the sun in the form of controlled nuclear fusion – a fashionable and potentially important aspect of modern research. But, like the original alchemists, this they refused to do except within the context of a view of nature which was both reverential and more important than their actual project.

If such attitudes still appear ridiculous in our objectivized society they will assuredly not remain so for long. In the words of the title to that television programme, 'Science is dead'; and at heart most of those who now practise it are well aware of the fact. Yet, as the subtitle paradoxically put it, 'long live science'. For ours is, beyond recall, a science-bound society; and if it is to have a healthy and assured future, the revolution will not be the political one promised us by the neo-Marxists but one of the scientific intellect. And that revolution must start from a re-evaluation of the role of the human spirit in human affairs.

We end as we began with a story from New Guinea.[5] Before the coming of Europeans in the 1880s, the hierarchy of Kanaka society ran from the idle and unambitious 'rubbish men' to the ambitious and successful 'big men' whose duties included the organization of the ancestor cults. For it was the ancestors who had shaped the traditions and social values of the Kanakas and it was their constant watchfulness from the world of the spirits which ensured the stability and smooth running of society. The coming of the white men changed everything. Their obviously superior power eroded the prestige of the big men; their new laws destroyed the old system and denied the ambitious the chance of winning status; and their very presence cast doubt on the whole cult of the ancestors. An immediate and colossal adjustment was called for.

The invaders' success seemed to rest on their possession of the Cargo, a range of material goods unknown to the ancestors and not, so far as the most thorough investigation could reveal, produced by the white men by working but delivered to them in regular shipments. The fact that the whites had Cargo and the Kanaka did not shattered their faith in their own culture. The problem was the more acute since the Europeans were clearly no better than the Kanakas. Among themselves they were no more honourable, loving or honest; towards the natives they were just as brutal and arrogant as any conquering tribe. Clearly the secret of Cargo had nothing to do with virtue—had, then, the ancestors got the myths wrong? How could it be that the traditional mode of life had been based, apparently, on total ignorance of one of the great principles of human existence?

The Kanakas did not shirk the issue. 'What is wrong?' islanders poignantly asked of one anthropologist. 'Why are we as we are —black, dirty, without learning, without cargo, without power?'[6] When the Europeans refused to disclose the secret of Cargo or, evading the issue, claimed that it was the work of white men overseas, the tribes drew on the only resources at their disposal—their religious and mythological imagination. A prophet proclaimed a new myth which told of two legendary brothers; one the ancestor of the Europeans, the other of the Kanakas. The second brother foolishly but excusably offended the Divinity and thus condemned his descendants to ignorance of the secrets of Cargo. However, the myth also showed how the good brother had helped the foolish brother and the Kanaka cults were first aimed at winning the co-operation of the Europeans, in the belief that they, like good brothers, would reveal the secrets of Cargo.

When the cults failed to move the white men, who continued as before to depise and bully the islanders, new prophets arose. The ancestors were not at fault; indeed it was the ancestors who actually produced the Cargo, it was claimed, intending it for their descendants. But, because of moral decline among the Kanaka, the evil white men had been able to intercept the ships bringing the Cargo and steal it from the islanders. These pirates would only be overcome when the Kanakas achieved moral regeneration under the guidance of new big men and by the performance of new rituals.

For the Kanakas, as for many primitive peoples, the most deep-working effect of the European incursion had been to eat into their native ethnocentrism. Any autonomous culture worthy of the name tends to look on alien cultures with a kind of pitying wonder that there are men who can be so plain silly. In the language of many remote tribes the name of the tribe itself is the same as the word for mankind. Even the Kanaka, at the very beginning of their contact period, looked on the white man as a poor kind of creature, ignorant of sorcery, ignorant of the Kanaka language and coming from a land apparently so miserable that he had fled from it. Tragically, this attitude soon changed into one of frank envy and admiration as the people found their natural pride demolished. In the words of Kenelm Burridge: ' ... when its myths are in issue all that a community lives by, holds dear and holds as self-evident, valid or true, is in issue also.'[7]

Such a crisis of self-confidence is settling in inspissated gloom upon the nations of the advanced world. For a century and more it has seemed that the whites' hot technology has secured for them the indisputable position as masters of this planet. But now, with a growing sense of unease, we begin to feel that the position is under heavy attack. For us the enemy is not another conquering race from without, disposing of a terrifying new capability or a futuristic technology. For us the enemy is within. For us the enemy is technology itself. Our ethnocentrism as very men is challenged. Now we stand, like New Guinea islanders, with a mixture of awe, admiration and apprehension before a principle of action which seems to promise much, but also threatens to submerge us. For technology takes no interest in our system of status or our code of values. And what is our response as we find ourselves forced to work in the plantations of this alien force? Like the Kanakas, we will not see that there are only two choices—either to submit to, or to expel, the invader. Like them, unwilling to do the one and unable to do the other, we exercise ourselves with ritual activity based on beliefs from the past.

We cling to our faith in a distant millenium when technology, placated by our co-operation and served by computerized robots, will act the part of the good brother in the story and leave us to discover the secrets of human happiness. But all this must wait on the day when the problems of industrialism have been solved, and in the meanwhile we do not realize what the pursuit of this millennium is doing to us. Already the most lauded quality in our society is efficiency. A man may be at peace with the world and his fellows, he may be loyal, he may be courageous, he may be loving, but if he is not also efficient he is a social liability.

At base, our contemporary crisis is one of the psyche, not of politics or the environment. Some people, being aware that the millennium like tomorrow never comes, are deserting the technological treadmill for more relaxed and humanly orientated modes of life. This book, we hope, will be a handbook of alternatives drawn from the accumulated experience of other societies. Its aim has been to suggest some ways in which denatured industrialized man might at last begin the trek back to social humanity.

Notes

Introduction

1. Bohannan, Paul, *Social Anthropology* (New York: Holt Rinehart & Winston, 1963).

1 The First Affluent Society

1. Morris, Desmond, *The Naked Ape* (London: Cape, 1967).
2. The publication of *Man the Hunter*, edited by Richard B. Lee and Irven deVore (Chicago: Aldine, 1968), was perhaps the public signal that the material aspects of primitive life were being revalued. A hunting people is here described for the first time as the original 'affluent society'.
3. Material on the :Kung Bushmen is to be found in Lee and deVore, op. cit., and in Vayda, Andrew P. (ed.), *Environment and Cultural Behavior* (New York: Natural History Press, 1969).
4. Grey, George, *Journals of Two Expeditions of Discovery in North-Western and Western Australia, during the years of 1837, '38 and '39* (London: T. and W. Boone, 1841).
5. Ford, C. Daryll, *Habitat, Economy and Society* (London: Methuen, 1934).
6. Lee and deVore, op. cit.
7. Woodburn, James, 'An Introduction to Hadza Ecology', in Lee and deVore, op. cit.
8. Sahlins, Marshall D., 'Notes of the Original Affluent Society', in Lee and deVore, op. cit.
9. Lee and deVore, op. cit.
10. Ibid.

11. Borgstrom, Georg, 'The World Food Crisis', in *Futures* (June 1969).

2 *Food Farmers and Dollar Farmers*

1. These criticisms are well summarized by Clifford Geertz and Harold C. Conklin in 'Two Types of Ecosystem' and 'An Ethnoecological Approach to Shifting Agriculture', in Vayda, Andrew P. (ed.), *Environment and Cultural Behavior* (New York: Natural History Press, 1969).
2. Conklin, Harold C., *Hanunóo Agriculture in the Philippines* (Rome: F.A.O., 1957).
3. Clark, J. G. D., *Prehistoric Europe; the economic basis* (New York: Philosophical Library, 1952).
4. Gourn, P., 'The Quality of Land Use of Tropical Cultivators', in Thomas, W. L. (ed.), *Man's Role in Changing the Face of the Earth* (University of Chicago Press, 1956).
5. For a good summary of this information, see Dumond, D. E., 'Swidden Agriculture and the Rise of Maya Civilization', in Vayda, op. cit.
6. 'The World Food Problem', a report of the President's Science Advisory Committee (Washington, D.C.: U.S. Government Printing Office, 1967).
7. Wokes, F., 'Proteins', in *Plant Foods for Human Nutrition* (I: 32, 1968).
8. Bradley, C. C., 'Human Water Needs and Water Use in America', in *Science* (138: 489, 1962).
9. Pirie, N. W., *Food Resources Conventional and Novel* (Baltimore: Penguin Books, 1969).
10. Schertz, Lyle p., 'The Economics of Protein Strategies', in *War on Hunger* (June 1971).
11. Borgstrom, Georg, 'Food and Ecology', in *Ecosphere* (2: 6, 1971).
12. Conklin, Harold C., 'An Ethoecological Approach to Shifting Agriculture' in Vayda, op. cit.
13. Odum, Howard T., *Environment, Power and Society* (New York: Wiley Interscience, 1971).

14. Ibid.
15. Productivity is now normally measured solely in terms of yield weight of the crop per acre. This has produced confusion as regards improvements made in modern agriculture because although high-yield varieties may produce more weight of crop from a given area, the proportion of protein in them is often lower than in the crop they replace. It has been said that a cheese sandwich today has the same protein value as the two pieces of bread without the cheese before the Second World War. For a good treatment of this and other aspects of modern food production techniques, see Francis Moore Lappe's *Diet for a Small Planet* (New York: Friends of the Earth/Ballantine, 1971).

3 More Than One Kind of Medicine

1. Dean of Engineering and Applied Physics at Harvard.
2. Beckwith, John, 'The Scientist in Opposition in the United States', in Fuller, Watson (ed.), *The Social Impact of Modern Biology* (London: Routledge, 1971).
3. Lévi-Strauss, C., *The Savage Mind* (London: Cape, 1966).
4. A good summary of this 'alternative' approach to medicine is Graham Chedd's 'Mental Medicine: Self-Help for your Insides?', in *New Scientist* (9 September, 1971).
5. Gilges, W., 'Some African Poison Plants and Medicines of Northern Rhodesia', in *Occasional Papers, Rhodes-Livingstone Institute* (No. 11, 1955).
6. Turner, V. W., 'An Ndembu Doctor in Practice', in Kiev, A. (ed.), *Magic, Faith and Healing* (The Free Press of Glencoe, Illinois, 1964).
7. Douglas, Mary, *Purity and Danger* (London: Routledge, 1966).
8. Livingstone, F. B., 'Anthropological Implications of Sickle Cell Gene Distribution in West Africa', in *American Anthropologist* (60: 533–62, 1958).
9. Quoted in Bunyard, Peter, 'Polynesian Blood Pressure', in *The Ecologist* (July 1971).

10. Lee, Dorothy, *Freedom and Culture* (Englewood Cliffs, N.J.: Prentice-Hall, 1959).
11. Neel, James V., 'Lessons from a "Primitive" People', in *Science* (170: 815, 1970).
12. Neel, J. V., *et al.*, 'Studies on the Xavante Indians of the Brazilian Mato Grosso', in *Amer. J. Hum. Gen.* (16: 52, 1964).

4 Population and Population Control

1. Lee, Richard B., 'What Hunters do for a Living, or, How to Make Out on Scarce Resources', in Lee, Richard B., and deVore, Irven (eds.), *Man the Hunter* (Chicago: Aldine, 1968).
2. Davies, David, 'A Shangri-La in Ecuador', in *New Scientist* (1 February, 1973).
3. Neel, James V., 'Lessons from a "Primitive" People', in *Science* (170: 815, 1970).
4. Bleakley, John William, *The Aborigines of Australia* (Brisbane: Jacaranda Press, 1961).
5. Firth, Raymond, *We, the Tikopia* (New York: American Book Company, 1936, and London: George Allen & Unwin, 1964).
6. Hardin, Garrett, 'Making Error Creative', in Wallia, C. S. (ed.), *Toward Century 21* (New York: Basic Books, 1971).
7. Lee, Richard B., 'What Hunters do for a Living, or, How to Make Out on Scarce Resources', in Lee and deVore, op. cit.
8. Neel, James V. and Chagnon, N. A., 'The Demography of Two Tribes of Primitive, Relatively Unacculturated American Indians', in *Proc. Nat. Acad. Sci.* (59: 680. 1968).
9. Salzano, F. M., 'Studies on the Caingang Indians', in *Hum. Biol.* (33: 110, 1961).
10. Neel and Chagnon, op. cit.
11. Neel, J. V. and Salzano, F. M., 'Further Studies on the Xavante Indians', in *Amer. J. Hum. Gen.* (19: 554, 1967).
12. Neel and Chagnon, op. cit.
13. Wagley, Charles, 'Cultural Influences on Population', in Vayda, Andrew P. (ed.), *Environment and Cultural Behavior* (New York: Natural History Press, 1969).

14. Whiting, John W. M., 'Effects of Climate on Certain Cultural Practices', in Vayda, op. cit.
15. Smith, Mary F., *Baba of Karo* (London: Faber, 1954).
16. Whiting, op. cit.
17. Birdsell, J. B., 'Some Environmental and Cultural Factors Influencing the Structuring of Australian Aboriginal Populations', in *The American Naturalist* (87: 171, 1953).
18. See also Stott, D. H., 'Cultural and Natural Checks on Population Growth', in Vayda, op. cit.
19. Wagley, Charles, 'Cultural Influences on Population', in Vayda, op. cit.
20. Douglas, Mary, *Population Control in Primitive Groups*, paper given to the Association of British Zoologists at the annual meeting on 8 January, 1966.
21. Douglas, Mary, *Purity and Danger* (London: Routledge, 1966).
22. Neel, J. V. *et al.*, 'Studies on the Xavante Indians of the Brazilian Mato Grosso', in *Amer. J. Hum. Gen.* (16: 52, 1964).

5 Primitive Man and Nature

1. Conklin, Harold C., *The Relation of Hanunóo Culture to the Plant World* (doctoral dissertation, Yale, 1954).
2. Ibid.
3. Conklin, Harold C., 'An Ethnoecological Approach to Shifting Agriculture', in *Transactions of the New York Academy of Sciences* (Series II, 17: 133–42).
4. Herskowitz, Melville J., *Economic Anthropology* (New York: Knopf, 1952).
5. E. Carpenter, quoted in Lévi-Strauss, C., *The Savage Mind* (London: Cape, 1966).
6. Roszak, Theodoro, 'Ecology and Mysticism', in *The Humanist* (May 1971).
7. Jenness, D., 'The Carrier Indians of the Bulkley River', in *Bulletin no. 133, Bureau of American Ethnology* (Washington D.C., 1943).

8. Brown, Joseph Epes, *The Sacred Pipe, Black Elk's Account of the Seven Rites of the Oglala Sioux* (University of Oklahoma Press, 1953).

9. Ibid.

10. Dorothy Lee has written one of the very few professional anthropological books to treat the primitive as anything else than an object for study: *Freedom and Culture* (Englewood Cliffs, N.J.: Prentice-Hall, 1959).

11. Mead, Margaret (ed.) *Co-operation and competition among the Primitives* (New York and London: McGraw-Hill, 1937).

12. Lanternari, Vittorio, *The Religions of the Oppressed* (New York: Mentor Books, 1953).

13. Redfield, Robert and Warner, W. Lloyd, 'Cultural Anthropology and Modern Agriculture', in the 1940 Yearbook of Agriculture (Washington, D.C.: U.S. Government Printing Office).

14. Thompson, Laura, 'The Hopi Crisis' (mimeograph 1946), quoted in Lee, Dorothy, op. cit.

15. The New Alchemy Institute issues both a newsletter and a bulletin available to associate members from N.A.I.–East, Box 432, Woods Hole, Mass., U.S.A.

16. McHarg, Ian, *Design with Nature* (New York: Natural History Press, 1969).

17. Moore, Omar Khayaam, 'Divination – a New Perspective', in Vayda, Andrew P. (ed), *Environment and Cultural Behaviour* (New York: Natural History Press, 1969).

18. Harris, Marvin, 'The Myth of the Sacred Cow', in Leed, Anthony and Vayda, Andrew P. (eds.), *Man, Culture and Animals* (Washington, D.C.: American Assoc. for the Advancement of Science publication no. 78, 1965).

19. The essence of this thesis is best found in Vayda, op. cit., and in Roy Rappaport's *Pigs for the Ancestors* (Yale University Press, 1968). See also Chapter 18 below.

20. White, Lynn, Jnr., 'The Historical Roots of our Ecologic Crisis', in *Science* (155: 203, 1967).

6 Man and the Group

1. Lee, Dorothy, *Freedom and Culture* (Englewood Cliffs, N.J.: Prentice-Hall, 1959).
2. Slater, Philip Eliot, *The Pursuit of Loneliness. American Culture at Breaking Point* (Boston, Mass.: Beacon, 1970).
3. Ibid.
4. Van Gennep, Arnold, *The Rites of Passage*, trans. from the French by Monika B. Vizedom and G. I. Caffee (London: Routledge, 1960).
5. Ibid.
6. Mair, Lucy, *Marriage* (Harmondsworth: Penguin Books, 1971).
7. Maddock, Kenneth, *The Australian Aborigines: A Portrait of their Society* (London: Allen Lane, 1972).
8. Radin, Paul, *Primitive Man as Philosopher* (New York: Dover, 1957).
9. Radin, Paul (ed.), *Crashing Thunder, The Antobiography of an American Indian* (New York: D. Appleton, 1926).
10. Lowe, Robert H., *Indians of the Plains* (New York: Natural History Press, 1963).
11. Maddock, op. cit.

7 Men and their Wives

1. Morgan, Lewis Henry, *Ancient Society* (New York: Henry Holt, 1877).
2. I Corinthians vii, vv. 1–2.
3. Leighton, Dorothy and Kluckhohn, Clyde, *Children of the People* (Harvard University Press, 1947).
4. Malinowski, Bronislaw, *Argonauts of the Western Pacific* (London: Routledge, 1922).
5. Evans-Pritchard, E. E., *Kinship and Marriage among the Nuer* (Oxford: Clarendon Press, 1951).
6. Richards, A. I., 'Bemba Marriage and Present Economic Conditions', (Livingstone: Rhodes-Livingstone Institute Papers No. 4, 1940).

7. Gough, E. Kathleen, 'The Nayars and the Definition of Marriage', in *Journal of the Royal Anthropological Institute*, Vol. 89 (London: 1959).

8. Lévi-Strauss, C., *La vie familiale et sociale des Indiens Nambikwara* (Paris: Soc. des Americanistes, xxxvii, 1948).

9. Mead, Margaret, *Coming of Age in Samoa* (London: Cape, 1929).

10. Mead, Margaret, *Growing Up in New Guinea* (London: Routledge, 1931).

11. Dennis, W., *The Hopi Child* (New York: Appleton-Century, 1940).

12. Leighton and Kluckhohn, op. cit.

13. Mitchell, J. Clyde, 'Marriage, Matriliny and Social Structure among the Yao of Southern Nyasaland', in Ishwaran, K. and Mogey, John, *Family and Marriage* (Leiden: E. J. Brill, 1963).

14. Evans-Pritchard, op. cit.

15. Leighton and Kluckhohn, op. cit.

16. Le Vine, Robert A. and Le Vine, Barbara B., 'The Nayansongo. A Gusii Community in Kenya', in Whiting, Beatrice B., *Six Cultures: Studies of Child Rearing* (New York: John Wiley, 1963).

17. Mitchell, op. cit.

18. Le Vine and Le Vine, op. cit.

19. Mitchell, op. cit.

20. Firth, Raymond, *We, the Tikopia* (New York: America Book Company, 1936, and London: George Allen & Unwin, 1964).

21. Reay, Marie, 'The Social Position of Women', in *Australian Aboriginal Studies. A Symposium ...* (Melbourne: Oxford University Press, 1963).

22. Lienhardt, Godfrey, *Divinity and Experience: The Religion oj the Dinka* (Oxford: Clarendon Press, 1961).

23. Reay, op. cit.

24. Leighton and Kluckhohn, op. cit.

8 Kin and Family and Individual

1. Mitchell, J. Clyde, 'Marriage, Matriliny and Social Structure among the Yao of Southern Nyasaland', in Ishwaran, K. and Mogey, John, *Family and Marriage* (Leiden: E. J. Brill, 1963).
2. Quoted in Hoebel, E. Adamson, *The Law of Primitive Man* (Harvard University Press, 1954).
3. Leighton, Dorothy and Kluckhohn, Clyde, *Children of the People* (Harvard University Press, 1947).
4. Le Vine, Robert and Le Vine, Barbara B., 'The Nyansongo. A Gusii Community in Kenya', in Whiting, Beatrice B., *Six Cultures: Studies of Child Rearing* (New York: John Wiley, 1963).
5. Firth, Raymond, *We, the Tikopia* (New York: American Book Company, 1936, and London: George Allen & Unwin, 1964).
6. Robert Irvine Smith, of the Department of Education, York University, in a personal communication to the authors.
7. Erikson, Erik H., *Youth, Change and Challenge* (New York: Basic Books, 1963).
8. Ibid.
9. Le Vine and Le Vine, op. cit.
10. Linton, R., 'Marquesan Culture', in Kardiner, A., *The Individual and His Society* (Columbia University Press, 1939).
11. Firth, op. cit.
12. Le Vine and Le Vine, op. cit.
13. Schapera, Isaac, *Married Life in an African Tribe* (London: Faber, 1940).
14. Leighton and Kluckhohn, op. cit.
15. Schapera, op. cit.
16. Goody, J. R., *Comparative Studies in Kinship* (London: Routledge & Kegan Paul, 1969).
17. Mead, Margaret, *Sex and Temperament in Three Savage Tribes* (New York: Morrow, 1935).
18. Le Vine and Le Vine, op cit.
19. Ibid.
20. Leighton and Kluckhohn, op cit.

21. Firth, op. cit.
22. Leighton and Kluckhohn, op. cit.
23. Erikson, op. cit.
24. Le Vine and Le Vine, op. cit.
25. Ibid.
26. Ibid.
27. Firth, op. cit.
28. Maranda, Pierre, *Introduction to Anthropology* (Englewood Cliffs, N.J.: Prentice-Hall, 1972).

9 Rules for the Anti-Social

1. Hoebel, E. Adamson, *The Law of Primitive Man. A Study in Comparative Legal Dynamics* (Harvard University Press, 1954).
2. Llewellyn, K. N. and Hoebel, E. Adamson, *The Cheyenne Way: Conflict and Case Law in Primitive Jurisprudence* (University of Oklahoma Press, 1941).
3. Malinowski, Bronislaw, *Crime and Custom in Savage Society* (London: Kegan Paul, Trench & Trubner, 1926).
4. Malinowski, Bronislaw, *Coral Gardens and their Magic* (London George Allen & Unwin, 1935).
5. Rasmussen, Knud, *Across Arctic America* (New York: Putnam, 1926).
6. Hoebel, op. cit.
7. Ibid.
8. Boas, Franz, *The Central Eskimos* (Washington, D.C.: Bureau of American Ethnology Annual Report no. 6, 1888).
9. Rasmussen, op. cit.
10. This account of Nuer procedure in disputes is based on Mair, Lucy, *Primitive Government* (Harmondsworth: Penguin Books, 1970).
11. Hammond, Peter B. (ed.), *Cultural and Social Anthropology, Selected Readings* (London: Collier-Macmillan, 1969).
12. Buxbaum, David C., *Traditional and Modern Legal Institutions in Asia and Africa* (Leiden: E. J. Brill, 1967).
13. Quoted in Buxbaum, op. cit.
14. Ibid.

15. Hoebel, op. cit.
16. Llewellyn and Hoebel, op. cit.
17. Ibid.
18. Ibid.
19. Barkun, Michael, *Law Without Sanctions* (Yale University Press, 1968).

10 The Problems of the Polis

1. Marshall, Lorna, 'The :Kung Bushmen of the Kalahari Desert', in Gibbs, James L. (ed.), *Peoples of Africa* (New York: Holt, Rinehart & Winston, 1965).
2. Lévi-Strauss, C., *Nambicuara*, quoted in Hammond, Peter B., (ed.), *Cultural and Social Anthropology, Selected Readings* (London: Collier-Macmillan, 1969).
3. Lévi-Strauss, op. cit.
4. Montaigne, quoted in Lévi-Strauss, op. cit.
5. Lévi-Strauss, op. cit.
6. Mair, Lucy, *Primitive Government* (Harmondsworth: Penguin Books, 1970).
7. Olivier de la Marche, *Memoires*, ed. H. Beaune and J. d'Arbaumont (Paris, 1883–8).
8. Quoted in Hammond, op. cit.
9. Epstein, T. Scarlett, *Capitalism, Primitive and Modern. Some Aspects of Tolai Economic Growth* (Manchester University Press, 1968).
10. Diamond, Stanley, 'The Search for the Primitive', in Montagu, Ashley (ed.), *The Concept of the Primitive* (New York: Free Press, 1968).
11. Crick, Bernard, *In Defence of Politics*, 2nd revised edn. (Harmondsworth: Penguin, 1964).
12. Lee, Dorothy, *Freedom and Culture* (Englewood Cliffs, N.J.: Prentice-Hall, 1959).
13. Ibid.
14. Diamond, op. cit.

11 A Mountain of Blankets

1. Geoffroi de Vigeois, *ca.* 1170, referred to in Marc Bloch, *Feudal Society*, trans. from the French by L. A. Manyon (London: Routledge, 1962).
2. The account of the Potlatch in this chapter is based on Drucker P. and Heizer, R. F., *To Make My Name Good* (University of California Press, 1967); Codere, Helen, *Fighting With Property* (Monograph of the American Ethnographical Society, XVIII, 1950); and Boas, Franz, *The Social Organisation and the Secret Societies of the Kwakiutl Indians*, the U.S. National Museum Report for 1895 (Washington D.C., 1897).
3. Boas, op. cit.
4. Drucker and Heizer, op. cit.
5. Codere, op. cit.
6. Boas, op. cit.
7. Codere, op. cit.

12 To Be or to Have

1. Malinowski, Bronislaw, *Argonauts of the Western Pacific* (London: Routledge, 1922).
2. Herskowitz, Melville J., *Economic Anthropology* (New York: Knopf, 1952).
3. Ibid.
4. Ibid.

13 Gifts Were Never Free

1. Mauss, Marcel, *The Gift*, trans. from the French by I. Cunnison (London: Cohen & West, 1954).
2. Ibid.
3. Herskowitz, Melville J., *Economic Anthropology* (New York: Knopf, 1962).
4. Programme on B.B.C. TV, Channel 2, 1972.

5. Thurnwald, Richard, *Economics in Primitive Communities* (London: O.U.P., 1932).
6. Our account of the *kula* trading complex is based on Malinowski, Bronislaw, *Argonauts of the Western Pacific* (London, Routledge, 1922).

14 A Proper Place for Money

1. Schapera, Isaac, *Married Life in an African Tribe* (London: Faber, 1940).
2. Kroeber, A. L., *Handbook of the Indians of California* (Washington, D.C.: Government Printing Office, 1925).
3. Ibid.
4. Douglas, Mary, 'Primitive Rationing', in Firth, Raymond (ed.), *Themes in Economic Anthropology* (London: Tavistock Publications, 1967).
5. Ibid.
6. Barth, Fredrik, 'Economic Spheres in Dafar' in Firth, op. cit.

15 Wealth for Whose Sake?

1. Quoted in Packard, Vance, *The Waste Makers* (Harmondsworth: Penguin Books, 1960).
2. Ibid.
3. Ibid.
4. Ibid.
5. Mauss, Marcel, *The Gift*, trans. from the French by I. Cunnison (London: Cohen & West, 1954).
6. Herskowitz, Melville J., *Economic Anthropology* (New York: Knopf, 1952).
7. Einzig, Paul, *Primitive Money* (London: Eyre & Spottiswoode, 1949).
8. Our account of the Tolai in this chapter is largely based on Epstein, T. Scarlett, *Capitalism, Primitive and Modern. Some Aspects of Tolai Economic Growth* (Manchester University Press, 1968).
9. Ibid.

10. Taussig, Frank William, *Principles of Economics*, 4th edn. (New York: Kelley, 1939).
11. Einzig, op. cit.

16 Oracles Ancient and Modern

1. Van Gennep, Arnold, *The Rites of Passage*, trans. from the French by Monika B. Vizedom and G. I. Caffee (London: Routledge, 1960).
2. Ibid.
3. Park, George K., 'Divination and its Social Contexts', in Middleton, John (ed.), *Magic, Witchcraft and Curing* (New York: The National History Press, 1967).
4. Parkinson, C. Northcote, *The Law and the Profits* (London: John Murray, 1962).
5. Radin, Paul, *Primitive Religion, Its Nature and Origin* (London: Hamish Hamilton, 1938).
6. Newspaper Report 1971.

17 A Proper Place for Men

1. Radcliffe-Brown, A. R., *Structure and Function in Primitive Society* (London: Cohen & West, 1952).
2. Quoted in Radcliffe-Brown, op. cit.
3. Ibid.
4. Quoted in Radcliffe-Brown, op. cit.
5. Lienhardt, Godfrey, *Divinity and Experience: the Religion of the Dinka* (Oxford: Clarendon Press, 1961).
6. Douglas, Mary, *Purity and Danger* (London: Routledge, 1966).
7. Winter, Edward H., 'Amba Religion', reprinted in Middleton, John (ed.), *Gods and Rituals* (New York: Natural History Press, 1967).
8. Doughty, Charles, *Travels in Arabia Deserta* (London: Murray, 1888).
9. Firth, Raymond, 'Offering and Sacrifice: Problems of Organisation', in *Journal of the Royal Anthropological Institute*, Vol. 93, pt. I (London: 1963).

10. Ibid.
11. Langer, Suzanne, *Mind, an Essay on Human Feeling* (Johns Hopkins University Press, 1967).

18 The Ancestors, Ecology and War

1. Roy Rappaport has published many papers on the Tsembaga rituals, of which the most complete is *Pigs for the Ancestors* (Yale University Press, 1968).
2. See Chapter 2.
3. Rappaport, Roy, 'Sanctity and Adaptation', in *Io* (7: 46–71, 1970).
4. Shantzis, Steven B. and Behrens, William W., III, 'Population control mechanisms in a primitive agricultural society' (M.I.T. System Dynamics Group mimeograph, 19 January 1972).
5. Ibid.
6. Ibid.
7. Ibid.
8. Quoted in Radcliffe-Brown, A. R., *Structure and Function in Primitive Society* (London: Cohen & West, 1952).
9. Rappaport, Roy, 'Nature, Culture and Ecological Anthropology', in Shapiro, H. (ed.), *Man, Culture and Society* (London: Oxford University Press, 1971).

19 Reality and Experience

1. Radin, Paul (ed.), *Crashing Thunder, The Autobiography of An American Indian* (New York and London: D. Appleton, 1926).
2. Radin, Paul, *The World of Primitive Man* (New York: Henry Schuman, 1953).
3. Castaneda, Carlos, *The Teachings of Don Juan* (Harmondsworth: Penguin Books, 1970).
4. Gislebert of Mons, quoted in Bloch, Marc, *Feudal Society* (London: Macmillan, 1962).
5. Mbiti, John S., *African Religions and Philosophy* (London: Heinemann, 1969).
6. Ibid.

7. Ibid.
8. Adiseshiah, Malcolm S. *Let My Country Awake* (Paris: Unesco, 1970).
9. Mbiti, op. cit.
10. Stanner, W. E. H. 'The Dreaming', in Hungerford, T. A. G., *Australian Signpost* (Melbourne: F. W. Cheshire, 1956).
11. Stanner, op. cit.
12. Radin, Paul, *Primitive Man as Philosopher* (New York: Dover Publications, 1957).
13. Ibid.
14. Parry, Milman, 'Whole Formulaic Verses in Greek and South Slavic Heroic Song', in *Trans. Amer. Philol. Assoc.*, No. 64 (1933).
15. Radin, *Primitive Man as Philosopher*, op. cit.
16. Rasmussen, Knud, *The Netzilik Eskimos* (Copenhagen: Nordisk Forlag, 1931).
17. Monod, Jacques, *Chance and Necessity* (London: John Murray, 1972).

20 *The Search for Vision*

1. Tertullian, *De Carne Christi* 5.
2. Roszak, Theodore, *Where the Wasteland Ends* (New York: Doubleday, 1971).
3. Maslow, Abraham, *The Psychology of Science* (New York: Harper & Row, 1968).
4. 'Science is dead: long live science', programme first shown on B.B.C. TV, Channel 2, 25 January, 1973.
5. Our greatly condensed account of the Cargo Cults of New Guinea is based on three books: Worsley, P. M., *The Trumpet shall Sound: A Study of Cargo Cults in Melanesia* (London: McGibbon & Kee, 1957); Burridge, Kenelm, *Mambu: a Melanesian Millenium* (London: Methuen, 1960); and Cochrane, Glynn, *Big Men and Cargo Cults* (London: Oxford University Press, 1970).
6. Burridge, op. cit.
7. Ibid.